VAGABOND LIFE

George Kennan in his Caucasian mountain garb.
Undated photo from Kennan archive; courtesy Library of Congress.

VAGABOND LIFE

THE CAUCASUS JOURNALS OF

GEORGE KENNAN

Edited, with an Introduction and Afterword,

by FRITH MAIER

With Contributions by Daniel C. Waugh

UNIVERSITY OF WASHINGTON PRESS

SEATTLE AND LONDON

This publication was supported in part by the Donald R. Ellegood
International Publications Endowment.

Copyright © 2003 by the University of Washington Press
First paperback edition 2015
Printed in the United States of America
Designed by Audrey S. Meyer

All rights reserved. No part of this publication may be reproduced
or transmitted in any form or by any means, electronic or mechanical,
including photocopy, recording, or any information storage or retrieval
system, without permission in writing from the publisher.

LIBRARY OF CONGRESS CATALOGING-IN-PUBLICATION DATA

Kennan, George, 1845–1924.
Vagabond life : the Caucasus journals of George Kennan / edited, with an introduction and afterword, by Frith Maier ; with contributions by Daniel C. Waugh.
p. cm.
Includes bibliographical references and index.
ISBN 978-0-295-99487-1 (alk. paper)
1. Kennan, George, 1845–1924—Journeys—Russia. 2. Caucasus—Description and travel. 3. Russia—Description and travel. I. Maier, Frith.
II. Waugh, Daniel Clarke.
DK509.K46   2003   2002072783
914.704/81—dc21

The paper used in this publication is acid-free and meets the minimum
requirements of American National Standard for Information Sciences–
Permanence of Paper for Printed Library Materials, ANSI Z39.48–1984.

CONTENTS

PREFACE vii

EDITORIAL NOTE xiii

ACKNOWLEDGMENTS xv

INTRODUCTION 3

CHRONOLOGY OF KENNAN'S 1870 TRAVELS 43

The Caucasus Writings of George Kennan

Journey to the Caucasus 49

Across the Main Caucasus Ridge, with Prince Jorjadze 89

Through the Lands of Chechnya to the Dagestan Highlands 162

APPENDIX 225

AFTERWORD 233

REFERENCES 247

INDEX 253

PREFACE

TRAVELERS' ACCOUNTS CAN WHET ONE'S APPETITE for exploration and, when used critically by scholars, may serve as important sources in reconstructing the past and learning about other cultures. The travel writings of George Kennan (a great-uncle of George Frost Kennan, the twentieth-century statesman[1]) are excellent examples. He acquired his reputation as one of America's first "Russia experts" from his adventures in Siberia, but few are aware he was the first American to cross the Caucasus from the Caspian Sea to the Black Sea. That trip in 1870 is the subject of this book.

I discovered Kennan when I was a student of Russian and devoured *Tent Life in Siberia*, his classic book about the 1866–68 telegraph enterprise that drew him to further exploration in Russia. In the course of my own career in "adventure travel," I repeatedly visited Kennan's Kamchatka,

---

1. George Frost Kennan (born in 1904) notes the curious coincidence that he was born on the same date—February 16—and given the same first name as his grandfather's cousin (born in 1845), who was "this country's leading Russian expert [...] before anyone ever went by that designation." *At a Century's Ending* (New York: Norton, 1996), 299. In order to avoid confusing the two men, this text refers to the younger as George *Frost* Kennan wherever he is mentioned.

and the Muslim regions of the Soviet empire claimed my soul for the same reasons that the Orient has always enraptured travelers—the storming of the senses, the escape from a familiar cultural milieu. I rediscovered Kennan in 1996 when filmmaker Christopher Allingham invited me to join him in coproducing a documentary film inspired by Kennan's pioneering Caucasus journey. As I explain in the Afterword, by visiting Kennan's old haunts and searching out local people whose relatives were on the scene when he passed through, we sought to tell a story about the modern Caucasus, and its traditions.

During the months we spent that autumn in Dagestan and Georgia, we carried with us the typed transcripts of Kennan's 1870 journals, which had been buried among the 47,000 items of his archive occupying 57 linear feet of shelf space in the Manuscript Room at the Library of Congress in Washington, D.C.[2] These pocket notebooks in Kennan's tiny, regular, but often inscrutable pencil handwriting were decipherable only with a magnifying glass. The journals had been discussed briefly by Kennan's meticulous biographer, Frederick Travis.[3] However, as George Frost Kennan wrote us: "the notes you have found in the Library of Congress holdings were, to my knowledge, previously virtually unknown. I find them of considerable importance."[4]

Kennan never published his Caucasus notes as a book, although he used the material in his popular public lectures and a number of magazine articles, often elaborating on the stories jotted down in the travel journal.[5] Kennan was a very thorough diarist, but it is important to realize that much of the journal was written days or even weeks after he had been in a particular location. The diary received attention in the brief idle moments just before starting on the trail in the morning or late in

---

2. The journals, in Kennan MSS, LC, Box 19, will hereafter be cited as "Journal."

3. Frederick F. Travis, *George Kennan and the American-Russian Relationship, 1865–1924* (Athens: Ohio University Press, 1990), 43–47.

4. 19 Aug. 1996 letter from George Frost Kennan to Frith Maier.

5. In these articles, some of the material clearly comes from his 1870 journal, supplemented by the greater understanding of the region that Kennan gained through his scholarship. Other material—in particular, the dialogues with Akhmet related in his two-part series for *The Outlook* ("A Tenth-Century Barbarian" and "Murder by Adat")—is only hinted at in his 1870 notes.

PREFACE

*Page 168 in George Kennan's Caucasus journal.
Courtesy Library of Congress.*

the evening when he was "tired as a dog." When he was short of time, he scribbled lists of places, people, events, and anecdotes in order not to lose the impressions that are so quickly buried by new observations when traveling. Then, when he had a chance, he would turn these cryptic notes into detailed journal entries. While there is good reason to think that his memory for detail was excellent, for significant stretches of his itinerary he is silent, and we cannot be sure how much may have been lost or misremembered. Kennan's archive contains letters from the Caucasus and unpublished lecture and reading notes, which along with published writings close critical gaps in his travel journals.[6]

This account of Kennan's Caucasus journey, which I developed initially as a master's thesis at the University of Washington, presents all but the last few pages of the never-published travel journal, interspersed with excerpts from his letters, articles, and lectures. I have tried to interweave the different source materials in a complementary way. Section 1 covers Kennan's journey to the Caucasus, in itself a significant travel feat. Section 2 chronicles his expedition across the Main Caucasus Ridge with the Georgian nobleman Prince Jorjadze. In section 3, he circles back through the lands of Chechnya to slip once again into the Dagestan highlands.

Kennan's journals tend toward descriptions of physical geography, while his articles detail more of the human encounters. The writing in the journals is uneven in contrast to the polished prose of the articles he wrote after his return. Yet the journals are refreshing in their matter-of-factness and lack of pretension, even if their observations might not stand the test of modern political correctness. We gain a sense of a man who could endure considerable hardships, cheerfully facing the challenge of what some people he met along the way considered a dangerous plunge into the unknown, and be able to preserve a sense of self-deprecating humor in moments such as this account of a seasick Muslim being given

---

6. Interestingly, he mailed these letters from Petrovskoe (Makhachkala), Vladikavkaz, and Tbilisi (Tiflis), and they evidently reached his family in Ohio—a degree of postal reliability one could not count on a century and a quarter later. In at least one significant case, we have what purports to be a letter home but in a published version, where clearly there has been much literary reworking. Unfortunately no manuscript original seems to have survived.

a verse from the Koran dissolved in water to drink for relief from his suffering:

My only regret as I watched this performance was that the Mohammedan method of administering sacred literature in solution was not in vogue in America during my youthful days. If I could only have had the proverbs of Solomon, hymns and the Westminster catechism written on a big platter and washed off with a tumbler of water so that I could have swallowed them at a draught—how many tearful hours I should have been spared.[7]

The published articles and public lectures reflect the fact that Kennan's serious study of the Caucasus took place after his travels there and was indeed a life-long project. It is important to remember that the last article was published more than forty years after the trip. His accounts written after his travels often contain stories and dialogue that cannot be substantiated from the journals (although that of itself does not make them improbable) and presumably reflect an effort to appeal to a popular audience. My introduction will discuss Kennan's career and his reliability as an observer, and provide a brief background on the Caucasus to aid in appreciating his writings.

Kennan never postured as a Caucasus expert. Yet on his return from Dagestan and Georgia he read everything about the Caucasus he could obtain, thereby becoming a serious scholar of the region at a time when relatively little information was available in English. His journals make a valuable American contribution to a body of late nineteenth-century Caucasus writing that is primarily Russian and British. Kennan's travel and exploration writings have been obscured by his high profile political reporting from the 1880s on, but he was truly an adventure travel paragon and an explorer in the greatest sense—a student and interpreter of cultures. Determined to learn as much as he could about the Caucasus, Kennan used the trip as an occasion to undertake much more serious study of Russian than he had previously done. He crammed page after page of incisive observations into his journal. He provides insight into the Caucasus at a pivotal point in its history—the period immediately

---

7. "Vagabond Life" lecture (undated, unpublished lecture), Kennan MSS, LC, Box 73.

following the Russian conquest—through the eyes of a man who would be recognized as America's leading expert on Russia in the last quarter of the nineteenth century.[8]

In our own time, the war in Chechnya has demonstrated that the Caucasus is a region of world importance that Russians—and the West at large—still have difficulty understanding. Kennan traveled through Samashki, the site of a brutal massacre of civilians by Russian troops in April 1995, and Groznyi, whose bombed-out ruins shown on front pages of newspapers around the world made Chechnya a household word in the mid-1990s. Kennan himself, in an eerie foreshadowing of the recent conflict, wrote (of the *nineteenth* century war against the Russians): "What made the Chechenses hold out so long and so desperately, suffering hunger and peril and hardship, dying, and sending their children to die, in battle? [. . .] It was the love of independence—the natural devotion of brave men who were fighting for their country, their honor and their freedom."[9]

In Kennan's time, travel was not undertaken frivolously. It took the young daredevil a full month of travel days from New York to reach Dagestan on the coast of the Caspian.[10] And when he completed his Caucasus odyssey, he still had to traverse all of Europe, arriving in London with only enough money for cab fare and a cigar, before being able to replenish his funds for the long trip home. During the half year Kennan was in Russia, Napoleon III had time to declare war on Prussia, and to lose that war. So these writings, more than just depicting a jaunt across the Caucasus, form a complete chronicle that conveys the *feeling* of traveling around the world to Russia in the second half of the nineteenth century. They should prove useful and intriguing to historians, anthropologists, travelers, and armchair adventure aficionados alike.

8. Norman Saul, *Concord and Conflict: The United States & Russia, 1867–1914* (Lawrence: University Press of Kansas, 1996), 395.

9. George Kennan, "Unwritten Literature of the Caucasian Mountaineers," *Lippincott's* 22 (November 1878): 581.

10. June 11–24, New York to Glasgow; June 30–July 6, Edinburgh to St. Petersburg; September 1–11, Moscow to Petrovskoe.

EDITORIAL NOTE

IN THE INTRODUCTION AND NOTES, MY STANDARD for the modern rendering of geographic names is the National Geographic *Atlas of the World, Sixth Edition* (e.g., Dagestan, not Daghestan—although many British publications use the latter), with the exception of names that have familiar popular spellings. The best maps for tracing Kennan's route are the Soviet General Staff 1:200,000 series, which has been consulted for modern toponyms of small places not shown in standard atlases. Since it can be confusing to use only the modern names in the introduction and notes, Kennan's usage is followed in those cases where the modern name is quite different from the earlier one. Equivalents are given in brackets as reminders where appropriate. Transliteration from Russian follows the modified Library of Congress system without the diacritical marks.

Kennan's own writings contain nonstandard spellings of foreign words, and his unpublished diary often lacks punctuation other than dashes. I have added commas, hyphens, and apostrophes where appropriate to make the material easier to read but did not edit foreign words that Kennan wrote in transliterated form himself. Ellipses in brackets indicate my omissions (in many cases these are single illegible words). For technical reasons as well as the schematic nature of the drawings themselves, the sketches in the text of his journals have not been reproduced, but a bracketed notation indicates where he placed them. In cases where Kennan used a variety of spellings for one and the same place name (e.g., Gunib and Goonib) or one and the same person (e.g., Djordjadze, Jorjadzi, Jorjadze), I elected the spelling that appeared most frequently or was closest to the spelling accepted today. I indicate standard forms or current usage in brackets the first time a word is used and explain meanings of words in notes. Two names merit particular attention because of the frequency with which they appear: Kennan's Timour Khan Shoura was more properly Temir Khan Shura but today is Buinaksk. His Petrovskoe or Petrovski is Makhachkala. In the rare instances where it is difficult to identify on a modern map places he mentions, explanations for my guesses will be found in the notes.

Kennan's dates are largely New Style (the Gregorian calendar), although halfway through his diary he begins to use the Russian Empire's Old Style (Julian calendar) dates, which in the nineteenth century were twelve days behind. Where he gives the dates in O.S., I provide the N.S. equivalent in brackets. Twice he refers to O.S. as R.S. (i.e., Russian Style).

For certain other problems with chronology, I refer the reader to my introduction in the separate Chronology, which reconstructs as closely as possible the complete trip. In the course of Kennan's narrative, I have also added notes to clarify his itinerary and occasionally have rearranged the entries so that material about one location or topic connects directly with another section dealing with the same. Since one goal here has been to bring together all of Kennan's Caucasus writings and integrate them sequentially as the trip unfolds, excerpts from his published writings are interspersed with the unpublished material. The source for each selection is clearly identified at its start. With the exception of the final pages as he is preparing to depart from Istanbul, I reproduce in virtually complete form his travel journal. I have tried to ensure that the journal and the other writings tell Kennan's story in his own voice.

ACKNOWLEDGMENTS

MY RESEARCH ON GEORGE KENNAN'S PAPERS AT the Library of Congress was facilitated by a grant from the Russian, East European and Central Asian Studies Program at the University of Washington's Jackson School of International Studies. That program also supported a summer of intensive Avar language study with a U.S. Department of Education Title VI FLAS award, in preparation for my research in Dagestan and Georgia during the autumn of 1996. The documentary film project there on Kennan's travels was possible thanks to the financial support of General Motors and Chevron, and to the dedicated organizational efforts of my friends Bagaudin Gadjiev and Beno Kashakashvili.

I am indebted to Mihkel Maier for transcription assistance and to Michael Duckworth at University of Washington Press for helping to shape the book. Debbie Newell drew the maps. Jere Bacharach, Robert Burrowes, John Colarusso, Austin Jersild, George Frost Kennan, Efim Melamed, Anthony Rhinelander, Norman Saul, Frederick Travis, and Ronald Wixman all generously fielded my research questions. The book has benefited from the comments of two anonymous reviewers.

To a considerable degree the responses to them have been the work of my collaborator, Daniel Waugh, who deserves more credit for the final product than he was willing to allow on the title page ("It's your book, Frith"). He provided academic guidance and encouraged me to proceed with the project. When my other commitments prevented me from doing the revisions, he took the manuscript in hand and made numerous and important contributions: substantial editing, compilation of the chronology, additions to the annotation, selection of illustrations, and rewriting, the latter especially in the final section of the introduction regarding the history of the Caucasus. As he reminds me—paraphrasing Tom Lehrer's words about Lobachevskii—with the credit goes the blame. Collectively we are responsible for any errors of commission or omission.

VAGABOND LIFE

INTRODUCTION

*Exploring the Caucasus had seemed
to me easy enough while I sat in my library
at home and traced out possible routes
on the map with my pencil.*

Kennan's Road to Dagestan

GEORGE KENNAN (1845–1924) HAD NO ROYAL COMmission or missionary appointment, nor was he seeking his fortune. He was born with the instincts of a world traveler a century before global travel for ordinary people became fashionable or practical. He simply found life on the road irresistible, and out of this passion developed a career he could hardly have anticipated. That his travels would include the Caucasus, barely pacified by Russia and virtually unknown to Americans in 1870, is equally unexpected. Well before the end of the century, Kennan had become a recognized expert on Russia, one whose views would have a significant impact on America's policy toward that country.

When Kennan was growing up in Ohio, for most Americans adventure beckoned west, toward the Pacific. As a boy he read travel books voraciously, fantasized about distant adventures, and agitated to be allowed to go camping in the nearby woods. Financial difficulties in his family forced him to leave school at age twelve to work as a messenger in the telegraph office of the Cleveland and Toledo Railroad Company, where he was soon promoted to operator and manager. Desperate to escape

INTRODUCTION

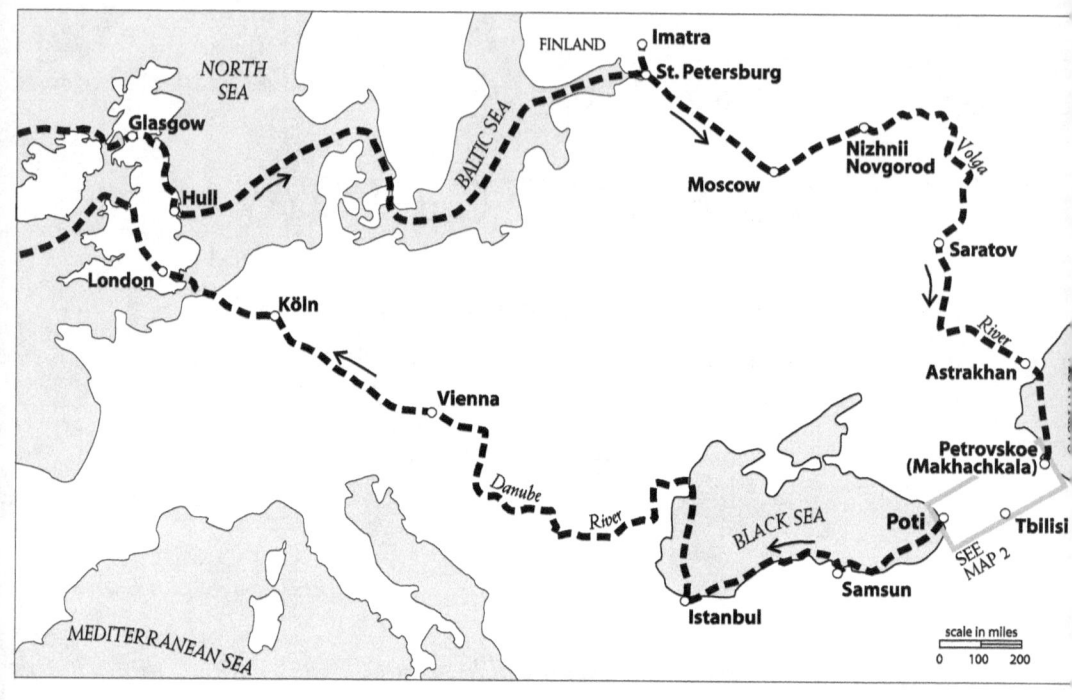

Map 1. Europe, with Kennan's route to and from the Caucasus.

INTRODUCTION

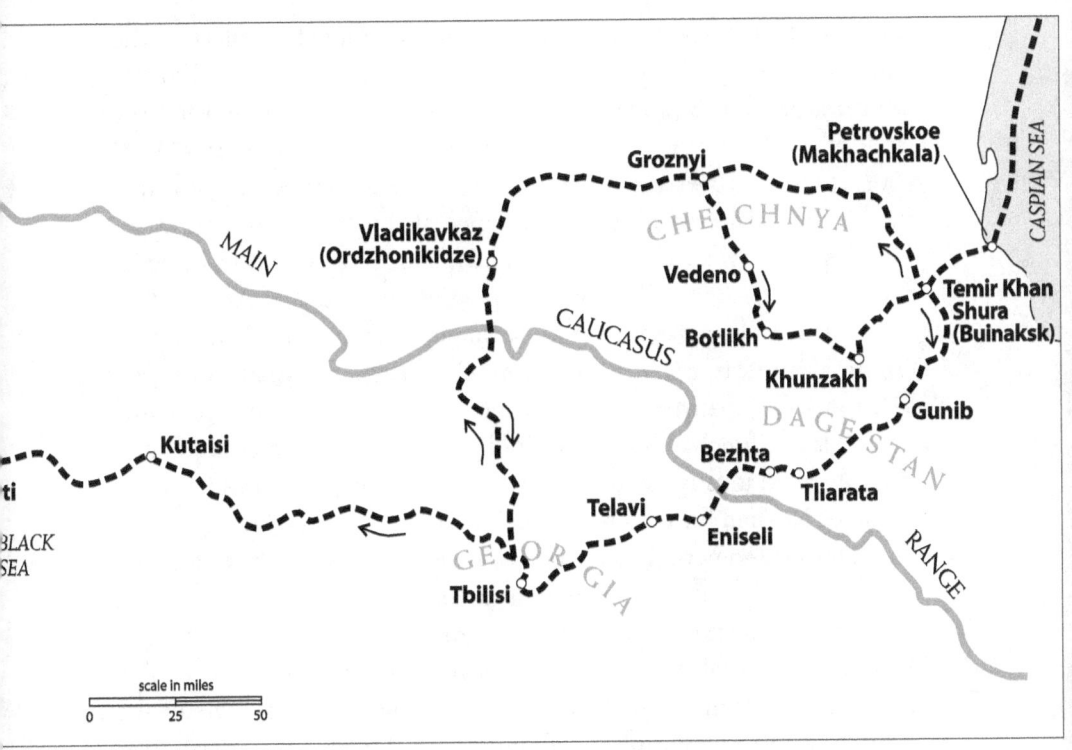

Map 2. Kennan's route through the Caucasus.

INTRODUCTION

his desk at Norwalk Station, the teenager attempted to enlist in the Military Telegraph Corps during the Civil War, but was obliged to stay at his telegraph post; capable operators were needed more in the large cities of the North than in the army. When Kennan learned in 1864 of plans to build an overland telegraph line from America to Europe across the Bering Strait and Siberia, he jumped at the chance for adventure, "offering his services as an explorer" and telling his superiors he could be ready in two hours to leave for Alaska—then still Russian America.[1]

Instead of being sent to Alaska, Kennan ended up in Russia's easternmost outposts in Asia in the employ of the Russian American Telegraph Company. For nearly two years, he tramped the mountainous wilds of Kamchatka and the Chukotka Peninsula, which were then still inhabited mostly by Koryaks and other native peoples and a smattering of Russian fur traders. In small parties of several men, the expedition traveled sometimes on reindeer, sometimes by skin canoe, camping out through the winters in temperatures down to 60 degrees below zero. It is difficult to imagine a harsher test for a city youth whose previous experience with wilderness had been gleaned primarily from books. The Russian-American telegraph was never completed (the success of the Atlantic Cable made it obsolete), but the explorer from Norwalk had been bitten by the travel bug.

Kennan made his way home from Kamchatka overland through St. Petersburg, where everyone spoke with excitement about the new "Russian Switzerland"—Dagestan.[2] Back in Ohio in 1868–69, he plotted how he might return to Russia, this time to the Caucasus. His interest in returning was surely fueled by the recognition he began to experience as a public lecturer and author of several articles on Siberia in *Putnam's*, which the publisher encouraged him to expand into a book. The result was *Tent Life in Siberia: Adventures among the Koraks and Other Tribes in Kamchatka and Northern Asia*, which he completed in St. Petersburg while already on his way to the Caucasus. The lasting success of the book might be partly attributed to his having "occasionally

---

1. Summarized from MS Autobiography, Kennan MSS, LC, Box 88: 31–73, and from George Kennan, *Tent Life in Siberia* (New York: Putnam's, 1889), i–10. For other details of Kennan's biography, I have drawn upon Travis, *George Kennan*.

2. MS Autobiography, 326.

6

deliberately altered the facts in order to increase the mood of imminent danger and create a more dramatic, gripping narrative."[3]

After attempts to line up a traveling companion fell through, Kennan sailed for Russia alone in June 1870, with $600 in his pocket. He spent July in St. Petersburg finishing his book on Siberia, working on his Russian, and acquiring books on the Caucasus. His plans to journey over the mountain range dividing the Caspian and the Black Seas struck his Russian friends as audacious and impossible. They warned that he would not make it through the wild, unmapped country where no American had ever been. Dagestan had not so much capitulated to Russian rule as been forced to its knees; it was a country exhausted by war, where the "victorious" Russians exercised only superficial control. When Kennan's St. Petersburg acquaintances said goodbye to him, they must have imagined he would never be heard from again.

Undaunted, Kennan took ship down the Volga, where he got his first introduction to Muslim life. "You won't find these places on any map," Kennan wrote his family when he landed at Petrovskoe. Indeed, from the perspective of a midwesterner in the nineteenth century, he might as well have fallen off the end of the earth.[4] Kennan's goal was "to gratify a love of rough travel and to skirmish with the difficulties of Caucasian exploration." He certainly found the reality of travel there less romantic than the stories circulating in St. Petersburg about "the Daghestan highlanders whose chivalrous and heroic courage had won the respect and admiration even of their enemies."[5] The conversational Russian he had picked up in Siberia turned out to be "next to useless," for Russian had not yet become the linguistic glue of the Caucasus.[6] After a week spent searching unsuccessfully for guides, transportation, and interpreters, the explorer nearly abandoned hope.

By chance, he met a Georgian nobleman, Prince Jorjadze, headed home to his estate in the Alazan Valley of the eastern Georgia kingdom

---

3. Travis, *George Kennan*, 42.

4. 12 Sept. letter home written from Petrovskoe, Kennan MSS, LC, Box 13, folder 1870–1878.

5. MS Autobiography, 326.

6. George Kennan, "An Island in the Sea of History: The Highlands of Daghestan," *National Geographic* 24 (October 1913): 1100.

of Kakhetia, across the rugged spine of the Caucasus mountains. The prince agreed to let the eager American tag along with his party. Day after day they traveled hard on horseback, but in the *auls*, or villages, where they stopped to spend the night, Kennan got a remarkable introduction to life in the highlands. The grueling two-week journey only whetted the adventurer's appetite for the highlands.

Kennan had arrived on the shores of the Caspian with no definite itinerary but a rough plan to make his way across the Caucasus to the Black Sea and then south to Armenia. He had a preliminary commitment to present a series of lectures on his return to the United States entitled "The Land of the Golden Fleece," focusing on Georgia's Black Sea coast.[7] But after crossing the Caucasus with Prince Jorjadze, he was so captivated by Dagestan that, following a brief respite in the lush Alazan Valley, he looped north through Chechen territory and headed back into the Dagestan highlands for another month. His Caucasus lecture would ultimately reflect the fact that he spent most of his time in the Muslim North Caucasus; it came to be called "Mountains and Mountaineers." In the space of ten weeks, he had described a rough circle about 600 miles in circumference in the middle of the Caucasus, encountering more than a dozen different languages as he moved from village to village, and crossing the Main Caucasus Ridge, the physical watershed and cultural divide between Christian Georgia and Muslim Dagestan. The substance of his observations and some basic historical background for appreciating his accounts will be treated in later sections of this introduction.

Kennan's Evolution from Cheerleader to Critic of the Tsar

FOR SEVERAL YEARS AFTER HIS RETURN FROM RUSsia in early 1871, Kennan struggled to find a career in which he was comfortable. He had little enthusiasm for his clerical jobs in banking and insurance, but finally in 1878 landed a position as an Associated Press reporter in Washington, D.C. He had continued to lecture on his Russian travels, having expanded his repertoire to include the Caucasus, and he

---

7. 16 Oct. 1870 published "letter home" from Caucasus, Kennan MSS, LC, Box 64.

contributed commentary on Russian affairs in letters to the editor published in prominent newspapers such as the *New York Herald*. In the same year that he headed off to the nation's capital he published two articles based on his experiences in the Caucasus, but he could not arouse publishers' interest in a book on the subject any more than he could in his translations of famous Russian writers. During that decade there was in fact still little evidence of how successful his journalistic career would eventually become, thanks largely to his experiences in Russia.

Successive disasters in American exploration of the Arctic (including areas north of the Bering Strait) provided a new opportunity for Kennan to capitalize on his Siberian expertise, in a widely publicized lecture for the American Geographical Society in February 1882. He devoted much of the talk to the Siberian exile system, in the process defending what he saw as its virtues. Kennan's lecture career really took off at this point, but his views on the subject of the Siberian exiles increasingly provoked criticism. This opened the opportunity he had been seeking to return to Russia, with the result that he became a much more sophisticated and critical observer of Russian policy and current events. A three-week trip to Russia in September 1884 had prepared the way for his ambitious journey across Siberia between May 1885 and August 1886 reporting for a series of articles in the magazine *Century* on political exiles. The articles subsequently appeared in his immensely influential book, *Siberia and the Exile System*. The journey was as rigorous as any of Kennan's previous travels, and his investigative journalism changed dramatically his own perceptions of democracy in Russia and in turn had a profound effect on public opinion in the United States.

Kennan's travels in Kamchatka and the Caucasus had left him impressed with Russian government policies, and he had subsequently publicly defended the tsar against criticism in the American press.[8] He was welcomed on the *Century* assignment by Russian officials, who saw in him a sympathetic mouthpiece for the tsarist government. He set off to Tomsk, Krasnoiarsk, Semipalatinsk, and dozens of other Siberian cities and towns firm in his pro-tsarist views, but fourteen months of research (ten months of it in Siberia, and some of the rest interviewing disaf-

---

8. Max M. Laserson, *The American Impact on Russia—Diplomatic and Ideological—1784–1917* (New York: Macmillan, 1950), 309; Travis, *George Kennan*, 77–78.

fected émigrés in London) convinced him he had been wrong about the system, and he now saw that the treatment of political dissenters proved the empire was rotten.[9]

In the United States, Kennan became a passionate crusader for Russian revolutionaries and a friend to émigré radicals including Catherine Breshkovskaia, Peter Kropotkin, and the terrorist Sergei Kravchinskii (aka Stepniak), helping them raise money for their cause and assisting them personally. Kennan was the most influential member of the Society of American Friends of Russian Freedom, railing against the tsarist government in prominent magazines such as *Century, The Outlook, The Nation,* and *Forum*.[10] In 1891, Kennan published the *Century* articles in book form under the title *Siberia and the Exile System*.[11] This material, and his outspoken stand against the monarchy, earned Kennan banishment from his beloved Russia; the last time he went there, in 1901, he was ordered to leave the country.

As a journalist and lecturer, Kennan reached a wide public. In the late nineteenth century, lectures served the purpose that educational television does today. Kennan was one of the most popular lecturers in the country for a time and got a great deal of exposure in the United States, as well as in Britain. During the 1890–91 season, he even set the record for the most consecutive appearances—two hundred evenings straight, except for Sundays![12] These lectures drew crowds of as many as 2,000 people.[13] He conducted lectures for over thirty years, all the while writing for popular magazines. Much of the responsibility for souring public opinion against Russia's tsarist government in the late 1800s belongs

---

9. "All my prepossessions were favorable to the Russian Government and unfavorable to the Russian revolutionists." Kennan, *Siberia and the Exile System*, vol. 1 (New York: Century, 1891), iv. For Kennan's "conversion" to critic of Russia, see Travis, *George Kennan*, chapter 4.

10. See Travis, *George Kennan*, chapter 6; also Taylor Stults, "George Kennan: Russian Specialist of the 1890s," *Russian Review* 29 (July 1970): 275–85.

11. Saul, *Concord and Conflict*, 282, notes that the series "would color the American perception of Russia for over a hundred years."

12. William Webster Ellsworth, *A Golden Age of Authors: A Publisher's Recollection* (Boston: Houghton Mifflin, 1919), 258. After this feat he collapsed from exhaustion and was forced to cancel his remaining engagements.

13. Stults, "George Kennan," 280.

INTRODUCTION

to Kennan.[14] *Siberia and the Exile System* had brought him prominence as a critic of the tsar and his secret police; his volunteer efforts on behalf of the revolutionaries further swung the perceptions of the American public which were trending toward radicalization.[15]

Kennan went so far as to oppose American food aid during the Russian famine of 1891, claiming that it supported despotism. He led a crusade in the United States in the early 1890s against ratification of an extradition treaty viewed as a threat to Russian revolutionaries who escaped to America,[16] and during the Russo-Japanese war of 1904–5 he orchestrated distribution of anti-tsarist propaganda among Russian soldiers. Kennan campaigned for three decades for the elimination of autocracy in Russia. However, Bolshevism was not the replacement system he had envisioned. He expected the Bolsheviks to be overthrown quickly; when they were not, he advocated U.S. military intervention to support the White Army.

While he reported primarily on events in Russia, Kennan's research interests were international in scope. He covered the Spanish-American War from Cuba, and wielded his anti-Russian pen in Tokyo during the Russo-Japanese War.[17] He wrote on subjects ranging from an account of the eruption of the island of Martinique in 1902, and a two-volume biography of railroad magnate E. H. Harriman, to translations from the Russian of folk legends about Napoleon's march to Moscow.[18] He was for ten years the Supreme Court reporter for the Associated Press. But Russia was his most abiding journalistic passion and he was one of few Americans reporting on Russia around the turn of the century. Kennan's views were listened to by policymakers in Washington and at his death

14. Laserson, *American Impact*, 304; Saul, *Concord and Conflict*, 311, 327, 357, 359. Saul actually labels "Kennanitis" the anti-tsarist sentiment current in America at the time, noting that Kennan was more critical than other observers in the United States.

15. Laserson, *American Impact*, 311, 316–17.

16. The extradition treaty was ratified despite opposition, but the tide of public opinion nonetheless had turned against Russia's government.

17. See Travis, *George Kennan*, chapter 7.

18. L[awrence] F. A[bbott], "Kennan, George (Feb. 16, 1845–May 10, 1924)," *Dictionary of American Biography*, vol. 10 (New York: Scribner's, 1933), 331–32. Travis provides an exhaustive bibliography of all Kennan's signed and unsigned writings. Travis, *George Kennan*, 388–403.

in 1924 he was eulogized as the "chief intellectual link between America, Europe and Russia for fifty years."[19]

The Caucasus through Kennan's Eyes

KENNAN'S LACK OF FORMAL EDUCATION AND HIS career as a popularizer, investigative journalist, and advocate may seem to put in doubt the objective value of his Caucasus writings. It is useful therefore to examine those writings in perspective by considering several of their important characteristics.

Kennan's view of the Caucasus in 1870 is complex, and reflects the ambivalent opinions of urban Russian society as well as what we might presume were interests of his editors and readers. He tended to "romanticize" and "orientalize" his subject most blatantly in what he wrote for publication, where he consciously articulated his search for "something distinctively Caucasian and oriental—something that should embody in material form the mystery and strangeness of the East and the adventurous romance of the Middle Ages," yet he also professed disappointment at not finding it.[20] His unpublished journals are more likely to romanticize landscape than people, although naturally his selection of detail in descriptions of the latter cannot be separated from his culturally conditioned responses to the unfamiliar. The extensive creation of dialogue in the published writings and lectures (largely absent in the notes he made while on the trip) reinforces the impression that he was trying to create narratives that would have particular resonance with an audience expecting a good story and a dose of exoticism. One of the best examples is his treatment forty-six years later of his translator and guide Akhmet, the "tenth-century barbarian," whose conversations about the harshness of customary law are absent from the travel journals.[21] Surely the actual words and at least some of the pertinent details were the prod-

---

19. David Fairchild, "George Kennan: The Inborn and Acquired Characteristics Which Made Him a Great Explorer of the Russian People," *Journal of Heredity* 15 (October 1924): 403.

20. Kennan MSS, LC, Box 64, envelope "Part of First Caucasus Article."

21. "A Tenth-Century Barbarian," *The Outlook* 113 (May 24, 1916): 201–7; "Murder by Adat," *The Outlook* 113 (June 28, 1916): 477–82.

uct of Kennan's imagination. The selections from Kennan's writings below will enable the reader to see the relationship between the scanty material in the journal and what are apparently the same incidents in their literary embellishment.

The same published materials and his unpublished autobiography show that he took careful note of the Russian infatuation with oriental style, and this in turn helped provide the context for Kennan's own take on the Caucasus:

Russian regimental bands were playing on the banks of the Neva the strange, wild music that they had learned on the coast of the Caspian; exquisitely wrought shirts of chain-mail and gold and silver hilted weapons made by the gortse were exhibited in the shop windows of St. Petersburg, and even the ladies showed their interest in the men whom their husbands and brothers had been fighting by adopting a part of the latters' picturesque costume and brightening the sidewalks of the Nevski Prospekt with the scarlet and white hoods of Circassian horsemen.[22]

Many of Russia's best-loved poets and novelists served in the Caucasus in the first half of the century—often as punishment for writings critical of the political establishment. Among these were Pushkin, Lermontov, and Tolstoi, whose travel journals, verses, and semifictional accounts portray Caucasians alternately as primitive fanatics and as noble savages.[23] Exotic romanticism was common to all these stories and the Caucasus literary genre continued throughout the nineteenth century, long after the end of the Muslim resistance. Kennan acquired Pushkin

---

22. "Island in the Sea of History," 1095.

23. Susan Layton has explored what she calls the "literary colonization" of the Caucasus in her *Russian Literature and Empire: Conquest of the Caucasus from Pushkin to Tolstoi* (Cambridge: Cambridge University Press: 1994). See also her "Nineteenth-Century Russian Mythologies of Caucasian Savagery," in *Russia's Orient: Imperial Borderlands and Peoples, 1700–1917*, ed. Daniel R. Brower and Edward J. Lazzerini (Bloomington: Indiana University Press, 1997), 80–99. One of the most striking manifestations of the Russian romance with the "noble primitivity" of the mountaineers was the adulation for the Muslim leader Shamil on his way to enforced exile in Kaluga. See Layton, *Russian Literature and Empire*, 254.

and Lermontov on his way to the Caucasus (which of their works is not specified), but at least at the time his interest in Tolstoi seems to have been confined to *War and Peace* (Journal, 50).[24]

The romantic enthusiasm for the Caucasus that Kennan encountered reflects the uniquely Russian strain of the imperial snobbery on which Edward Said has focused attention with his criticism of Orientalism.[25] Russians themselves had long desired to be as European as the rest of Europe and their campaigns in the Caucasus can be explained in part by a psychological need to play the role of the conquering European power and "enlighten some savages," the language of liberation in which imperialist missions of the day were cloaked. The Russians stereotyped the Caucasians as savages in part as a way to emphasize that they *themselves* were civilized. There was wide acceptance for the idea that being subjects of Russia was in the best interests of the Chechens, Avars, and others, and that they would be grateful for the tsar's protection if they were not being agitated to "holy war" by the Imam Shamil. However, as Susan Layton has pointed out, Said's analysis is of somewhat limited value for understanding the varieties of Russian Orientalism, which also included a strain of admiration for those "noble savages" as a foil to the ignoble oppression by Russian officialdom and an inspiration for Russians, who lacked the same spirit of freedom that was seen among the Caucasus highlanders.[26]

Young George Kennan was taken primarily by the image of the romantic savage and seems to have assumed it was one that would appeal to his readers. In particular, the image emphasized the antithesis between fanatical Muslims and virtuous crusaders, a view that now seems antiquated. His articles and lectures played up those elements in Dagestan and painted colorful fantasies:

---

24. In 1877, he translated Lermontov's "Kozach'ia kolybel'naia pesnia" as "Cradle Song of the Line Cossacks," but it was never published. See "Chronology" of Kennan's life prepared by his wife, Emiline Rathbone Weld Kennan, Kennan MSS, LC, Box 88, 5.

25. A term carrying all the baggage of the West's approach to the Orient and "that collection of dreams, images and vocabularies available to anyone who has tried to talk about what lies east of the dividing line." Edward Said, *Orientalism* (New York: Vintage, 1979), 73.

26. Layton, "Nineteenth-Century Russian Mythologies," 82.

[A]s the clear, excellent strains of the savage battle hymn came echoing back from the mountain cliffs under which we rode mingled with the clattering of a hundred hoofs and the sharp clank of sabres against ringing stirrup-irons, I half imagined myself a moss-trooper, or a knight of the fourteenth century making a raid into the territories of a hostile baron. The whole atmosphere seemed filled with the warlike, adventurous spirit of the Middle Ages; and if Prince Djordjadze had only suggested making an attack upon the very next village we came to, I was just in a state of mind to draw my revolver and dash into the fray with all the enthusiasm of a crusader.[27]

KENNAN'S PRO-RUSSIAN BIAS

Any world traveler can identify with Kennan's giddiness at being on the go, but the flip side of this youthful enthusiasm is that the journal is not always well-informed. Kennan's blindly pro-Russian bias stands in stark contrast to his later objective and critical journalistic reporting. His sympathies with Russian policy skewed his writing at the time he traveled the Caucasus and for a decade afterwards. In 1877, when Russia was at war once again with the Ottoman Empire, Kennan wrote a letter to the editor of the *New York Tribune* in response to an article noting insurrection among the Chechens and the reported cooperation of the highlanders with the Turks.[28] Kennan expressed the opinion that widespread uprisings among the peoples of Chechnya and Dagestan were unlikely because of what he called Russia's "enlightened policy" toward these people. After the capture of Shamil, he wrote, "Russia strove by every possible means to win over the most prominent men—men who might become leaders of another insurrection—and to open to them a new career." Kennan was impressed by the Russians' zeal to educate highlander boys in Russian schools and saw the Russian influence as a civilizing one.

Kennan's support for Russian actions in the Caucasus, and Russian foreign policy in general, was in line with popular sentiment in America during that decade. The countries of Western Europe were critical of Russian expansionism: just fourteen years before Kennan arrived on the

---

27. George Kennan, "The Mountains and Mountaineers of the Eastern Caucasus," *Journal of the American Geographical Society of New York* 5 (1874): 177–78.

28. June 1877 letter titled "On Russian policy in Caucasus," Kennan MSS, LC, Box 64.

INTRODUCTION

shore of the Caspian, Britain and France had teamed up with the Turks in the Crimean War to defend the territorial status quo and quell Russia's ambitions against the Ottoman Empire. The Caucasian Wars were in full swing, but the Crimean War was not a mission of mercy by Britain, France, and the Ottomans to assist the Caucasians in their resistance to Russian colonization. Nonetheless, the struggle of Shamil and his fighters was widely publicized, especially in England.[29]

Kennan's lack of sympathy for Shamil's war of independence in part may reflect sour Anglo-American relations. He was disinclined to be partial to Shamil specifically *because* the British championed the mountaineers' cause. Relations between Great Britain and the United States had yet to thaw; in fact, in the years immediately following the Civil War, Americans despised Britain.[30] The United States, not yet a Great Power player and not involved in the nineteenth-century skirmishes with the Ottoman Empire, publicly opposed Britain on the Eastern Question, the paramount diplomatic problem of the day. Following the axiom "the enemy of my enemy is my friend," when it came to the conflicts between Russia and the Ottoman Empire, the United States until the end of the nineteenth century tended to take the part of Russia in order *not* to be aligned with Britain.[31]

Kennan's uncritical advocacy of Russia's presence in the Caucasus seems particularly naive considering that just a few years before he set off for Dagestan, upwards of a million Adyge (also referred to as Cherkass or Circassians) had been forced by the Russians' scorched earth policies to abandon their ancestral lands north of the Terek River and in the Black

---

29. "Abroad Shamil was at least the second most famous person in the Russian Empire—he had reached almost legendary status in the West by the time of his capture." Thomas M. Barrett, "The Remaking of the Lion of Dagestan: Shamil in Captivity," *Russian Review* 53 (1994): 358. Thirty-eight books on Shamil appeared in Europe and America in a six-year period (ibid., 359).

30. Charles Campbell, *The Transformation of American Foreign Relations, 1865–1900* (New York: Harper and Row, 1976), xvii.

31. In *The Limits of American Isolation: The United States and the Crimean War* (New York: New York University Press, 1971), 87, Alan Dowty quotes the *New York Herald* explaining that public opinion favored Russia because people "hated her less than the Allies." Saul, *Concord and Conflict*, 120, notes that during the 1877–78 Russo-Turkish war, American reporters generally supported the Russian, "Christian" side.

INTRODUCTION

Sea valleys between Sukhumi and the Crimean Peninsula, fleeing to the Ottoman Empire with hundreds of thousands dying en route.[32] The dislocation and exodus of North Caucasian peoples, including Chechens to Jordan, Syria, and Iraq, continued through the turn of the century.

But Kennan, born in 1845, was a young boy at the time of the Crimean War, and evidently not well informed about the details of the decades-long Caucasian conflict when he went there. The U.S. press published little on the Caucasus in the years immediately preceding Kennan's journey[33] and what little reporting there *had* been of the Caucasian Wars dismissed the Muslim resistance as "the battle of semi-barbarism against the advancing column of Muscovite colonization."[34] During his travels in the Caucasus, Kennan's sources were limited to Russian army officers because few highlanders spoke Russian, not to mention English; presumably this further contributed to his pro-Russian bias. Apart from everything else, the lack of any real American strategic interest in the Caucasus could explain his lack of sympathy for the fate of its indigenous peoples.

ATTENTION TO DETAIL

Travel diarists sometimes skip over descriptive details in the rush to convey the novelty of pioneering. Kennan resists this tendency with his attention to minutiae ranging from details of clothing and household furnishings to the inventory of stores. Often he provides important insights into the contacts between ostensibly inaccessible villages and the outside world and the changes which undoubtedly were under way in traditional life. We are struck by his discovery in the highland aul of Khunzakh of "Longfellow's *Evangeline* . . . as well as Thiers' *Consulate*

---

32. Paul B. Henze, "Circassian Resistance to Russia," in *The North Caucasus Barrier: The Russian Advance towards the Muslim World*, ed. Marie Bennigsen Broxup (London: Hurst, 1992), 103. For details of the mass emigrations and their disastrous consequences, see *Istoriia narodov Severnogo Kavkaza (konets XVIII v.–1917 g.)*, ed. A. L. Narochnitskii (Moscow: Nauka, 1988), 202–12.

33. Between 1865 and 1870, there was not a single article or editorial about the Caucasus in the *New York Times*. Even the London *Times* during this period published only three articles about politics in the region.

34. "The Fall of Schamyl," *New York Times*, October 6, 1859, 4, col. 3.

and Empire and Buckle's *History of Civilization in England*" (Journal, 259), although unfortunately we never learn who owned them. He notes in the stores of Temir Khan Shura (Buinaksk) "a very good assortment of European dry goods, knicknacks, and jewelry, but not much that is peculiarly Caucasian" (Journal, 105). He also notes that Russian paper currency was in general circulation deep in the mountains of Dagestan. These kinds of observations provide insight into how the economy was in transition in this decade following the conquest.

Some of his records remind us that modern perceptions of the past may not in fact correspond to reality. In Bezhta, on Dagestan's border with Georgia, Bezhtans today brag that they always enjoyed a superior position vis-à-vis their neighbors across the mountains.[35] Yet when Prince Jorjadze "heard complaints" in Bezhta, the conversation was carried on in Georgian (Journal, 152). There is much more in the Journal to suggest that the histories of Georgia and Dagestan were very much interconnected, at least in 1870.

Kennan tells the reader a lot about patterns of daily life, religion, etiquette, and local government.[36] He took a particular interest in Dagestani customary law, *adat,* the pre-Islamic code that orders society by mandating property rights, dispute resolution, and the punishment for crimes. Islam came slowly and late to the Caucasus, and Dagestan adopted the faith of the Prophet more as a way to worship than as a script for how to live. Even after all the Christian and animist villages had been converted, *adat* continued to coexist alongside *sharia.*[37]

---

35. The history teacher in the Bezhta school insisted to me that Kakhetia paid tribute to the free society of Bezhta.

36. For those wishing to compare Kennan's observations with ethnographic studies based on more recent observations, the most detailed treatment currently available in English on Dagestani culture is Robert Chenciner, *Daghestan: Tradition and Survival* (Richmond, Surrey: Curzon, 1997). Although heavily anecdotal, it is based on extensive fieldwork and research in published sources. A good overview of selected topics and introduction to the literature can be found in the recent series *Narody Kavkaza,* esp. book 3: Ia. S. Smirnova and A. E. Ter-Sarkisiants, *Sem'ia i semeinyi byt,* part 1, *Formirovanie, tip i struktura* (Moscow, 1995); and book 4: S. A. Arutiunov, G. A. Sergeeva, and V. P. Kobychev, *Material'naia kul'tura: Pishcha i zhilishche* (Moscow, 1995).

37. Alexandre Bennigsen and Chantal Lemercier-Quelquejay, *Islam in the Soviet Union* (New York: Praeger, 1967), 20.

INTRODUCTION

Russian administrators promoted adat over sharia courts, seeking to weaken the authority of spiritual leaders and only gradually attempted to introduce European legal procedure following the Russian judicial reform of 1864.[38] While a substantial portion of his material on adat was written only well after the trip, Kennan's journals contain enough to suggest he developed a specific interest in the subject while in Dagestan. But in the case of adat, as in instances where he describes religious belief and practice, he seems commonly to have relied on secondhand information.

READING BETWEEN THE LINES

Subjects missing from the journals also intrigue. I found little commentary about education. Kennan evidently never visited a school, which would have been an interesting glimpse into the changing times. The use of classical Arabic for religious study and practice was still widespread; Russian-language schools had not yet begun to replace the madrasas.[39] Kennan's only mention is of "boys keeping house together for themselves in the mosque, where they are taught by the moolah or village priest." His journey did not produce a comprehensive picture of Dagestan and Georgia: for all his interesting stories about the auls

---

38. Bariatinskii, Vorontsov's successor as viceroy, particularly favored limiting sharia influence; criminal prosecution and cases involving landownership were removed from sharia jurisdiction. Semen Esadze, *Istoricheskaia zapiska ob upravlenii Kavkazom*, vol. 2 (Tbilisi, 1907), 111, 114, 127. In general though, Russian efforts to limit the influence of Islam and to convert the Caucasus Muslims were a failure. See Firouzeh Mostashari, "Colonial Dilemmas: Russian Policies in the Muslim Caucasus," in *Of Religion and Empire: Missions, Conversion, and Tolerance in Tsarist Russia*, ed. Robert P. Geraci and Michael Khodarkovsky (Ithaca: Cornell University Press, 2001), 229–49. On the implementation of administrative and legal reform, see *Istoriia narodov Severnogo Kavkaza (konets XVIII v.–1917 g.)*, 277–82.

39. Austin Jersild notes that in 1880 the nine districts of Dagestan Oblast had only five Russian schools with a total of 159 students, while more than 5,000 students attended madrasa. "Who Was Shamil? Russian Colonial Rule and Sufi Islam in the North Caucasus, 1859–1917," *Central Asian Survey* 14/2 (1995): 223, citing Rossiiskii gosudarstvennyi istoricheskii arkhiv, f. 932, op. 1, 1880–1882, d. 292 (Delo "Otchet nachal'nika Dagestanskoi obl. Namestnika na Kavkaze o politicheskom i ekonomicheskom sostoianii kraia . . . "), fol. 15.

he visited, there were hundreds more auls Kennan never saw, many of them with practices and traditions totally different from any he described. His journals tell us nothing of Dagestan's legendary craftsmen, in part because the skills of carpet weaving, pottery making, and metalwork were more developed in the southern part of the republic. He did not make it as far south as Derbent, the city that put Dagestan on the map of antiquity, and he devoted little space to Georgia and its rich culture, so different in many ways from what he saw in the Dagestani highlands. Much of what he *did* write about Georgia was so focused on dramatizing his frustration with petty bureaucrats in Tbilisi that he invented an extra week of his struggle to obtain travel permits. He traveled through Chechnya on his way to and from Dagestan, but did not stop for long, and his description is limited to the logistics of transportation.

Even the passages of Kennan's writing that were misinformed, or which are considered inaccurate based on more recent historiography, are revealing. Because the highlanders are light-skinned, Kennan concluded they must be the descendants of the Crusaders—a common view in the literature of the period, but one that is not supported by historical evidence. He was confused about the ethnicity of the Caucasian peoples he came in contact with—but then, the Russians were confused too, and these peoples identified *themselves* by their clan or aul, rather than as members of an ethnic group.[40]

Kennan's Caucasus journals overall reflect a remarkable openness to the people and customs he encountered. Curiously, although Kennan had been raised in a rigidly religious home,[41] neither Calvinism nor his pro-Russian views obscured his ability to observe Muslim culture without religious bias. His objectivity may be partly attributable to his youth—he was neither professional scholar nor professional explorer—and the fact that he came from America, where people knew little and cared less about the Caucasus. At times, though, the cultural biases of his time are evidenced in remarks like these:

---

40. Ronald Wixman, *Language Aspects of Ethnic Patterns and Processes in the North Caucasus*, University of Chicago Department of Geography Research Paper 191 (Chicago, 1980), 100–101.

41. Travis, *George Kennan*, 5.

INTRODUCTION

There is no reason to doubt that the innate capability of these wild Lezgin mountaineers is equal to that of the average Englishman or American and the only difference between them arises out of the circumstances in which they are respectively placed. ... One grows up an intelligent, thinking reasoning human being and the other a mere wild animal. [Journal, 155]

LANGUAGE AND SCHOLARSHIP

An important factor influencing the substance of any traveler's narrative is language. All too frequently the explorer has no functional ability in the vernaculars of the areas he or she visits. When he first arrived in Dagestan, Kennan lamented: "The language I no longer understand, the geography of the country with the outlandish Tartar and Chechense names is entirely unknown to me, and I feel as much at a loss as if I had been set down suddenly in the middle of China or in Central Africa."[42] Later in the mountains Kennan readily admitted being left out of conversations in Avar or Georgian. Much more intriguing is his admission (in his 16 October 1870 "letter home" writing about his experiences in Tbilisi) that he does not write Russian. Certain words written in Cyrillic in the journal make it clear that he *could* write, but he may not have felt competent to compose the official statement the Tbilisi bureaucrats demanded of him. Or perhaps he simply stressed the point in this published piece to underscore how helpless he was before the Russian bureaucracy. His unpublished autobiography in the Library of Congress explains that he shunned Russian grammar and chose to get by with simplified conversational forms.[43] In St. Petersburg, Kennan devoted a part of every day to the study of Russian:

The knowledge that I had of it when I returned from Siberia was very imperfect and inadequate, and had been gained, almost wholly, by listening to the talk of Cossack and Kamchadal dog-drivers by the camp-fire. The best I could do was to make a vocabulary and grammar of my own by writing down in English letters the words that I heard, and then framing rules for the inflections by a rude process of observation and induction. I did not even know

---

42. 12 Sept. 1870 letter home from Petrovskoe, Kennan MSS, LC, Box 13, folder 1870–1878.

43. MS Autobiography, 357–61.

the Russian alphabet, and it was weeks after my arrival in St. Petersburg before I could find a word in the dictionary or give more than a guess at the proper way to spell it.[44]

These statements raise questions about how well Kennan knew Russian. He later translated into English Turgenev and other Russian authors. One assumes that he must have become proficient at reading and writing Russian in order to translate novels, but, on the other hand, these translations were never published.[45] None of the biographical material on Kennan satisfactorily resolves the question of his Russian fluency. The journals, however, make it clear that in 1870 his spoken Russian was sufficient to gather information about many aspects of daily life in the Caucasus. By the end of the trip, even after he left the Russian-speaking environment, he would, perhaps unconsciously, lapse into Russian usage. The fact that he learned Russian entirely through self-study is impressive, although not surprising from a man who never went to high school or college but nonetheless became an astute, widely respected journalist.

Kennan was also self-taught about the Caucasus, acquiring his book knowledge over the years after he returned home. His first references to other Caucasus travelers apparently derived from what he was told in Temir Khan Shura by a correspondent for a Moscow newspaper (Journal, 110); his references to what Strabo and Plutarch had to say about the Georgians seem to have come from Prince Chevchavadze's adjutant (Journal, 238). After his return, he kept an extensive card file of references for his study of the Caucasus (as well as similar card files for other topics of research). Kennan's card catalog and his library reflect the fact that he made a lifelong study of the history as well as the folklore of the Caucasus. By the time he published his first article on the Caucasus in

---

44. Ibid., 358–59.

45. Kennan publicly skewered the literary translations from Russian of Eugene Schuyler, his fellow Russophile, but Schuyler's translations, unlike his own, were published to good reviews—a fact that evidently gave Kennan more reason to resent his contemporary. See Travis, *George Kennan*, 78–79; Saul, *Concord and Conflict*, 320–21.

1874, he had obviously acquired systematic information about Caucasus geography and history, and he could take issue with authors such as Richard Burton and Arthur Cunynghame.[46] Among the books to which Kennan turned at one time or another for information about the region were James S. Bell's *Journal of a Residence in Circassia,* Rawlinson's *Herodotus,* François Lenormant's *Ancient History of the East,* and the multivolume *Sbornik svedenii o kavkazkikh gortsakh.*[47] This last work was published in Tbilisi about the time Kennan traveled there, a product of the Imperial Russian Geographic Society's Caucasian Section.

The Caucasian Section counted among its members General Petr Uslar, a man whom Kennan met in Temir Khan Shura and who provided Kennan with valuable materials for his future studies. Uslar, a military engineer sent to the Caucasus in 1837 to serve in the Russian Army, was commissioned twenty years later to write a history of the Caucasus. He took a remarkable approach to the assignment, deciding that since most of the native languages of the Caucasus were not written, the first step to a history—and a necessary groundwork for future ethnographic work—was to create writing systems for them. Uslar spent the remainder of his life studying and publishing grammars for Abkhaz, Chechen, Avar, Lak, Dargin, Lezgin, and Tabasaran, a colossal body of work considering that these languages belong to different branches of the Caucasian languages group, which are in turn distinct from the major language families. Although Uslar conceded that the Georgian alphabet ("in which every sound can be expressed with a specific letter and every letter always has the same sound") would lend itself best to writ-

---

46. The flamboyant Burton became known for his visit to the Muslim holy cities in disguise, for his explorations in Africa, and for publication of oriental erotica. It is not clear to which of his publications Kennan may have referred, although presumably Burton commented on the Circassians (who were one source of slave soldiers) in one of his writings about the Middle East. Arthur Cunynghame visited Dagestan the year after Kennan was there. Undoubtedly Kennan read his *Travels in the Eastern Caucasus, in the Caspian and Black Seas, Especially in Daghestan, and on the Frontiers of Persia and Turkey, During the Summer of 1871* (London: J. Murray, 1872).

47. List of books in Kennan library, Kennan MSS, LC, Box 88.

ing the mountain languages of the North Caucasus, he chose to write them with the less expressive Cyrillic alphabet. Russia had, after all, just planted its victor's boot firmly on these territories.[48] Part of the agenda was to provide the means to educate the highlanders in their own languages but thereby contribute to their integration into the non-Muslim secular culture of the Russian Empire.[49] In a curious paradox, Uslar, the conqueror's designated chronicler, made a unique contribution to serious study of Caucasian language and culture. It was Kennan's good fortune to cross paths with him.[50]

Vocation: Vagabond

THIS BOOK, THOUGH, IS A TESTAMENT NOT TO AN influential international journalist or scholar, but to an indomitable adventurer. In the late nineteenth century, few Americans traveled abroad, and those who did rarely ventured farther than Western Europe. Not only was Kennan apparently the first American to visit Dagestan and cross the Caucasus, but he was one of only a handful to travel beyond Russia's main cities at all.[51] George Ditson traveled along the Black Sea coast and in Georgia in the late 1840s. He went in the company of Georgians and took a dark view of Dagestan—perhaps understandably, for in his book about the adventure he describes how his party was attacked by

---

48. Uslar's biographical information has been summarized from A. A. Magometov, "P. K. Uslar—Kavkazoved," appended to a previously unpublished manuscript Uslar was working on when he died in 1875: *Etnografiia Kavkaza: Iazykoznanie VII, Tabasaranskii iazyk* (Tbilisi: Metsniereba, 1979), 1046–68.

49. See Austin Lee Jersild, "From Savagery to Citizenship: Caucasian Mountaineers and Muslims in the Russian Empire," in Brower and Lazzerini, eds., *Russia's Orient*, 107–8.

50. Kennan acknowledges his debt to Uslar and Prince Jorjadze for sharing with him materials they'd collected on Dagestan. See "Unwritten Literature of the Caucasian Mountaineers," *Lippincott's* 22 (October 1878): 440; see also Journal, 109.

51. An article in the journal of the Russian Imperial Geographic Society on foreign travelers mentions a single American: George Kennan. See "Angliiskie i amerikanskie puteshestvenniki v Rossii," *Izvestiia Imperatorskogo Russkogo geograficheskogo obshchestva* 10/3 (1874): 143.

"Lezgins."[52] The British had the longest interest in the Caucasus. Several Englishmen had lived among the peoples of the North Caucasus in the 1830s, notably James Bell, a merchant who also actively supported the locals' independence struggle.[53] Bell's books leave no doubt that he considered the Russian influence a negative one. "The trade of Georgia has been ruined since she was treacherously annexed to the empire;" he wrote, "and, what is infinitely worse, the virtue of the female part of her population has been destroyed by the hosts of Russian military."[54] The most famous foreign visitor to the Caucasus was the author Alexandre Dumas, who traveled there in 1858.

A British team led by Douglas Freshfield made the first serious mountaineering expedition in the Caucasus two years before Kennan, and in the decade between 1886 and 1896, most of the major Caucasus summits were climbed by British alpinists.[55] Freshfield and his countrymen were without question the mountaineering pioneers of the range, but they weren't necessarily interested in local people or customs, tending to treat them as stepping stones—or obstacles—to accomplishing their climbing feats. Kennan stood out among early foreign travelers to the region for his determination to learn and record as much as he could about the beliefs, rituals, celebrations, and social organization of Dagestan. But he went because he was footloose and he argued passionately for the legitimacy of travel for its own sake.

The gratification of one's curiosity is nothing more nor less than the acquisition of knowledge for which the mind has a craving. I don't believe that my reputation as a respectable citizen will suffer if I admit that I travel for the gratification of my curiosity.... I traveled through the Caucasus like a per-

---

52. George Leighton Ditson, *Circassia, or, A Tour to the Caucasus* (New York: Stringer and Townsend, 1850), 234–36. Kennan never mentions this book, although he must have been familiar with it.

53. Paul Henze, "Circassian Resistance," in *The North Caucasus Barrier*, 84.

54. James Stanislaus Bell, *Journal of a Residence in Circassia during the Years 1837, 1838 and 1839*, 2 vols. (London: Edward Moxon, 1840), 2:140.

55. Audrey Salkeld and José Luis Bermúdez, *On the Edge of Europe: Mountaineering in the Caucasus* (Seattle: The Mountaineers, 1993), 7. Freshfield's 1896 two-volume *Exploration of the Caucasus* is another classic adventure tale.

fect vagabond, living one day with a prince, riding the next on a load of flour with a miserable Jew, sitting down one day to a table covered with silver plate, and making a dinner the next out of salted cheese, raw turnips and black bread begged from soldiers! And was there anything disgraceful in it? Not a bit![56]

Kennan's defense of "vagabonding" may sound quaint *now*, but he was pleading the virtues of adventure travel nearly a century before it became mainstream. His Caucasus journey, against the grain of the times, stands out as a pure celebration of the peripatetic spirit. The charm of Kennan's journals lies in the grafting of scholar on adventure pioneer. One of his most popular lecture offerings was on "Vagabond Life," and it provides insight into his very progressive approach to travel. In the lecture, he took issue with Oliver Goldsmith's dismissive comment that "one who rambles from country to country guided only by the blind impulse of curiosity is nothing but a vagabond."[57] Kennan justified the right to roam just for the fun of it:

A vagabond then is primarily a man who travels without any definite utilitarian aim. He does not go abroad expecting to bring about the millennium by impressing upon the world his own opinions and prejudices, neither does he ramble from Country to Country collecting statistics and accumulating information as a pure matter of mental discipline. He is content to be a simple observer in the great world of God—studying those things which interest him for no other reason than because they do interest him.... [A] vagabond seeks to know the world and its people as they are, and in order to acquire that knowledge he is ready to become all things with all men and to make himself equally at home in all places. In this sense of the word I do not hesitate to avow myself a vagabond of the most pronounced type.[58]

Kennan's threw himself into the role of lecturer and journalist, but it would be a mistake to think he outgrew his taste for adventure. In a

---

56. 19 Nov. 1872 letter, Kennan MSS, LC, Box 13, folder 1870–1878.

57. Oliver Goldsmith's *The Citizen of the World, or, Letters from a Chinese Philosopher, Residing in London, to His Friends in the East,* first published in 1762, was immensely popular.

58. "Vagabond Life" lecture, Kennan MSS, LC, Box 73.

letter to his mother after returning home from Dagestan, Kennan confessed that "working at a desk doesn't agree with me as well as knocking around in the mountains of the Caucasus."[59] To set the stage for what the avowed vagabond will tell us in his own words, let us now look briefly at the geography and history of the Caucasus up to 1870, focusing especially on Dagestan and its immediate neighbor Georgia.

The Caucasus up to 1870

WHEN KENNAN ARRIVED IN THE CAUCASUS IN 1870, the Russian authorities were just embarking on a task which a knowledge of the region's history and geography would have revealed to be impossible: gaining acceptance and loyalty to a single political entity and breaking down the vastly diverse cultural and linguistic barriers. The Caucasus had never been unified except as a geographic concept applied to the territory between the Black and Caspian Seas, bordered on the north where the inland sea of the steppe breaks against a mountain barrier and on the south, rather more vaguely, by the plateau of what is now northern Iraq and Iran. A mosaic of independent kingdoms, khanates, and much smaller entities, often not extending beyond the boundaries of a valley or a few mountain villages, the Caucasus had the misfortune of lying in the path of expanding empires—the Russians were, after all, not the first. However, none of them could hold more than part of the territory for long, even though, as their empires ebbed, they left an imprint on the cultures that survived them. Witness to the turbulent history of internal strife and external invasion are the three- and four-story stone towers that still dot the crags and give a kind of medieval aura to mountain villages. Reinforcing this image of feudal disunity are the suits of mail that still were worn in some places in the nineteenth century. It is no wonder that myths of descent from crusading knights were still alive and Prince Chevchavadze could attempt to purchase what was purportedly a crusader's sword (Journal, 238). Yet for all the evidence of human and physical barriers to peaceful intercourse, the history of the region continually reminds us of how the culturally different regions were interdependent.

59. 1 Oct. 1871 letter, Kennan MSS, LC, Box 13, folder 1870–1878.

DAGESTAN

The Arab writer Mas'udi in the tenth century called the Caucasus the "mountain of languages." He wrote "it contains many kingdoms and nations and each of them has a king and a language different from that of the others."[60] These are mutually unintelligible languages, not dialects, although of themselves historically they tended not to define anything like a modern concept of ethnic identity.[61] Even in the twentieth century the Caucasus had a greater diversity of languages and races than any comparable territory anywhere else in the world.[62] Kennan landed in Dagestan, the very heart of this ethnic mosaic, which today claims at least forty distinct languages grouped into three main families—Caucasian, Altaic, and Indo-European.[63] The very name of Dagestan, formed from the Turkic root "dag" (mountain) and Persian word "stan" (a land or territory), attests to the the mixed ethnic and linguistic influences in the region.

Lying just north of Azerbaijan, Dagestan occupies about one-seventh of the coastline of the Caspian Sea. Although a little smaller than West Virginia, the territory's physical geographically is quite varied, with the

---

60. V. Minorsky, *A History of Sharvan and Darband in the 10th–11th Centuries* (Cambridge: W. Heffer and Sons, 1958), 143. Among the most useful, broadly conceived histories of Dagestan is M. G. Gadzhiev, O. M. Davudov, and A. R. Shikhsaidov, *Istoriia Dagestana s drevneishikh vremen do kontsa XV v.* (Makhachkala, 1996), which repeats to a considerable degree the early material in Akademiia nauk SSSR, *Istoriia Dagestana*, 4 vols. (Moscow: Nauka, 1967–69), but at least begins to move away from the distortions imposed by Soviet Marxist historiography which are so prominent in the latter. Such distortions diminish the otherwise very informative material in the relevant sections of the two volumes of *Istoriia narodov Severnogo Kavkaza* edited by A. L. Narochnitskii: *Istoriia narodov Severnogo Kavkaza s drevneishikh vremen do kontsa XVIII v.*, ed B. B. Piotrovskii (Moscow: Nauka, 1988); and *Istoriia narodov Severnogo Kavkaza (konets XVIII v.–1917 g.)*, ed. A. L. Narochnitskii (Moscow: Nauka, 1988).

61. Wixman, *Language Aspects of Ethnic Patterns and Processes in the North Caucasus*, 100.

62. Richard Pipes, *The Formation of the Soviet Union: Communism and Nationalism, 1917–1923* (Cambridge: Harvard University Press, 1964), 16, cited in Wixman, *Language Aspects*, 5.

63. For a map, see Chenciner, *Daghestan*, 302.

regional differences in part explaining the historic patterns of cultural diversity. The flatlands of northern Dagestan, which narrow to a ribbon along the southern coast, have invited invasion and settlement by Turkic peoples from the steppe; the first of those empires to compete for control of the territory was the Khazar state in the seventh century. The Khazars' main rivals in the Caucasus were the Arabs, but like subsequent invaders from the south, they were hindered by the mountains, which cut across the Caucasus practically to the shores of the Caspian. In the thirteenth and fourteenth centuries, the Mongols of the Golden Horde in the North competed successfully with the Mongol Ilkhanid State in the Middle East for control of Dagestan. With the disintegration of the Mongol empire, the Caucasus next became a battleground between the Ottoman and Safavid empires. By the beginning of the second half of the sixteenth century, when it had conquered down to the mouth of the Volga River, Muscovite Russia also became involved in North Caucasian politics.

What did all this mean for the peoples of the North Caucasus? To a considerable degree they were able to maintain at least political autonomy. The Turkic Kumyks established local power in the northern coastal regions of Dagestan by the beginning of the sixteenth century and attempted to extend their control into the highland interior. The Kumyks had a complex feudal system consisting of a princely clan—the *shamkhal*—and their vassals, the free, noble agriculturists, or *uzden*. Below them were nonnoble peasants assembled into so-called free societies (*jamaat*) and, at the bottom of the heap, slaves.[64] According to the mid-seventeenth century Ottoman traveler Evliia Chelebi, the shamkhal's Dagestan included seven khanates.[65] As the Safavids and Ottomans both discovered, the mountainous terrain of the region effectively precluded any outside power from gaining control. The shamkhal's capital of Tarku

---

64. This brief summary follows closely Chantal Lemercier-Quelquejay, "Cooptation of the Elites of Kabarda and Daghestan in the Sixteenth Century," in Broxup, ed., *The North Caucasus Barrier*, 31.

65. Evliia Chelebi, *Kniga puteshestviia (Izvlecheniia iz sochineniia turetskogo puteshestvennika XVII veka): Perevod i kommentarii*, part 2, *Zemli Severnogo Kavkaza, Povolzh'ia i Podon'ia,* Pamiatniki literatury narodov Vostoka, Perevody 6 (Moscow: Nauka, 1979): chapter 4.

on the coast (near Kennan's Petrovskoe, the Makhachkala of today), was modest by the standards of major contemporary Muslim cities; the Sunni Muslim religious authorities exercised considerable power and enforced a kind of puritanism that discouraged lavish court display and focused the ruler's attention on defending the faith, especially against the Persian Shiites. Although the enemy was different, perhaps one can see in a foreshadowing of the situation that would develop under the so-called Murids, the Muslims who led the fight against Russian control in the nineteenth century.

Just as the terrain could help the shamkhals defend Dagestan against exterior foes, it also could limit the degree of their control within the region. Even though they were relatively accessible from the coast, the highlands formed a distinct region politically and culturally. Evliia Chelebi may have been misled by his focus on the shamkhal and his capital, for by the early seventeenth century, at best he exercised nominal control over the khanates of the interior. The most important were the Avar khanate, with its capital at Khunzakh (visited by Kennan in 1870), and the Kaitag and Tabasaran khanates in the south.[66] But their power was so limited that the Avars, based along the Avarskoe Koysu River, could not even control Andi, just north of the next major river, the Andiiskoe Koysu, and in peacetime probably even then only two to three days' journey away (as it was in Kennan's time). Indeed, to cross two ridges and a river put one in a different world. At the same time though, Dagestanis have many affinities with the other mostly Muslim peoples of the North Caucasus—the Chechens, Ingush, Adyge and Balkars. These connections would become particularly important during the wars against the Russians in the nineteenth century.

With the exception of a small community of Tats, so-called "Mountain Jews," who apart from religion have much in common culturally with their neighbors, Dagestan is overwhelmingly Muslim. The process of Islamization was a gradual one: it took from the first Arab incursions in the eight century until the fifteenth century for Islam to spread throughout Dagestan, but even then there were substantial regional differences in religious practice. There are even reports of several of the khans worshipping one day with the Christians, the next with the Mus-

66. Lemercier-Quelquejay, "Cooptation of the Elites," 33–34.

lims, and the next with the Jews.[67] Religious traditions deep in the mountains were largely unaffected by Islam; syncretism between Islam and pre-Islamic tradition was common. If there was religious friction, often it was stronger between Muslims of different persuasions than between Muslims and non-Muslims. To the degree that there was any written language in Dagestan which cut across linguistic and cultural barriers, it was Arabic, but most of the peoples of the region remained without their own written language until modern times.

It is important not to read the earlier history of Dagestan and its relations with its neighbors through the lens of the nineteenth-century Russian wars with the Murids or late twentieth-century propaganda about Muslim fundamentalism in the context of the Chechen war. The lines of division and alliance in the Caucasus did not consistently follow boundaries between faiths. The example of the relations between Christian Georgians and the people of Dagestan is a case in point and very relevant to what Kennan witnessed.

GEORGIA AND DAGESTAN

There are many similarities between the political history of Georgia and that of Dagestan, since what we may now perceive as a single independent state with a sense of national identity in fact historically has been a political and cultural mosaic. In the case of the Georgians, their location south of the Main Caucasus Ridge (in what we term Transcaucasia) helps to explain much of their history down to modern times, for they were continually involved with the empires to the south and west. It was only on the eve of the modern era that Russia became an important factor in their history.

Georgians have tended to think of themselves as a Christian outpost beset by hostile Muslims, although history suggests that the situation is substantially more complex. The Georgians adopted Christianity in the fourth century (more than half a millennium before the ancestors of the Russians converted!) and came to recognize the Orthodox supremacy of Byzantium. Their unique alphabet was developed apparently as a means

---

67. Minorsky, *A History of Sharvan*, 168; W. Barthold and A. Bennigsen, "Daghistan," *Encyclopaedia of Islam*, vol. 2 (Leiden: E.J. Brill; London: Luzac, 1965), 85–89.

to help them combat the cultural influence of Sasanian Iran; thus they became one of the first peoples in the Caucasus with a written literature. The medieval Georgian kingdom reached its peak in the early twelfth century under King David the Builder, who even managed to extend his dominions from eastern Anatolia to the shores of the Caspian at Derbent, the fortified key to the passage from Persia into southern Dagestan.[68] Georgian culture, as consolidated in that period, had "affinities to both the Byzantine West and the Iranian East," and the towns in particular were cosmopolitan centers.[69] At the time David conquered Tbilisi (the modern capital), it had been a Muslim town for four centuries.

Political unity crumbled in the aftermath of conquest by the Mongols in the thirteenth century, and by the end of the fifteenth century the country was divided into three main kingdoms and many smaller principalities. It should not surprise us that the subsequent fate of the easternmost of these kingdoms, Kakhetia, was most frequently tied to Persia, since Georgia's eastern kingdoms geographically connect most logically not with the Black Sea but with the Caspian. Although there were periods of Ottoman Turkish domination, "Iranian power and cultural influence dominated eastern Georgia until the coming of the Russians" at the beginning of the nineteenth century, and we even see instances of conversion to Islam by members of Georgian noble families.[70] An important aspect of this eastern orientation was the close connection of eastern Georgia with the flourishing trade through the silk-producing centers of nortwestern Iran and up along the Caspian shores, a trade which often ensured the prosperity of eastern Georgia at times when the rest of the country struggled.

The eastern orientation of Kakhetia was mirrored in a western orientation of the western highlands of Dagestan, although modern histories often distort the relations between Georgia and Dagestan in curiously opposite ways.[71] The Georgians emphasize hostilities and terrorization

---

68. David Marshall Lang, *The Georgians* (New York: Praeger, 1966), 111–13.

69. Ronald Grigor Suny, *The Making of the Georgian Nation*, 2d ed. (Bloomington: Indiana University Press, 1994), 38.

70. *Ibid.*, 48.

71. See, for example, the sweeping claim by David Marshall Lang (*The Last Years of the Georgian Monarchy, 1658–1832* [New York: Columbia University Press, 1957], 188)

of Georgian Kakhetia by Dagestani slave raiders and even today look down on Dagestanis as primitive and backward Muslims, an attitude that Kennan clearly encountered. Soviet-era histories were prone to emphasize brotherhood of Caucasian peoples against the outside forces that wished to subject them.[72] The real history probably is a mixture of both.

Over the course of their long histories, these neighbors have traded with each other and interacted extensively. Metalwork and carpets from Dagestan could be found in the bazaars of Tbilisi, a great commercial city in the early medieval period.[73] From the time of David the Builder, Georgian currency was traded in Dagestan; his coins, uncovered by archaeologists, can be seen today in Makhachkala museums. Dagestani trade with Georgia followed two main routes, one being to the south along the Caspian to Derbent and then west, avoiding the mountain highlands.[74] For western Dagestan though, Kakhetia was a much closer trading partner than were the Caspian towns of Dagestan. Most trade between Kakhetia and western Dagestan went over the Vartashan and Kodor passes. The Bezhtans traded meat and dairy products for, among other things, salt, corn, wheat, and fresh produce.[75]

For centuries Georgian culture was a major force in Dagestan. At least up to the fourteenth century, Georgian Orthodox Christianity was expanding into Dagestan, spread through schools established by Georgian missionaries.[76] Its replacement by Islam was a slow process extending over several centuries. The Georgian language became a lingua franca of the area of western Dagestan bordering on Georgia, where the resi-

---

that raids from Dagestan "reduced the population of Georgia by 50%." Lang dwells on the raids to the exclusion of any other discussion of Dagestan-Georgian relations. Clearly there *was* a slave trade, which could reach massive proportions as a consequence of war. See Lemercier-Quelquejay, "Cooptation of the Elites," 31; also, see below. Contrast the Makhachkala-published history of Dagestan, which skates over the subject of the raids: Gadzhiev et al., *Istoriia Dagestana*, passim.

72. See, for example, the two-volume *Istoriia narodov Severnogo Kavkaza*.
73. Lang, *The Georgians*, 104.
74. Gadzhiev et al., *Istoriia Dagestana*, 368.
75. AN SSSR, *Istoriia Dagestana*, 1:386.
76. Even today, in Bezhta, near the Georgian border, crosses can be found on old graves in the cemetery. Minorsky cites sources supporting the theory that Christi-

dents of various auls spoke languages so different they could not understand each other.[77] Even in the Avar areas of Dagestan that are now Muslim, Georgian influence can be seen in the roots of personal names, and a number of distinguished Georgian families trace their lineage to Dagestan.[78]

The major shift in this pattern of mutually beneficial interactions seems to have begun in the seventeenth century, when the Georgians attempted to free themselves of Safavid control. The Persian response was to crush the rebellion with help from their Dagestani Muslim allies. The major blow fell in 1615, resulting in tens of thousands of Georgian deaths and some 100,000 of the inhabitants of Kakhetia being taken off to Persia in captivity.[79] In the aftermath of this disaster, increasingly for the Georgians the support of Orthodox Russia came to be seen as the means to free themselves from Muslim rule.

RUSSIA COMES TO THE CAUCASUS

The history of Russian expansion to the south has often been distorted by the lens of the kind of anti-Russian sentiment that George Kennan first attempted to combat and then helped propagate during his career. In the conventional telling, Russian expansion was the result of carefully planned policies guided by the center, resulting in the subjection of peoples on the periphery who played no role in determining their own fate. As we are increasingly appreciating, the creation of empire was fraught with uncertainties, the center often did not control very well even its own officials on the periphery, and the whole process was very much one of negotiation.[80] The establishment of Russian control in the Caucasus is an excellent example.

---

anity survived among the Avars down to the fourteenth and fifteenth centuries (*A History of Sharvan*, 99), while according to the *Encyclopedia of Islam*, Kubachi "preserved traces of Christianity until the end of the eighteenth century" (Barthold and Bennigsen, "Daghistan," 86). See also Gadzhiev et al., *Istoriia Dagestana*, 339, 365–68.

77. Wixman, *Language Aspects*, 112.
78. AN SSSR, *Istoriia Dagestana*, 1:215.
79. Suny, *Making of the Georgian Nation*, 50.
80. See, for example, Thomas M. Barrett, "Lines of Uncertainty: The Frontiers of the North Caucasus," in *Imperial Russia: New Histories for the Empire*, ed. Jane

INTRODUCTION

Russia first gained a foothold in the North Caucasus some decades after the taking of strategically important Astrakhan, which controlled the outlet of the Volga River to the Caspian Sea. Russian forts were established on the Terek River in 1587, on the northern border of Dagestan, the Sunja, in 1590, and the Sulak in 1591. The first Russian military actions against Dagestan came at the request of neighboring Georgia—ironically, because Georgia would itself be subsumed eventually by Russian power. Tsar Feodor in 1594 responded to the plea of King Alexander II of Kakhetia and sent 7,000 men against the shamkhal of Tarku. The tsar's troops were cut to pieces, as were two forces sent ten years later by Boris Godunov, with the result that the Russians withdrew to Astrakhan.[81] For the rest of the seventeenth century, the Russians provided at best moral support and political refuge for Georgian princes, since the empire had many more pressing concerns.

It was only after he had successfully concluded his war against Sweden that Emperor Peter the Great turned toward the Caspian. In 1722, he personally led a campaign that seized Derbent, Tarku, and Baku, and in 1735 a Russian fort was established at Kizlyar. Later that same year Empress Anne, Peter's niece, withdrew her forces to the northern bank of the Terek at Mozdok, north of present-day Groznyi, but from that point on the Russians would never take their eyes off the Caucasus.

Burbank and David L. Ransel (Bloomington: Indiana University Press, 1998), 148–73 (reprinted from *Slavic Review* 54 [1995]: 578–601), and idem, *At the Edge of Empire: The Terek Cossacks and the North Caucasus Frontier, 1700–1860* (Boulder: Westview, 1999). Sean Pollock's soon-to-be-completed Harvard Ph.D. thesis on Russian-Georgian relations in the late eighteenth and early nineteenth century, previewed in a paper at the 2000 Annual Convention of the American Association for the Advancement of Slavic Studies, develops in important ways some of these themes.

81. Moshe Gammer, *Muslim Resistance to the Tsar: Shamil and the Conquest of Chechnia and Daghestan* (London: Frank Cass, 1994), 1. A useful overview of key phases in Russian relations with the North Caucasus is Marie Bennigsen Broxup, "Introduction: Russia and the North Caucasus," in *The North Caucasus Barrier*, 1–17. Lemercier-Quelquejay sees in the aftermath of the disaster of 1604 the beginning of the Sunni Muslim *jihad*, or holy war, against the Russians, their Georgian allies, and, the Shiite Persians(!), although one may wonder whether finding the roots of the confrontations of the late eighteenth and early nineteenth centuries is justified in the given instance. See Lemercier-Quelquejay, "Cooptation of the Elites," 41.

They picked off Dagestan's northern neighbors one by one. Those they were not able to coopt and force off their lands by resettling Cossacks on them, they destroyed and drove into exile by scorched earth warfare. From the conquest in the 1770s of the Nogai people who lived in the steppes, the Russians maintained steady pressure against the inhabitants of the North Caucasus until they caved in one after another.[82] It is questionable whether Russia could have subdued the Caucasus had there been a unified Caucasian resistance, but there never was. Instead, there were separate resistance movements of the principal ethnic groups.[83]

By the end of the eighteenth century, incursions from both the Avars of Dagestan and the Persians to the south squeezed the Georgian kings reluctantly into Russian arms. In 1800, King Giorgi XII of Kartlo-Kakhetia appealed to the Russian emperor to accept direct authority over his kingdom. In the space of the next decade, the other Georgian kingdoms of Mingrelia, Imeretia, and Guria become Russian protectorates.

THE MUSLIMS OF THE NORTH CAUCASUS CONFRONT THE RUSSIANS

While the Russians and Georgians negotiated the latter's acceptance of Russian sovereignty, in Dagestan and the neighboring Chechen regions to its north a coalition of fighters known as Murids tenaciously resisted the tsar's armies through the middle of the nineteenth century.[84] Lieutenant-General Grabbe, posted to the Caucasus in 1838, boasted that the armies under his command would defeat these mountain peoples "no matter how dear our troops have to pay for it."[85] They paid dearly.

The Murid resistance began as a religious movement intended to

---

82. John F. Baddeley, *The Russian Conquest of the Caucasus* (London: Longmans, Green, 1908), 45.

83. Pipes, *Formation of the Soviet Union*, 17.

84. The word "murid" refers to a disciple of a Sufi sheikh or elder; its generalization to all the peoples of the North Caucasus who fought the Russians is misleading. See Gammer, *Muslim Resistance*, 315 n. 17.

85. Moshe Gammer, "The Siege of Akhulgoh: A Reconstruction and Reinterpretation," *Asian and African Studies* 25 (1991): 104.

establish a purified version of Islam. Although Sufis (Sunni Muslims practicing a mystical form of Islam) had long been established in parts of Transcaucasia, the most important period of their expansion in the north was marked by the uprising led by Sheikh Mansur in 1785–91.[86] A Chechen, he proclaimed himself a Sufi leader or imam, and declared a jihad that for a time united much of the Muslim North Caucasus before he was finally captured by the Russians. Tradition (probably inaccurate) attributes to Sheikh Mansur the spread of the most important Sufi orders in Dagestan, the clandestine and strictly orthodox Naqshbandiya. There is good reason to believe that this order's success was in large part a response to the brutal policies of the Russian General Ermolov, who was appointed Viceroy of the Caucasus in 1816 and whose campaigns against the mountain peoples illustrated all too well the second half of his oft-quoted and contradictory self-assessment: "Out of pure humanity I am inexorably severe."[87]

Shamil, the most famous and successful of the Naqshbandi imams, or spiritual leaders, proved to be a military mastermind.[88] A native of Vedeno, through which Kennan would pass on his return to Dagestan,

---

86. For a brief account, see John B. Dunlop, *Russia Confronts Chechnya: Roots of a Separatist Conflict* (Cambridge: Cambridge University Press, 1998), 9–13; for details, Alexandre Bennigsen, "Un mouvement populaire au Caucase à XVIII siècle: Page mal connue et controversée des relations russo-turques," *Cahiers du monde russe et soviétique, 5/2 (1964): 159–205*. The history of Sufism in the Russian Empire and Soviet Union is only beginning to be properly studied. For a rather dated but pioneering treatment, see Alexandre Bennigsen and S. Enders Wimbush, *Mystics and Commissars: Sufism in the Soviet Union* (London: C. Hurst, 1985).

87. Baddeley, *Russian Conquest,* 97. As Gammer puts it, "Ermolov pushed the Mountaineers into the arms of the Sufi order, which would unite and lead them in a thirty-year-long struggle against the Russians" (Moshe Gammer, "Russian Strategies in the Conquest of Checnia [sic] and Daghestan, 1825–1859," in Broxup, ed., *The North Caucasus Barrier,* 49). For the early history of the Naqshbandiya in the North Caucasus, see Gammer, *Muslim Resistance,* chapters 5–7. Gammer stresses that the early Naqshbandi leaders were initially less interested in a jihad against the Russians and more concerned about strengthening true Islam among the mountain peoples.

88. The most thoroughly documented account of Shamil's rule and the Russian campaigns is that by Gammer, *Muslim Resistance.*

INTRODUCTION

Shamil narrowly escaped death in 1832 while fighting for the first of the imams against the Russians.[89] Two years later, the second imam was assassinated, and Shamil succeeded him. It was with the authority of rigid interpretation of *sharia* (Muslim law) that Shamil enforced discipline among the villages and towns. He burned villages that failed to unite behind him. He had his own mother flogged (saying Allah told him to do it) when she relayed the plea of war-exhausted Chechen villagers to allow them to make peace with the Russians, but insisted on absorbing most of the punishment himself when she fainted after the first five strokes.[90] In paranoia, he put out a contract on the life of his deputy Haji Murat.[91] With his harsh modus operandi, Shamil managed to ally the numerous hostile khanates against a common enemy. In desperate battles waged from the precipitous mountains and gorges, with partisan strategy and hand-to-hand fighting, over the span of more than twenty years Shamil's Murids repulsed Russian forces that hugely outnumbered them.

One of his most publicized exploits was a raid in 1854 across the mountains into the Alazan Valley of Georgia, where he captured the great-granddaughters of the last king of independent Georgia and took them back to Vedeno.[92] Although the princesses were exchanged for ransom, this event alienated potential support Shamil might have had from Britain, Russian's enemy in the Crimean War. Vedeno would be one

---

89. Vedeno seems to breed Caucasian military leaders. In recent times it has been the home of both Chechen leaders fighting against the Russians and Chechen commanders fighting for them. See Patrick E. Tyler, "Chechen Warlord Fights Rebels for Mother Russia," *New York Times,* National ed., July 18, 2001, A4.

90. Gammer, *Muslim Resistance,* 239–40.

91. See Gammer, *Muslim Resistance,* 216, who suggests that Haji Murat's military victories may have gone to his head and thus provoked Shamil's decision. Haji Murat had served the Russians before becoming one of Shamil's most successful commanders, and he now fled back to them in 1851. He is perhaps best known from Tolstoi's romanticization in his beautifully written novella *Hadji Murat,* which condemned the Russian war for conquest. Regarding it, see Layton, *Russian Literature and Empire,* chapter 15. On Shamil's dealings with his subordinates and allies, see the summary comments in Gammer, chapter 22.

92. See Baddeley, *Russian Conquest,* 449–55; Gammer, *Muslim Resistance,* 270–74. The account of the princesses' captivity, originally published in Russian, appeared as well in English and French.

INTRODUCTION

*The storming of Shamil's fortress, Gunib, in 1859.
Painting by Gruzinskii. Evgenii Markov,* Ocherki Kavkaza.
Kartiny kavkazskoi zhizni, prirody i istorii, *2nd ed. (St. Petersburg
and Moscow: M. F. Vol'f, 1904): following p. 512.*

of the last of Shamil's strongholds to fall in the final Russian campaign which led to his capture in 1859. His surrender at Gunib (another of the places Kennan visited) is widely considered the end of the Caucasian Wars, even though in subsequent decades there were outbreaks of rebellion. Although it is no more than chronological coincidence, Kennan's venture into Dagestan coincided with Shamil's last journey, when he was allowed by the Russian authorities in 1870 to make the pilgrimage to Mecca. He died in the holy city of Medina a few months after Kennan had returned to the United States.

INTRODUCTION

ALL THE TSAR'S MEN

The 1840 edict establishing a Russian provincial government in the Caucasus abolished local laws, and decreed that all business would be conducted in Russian, and all positions of authority filled by Russians.[93] This attempt at centralized administration failed miserably. In 1844, Tsar Nicholas I appointed Mikhail Voronstov "Viceroy (*namestnik*) of the Caucasus." Vorontsov, in contrast to the heavy-handed and disorganized administrators who preceded him in the Caucasus, proved a practical and flexible administrator who sought to adjust imperial rule to local conditions.

Kakhetia and the other Georgian kingdoms all had large classes of landed aristocrats. The Russian imperial state sanctioned serfdom and recognized these local nobilities. A cornerstone of Vorontsov's policy was to forge bonds with the Georgian elite by assimilating them into the imperial leadership, and he replaced many Russian officials in the Caucasus with locals.[94] Russia ran its operations in the region from Tbilisi, and viewed Georgia, a Christian nation, as a natural ally in its struggle to subdue the Muslims of the North Caucasus. Many Georgians fought with the Russians against the mountain peoples. Vorontsov's policy of appointing Caucasian officials was continued after his tenure, and a large number of Georgians worked in the Russian territorial administration. Grand Duke Mikhail Nikolaevich, younger brother of Tsar Alexander II, held the post of viceroy from 1862 to 1882. Kennan's arrival in Temir Khan Shura in 1870 coincided with a visit by the Grand Duke, which meant that Kennan had difficulty finding lodging there.

A KAKHETIAN FAMILY

In Dagestan following the Russian conquest, there were more Georgian administrators than Russians. Prince Giorgi Davidovich Jorjadze and his elder brother Dimitri were two of those nobles in the service of the

---

93. L. H. Rhinelander, "Russia's Imperial Policy: The Administration of the Caucasus in the First Half of the Nineteenth Century," *Canadian Slavonic Papers* 17/2–3 (1975): 231.

94. L. H. Rhinelander, *Viceroy Vorontsov's Administration of the Caucasus*, Occasional Paper 98 (Washington: Kennan Institute for Russian Studies, 1980), 2–3, 17.

tsar. The Jorjadze brothers had a house in Temir Khan Shura,[95] then the most important town in Dagestan, and Prince Giorgi Jorjadze happened to be setting out for Kakhetia the same week Kennan was searching for guides there. The prince initially resisted taking Kennan along, expressing concern that he would not be up to the difficult route across the crest of the Caucasus. The young adventurer told him he had weathered rough travel in Siberia and Kamchatka and persuaded him to change his mind. Kennan admired the older man and was grateful to him for letting him join his party. He did his best to make a good impression, even when he suspected the prince was testing his courage by declining to dismount on narrow mountain trails where a fall would mean death for both horse and rider.

Locals exceeded their usual generous hospitality, greeting the prince with special pomp and ceremony and providing abundant meals and boisterous entertainment. Kennan observed Prince Jorjadze perform his official function hearing and mediating disputes.[96] Traveling in his entourage allowed Kennan to "get inside" the communities they stopped at, particularly as the prince willingly explained local customs to the curious American. Since he need not worry about the exhausting travel tasks of finding lodging and horses and planning the next leg of the journey, Kennan could spend his energies studying local culture.

The first snows caught them on the Dagestan side of the Caucasus crest, and their final day over the mountains was a cold and trying one.

---

95. His gravestone in Gremi church states that Dimitri Davidovich Jorjadze, 1821–1883, was a *Tainyi sovetnik* (privy councillor) to the tsar. According to Glavnoe arkhivnoe upravlenie pri Sovete ministrov SSSR et al., *Lichnye arkhivnye fondy v gosudarstvennykh khranilishchakh SSSR*, vol. 1 (Moscow, 1963), 232, Dimitri Davidovich was chief of staff to the head of civil services for Dagestan Oblast and a member of the Council of the Chief Administration for the Caucasus. Although on page 119 of the journal Kennan mentions calling on Jorjadze and his brother, it is not clear whether the latter is Dimitri and whether they actually met. Given the presence of the Grand Ducal party in town at the time, Dimitri likely was there. *Lichnye arkhivnye fondy* also lists possible sons of Giorgi Davidovich—Dimitri Georgievich and Il'ia Georgievich—estate owners in Tbilisi Province (1:233).

96. Kennan notes that in Bezhta, the prince communicated with locals in Georgian. It is not clear whether he used Georgian throughout Dagestan, spoke local languages himself, or relied on interpreters.

INTRODUCTION

Reaching the top of the Caucasus, Kennan looked down to the west at the warm, inviting Alazan plain and the cluster of three villages that were traditionally Jorjadze lands: Eniseli, Gremi, and Sabue. He thought he was seeing heaven.

If ever there was a land meant for growing wine it is Kakhetia. All local families produce their own wine, storing it in great clay vats dug into the earth and ladling it into jugs for drinking with meals. The Jorjadze clan was instrumental in establishing the vintner's craft on a scale larger than the traditional local production of wine for one's own household and friends. Several Jorjadzes traveled to France for apprenticeships, bringing European winemaking practices back to the abundant valley. At least one of them married a Frenchwoman.[97] At Prince Jorjadze's estate, where "wine flowed like water," Kennan relaxed for five days before traveling on alone. The journal is the richer for his having journeyed with the Georgian nobleman and personally experiencing the Dagestan-Georgian divide—the Muslim-Christian watershed that has figured so prominently in the history of the Caucasus.

97. Liziko Bagration, 1996 interview. Six-page memoir handwritten by Nina Jorjadze (daughter of Zakaria Jorjadze) at Kvareli museum.

CHRONOLOGY OF KENNAN'S 1870 TRAVELS

THIS IS BASED IN THE FIRST INSTANCE ON KENNAN'S unpublished journal, since the chronology in his later writings, both published and unpublished, is often misleading and can be presumed to be less accurate. Even in the journal there are problems, especially at the start, with days of the week and dates not always seeming to match. More often than not it is days or even weeks later that he records information about a location through which he had passed earlier. In some instances, his record of a visit to a particular village occupies entries written in the course of several days as he moves on. In transcribing his journal, I have left the "datelines" for the entries as he gives them. As my annotation indicates, in most cases they tell us where he wrote the entry, not the place about which he is writing.

Once Kennan set out with Prince Jorjadze from Temir Khan Shura, the party seems to have moved rapidly, only occasionally spending more than one night in a single location. Nearly a week is unaccounted for between the earliest possible date of his departure from Temir Khan Shura and his presence in Gunib. The distance presumably could have been covered in two to three days. His indication that the prince expected him to leave on short notice, the very next day after they met, may be an exaggeration, since he wrote that decades after the event. Very likely he spent the additional days in Temir Khan Shura rather than spending several days in Gunib. In his later writings about his time in Tbilisi, he seems deliberately to have conveyed needing an extra week there than in fact he actually spent, since this reinforced his dramatization of his struggle with the local bureaucrats.

In addition to the journal, I have consulted the typescript "Chronology" of Kennan's life compiled by his wife, Emiline Rathbone Weld Kennan, Kennan MSS, LC, Box 88 (see Travis, *George Kennan*, 27–28 n. 7), which is not always reliable regarding dates for the Caucasus trip.

June 11, 1870	Leaves New York on steamer *Cambria*.
June 23	Arrives Ireland.
June 24	Arrives Glasgow.
June 30	Leaves Scotland for St. Petersburg on the *Thomas Wilson*.
July 6	Arrives St. Petersburg.
Aug. 21–24	Visits Finland and waterfalls at Imatra, returning to St. Petersburg at midnight on Aug. 24.
Aug. 27	Departs for Moscow, arriving next morning.
Sept. 1	Departs for Nizhnii Novgorod on train, apparently arriving Sept. 2.
Sept. 5	Leaves Nizhnii on river steamer *Tsesarevna Mariia*.
Sept. 7	Samara.
Sept. 8	Saratov. Writing about stop in Samara.
Sept. 9	Passes Chernyi Iar.
Sept. 10	Arrives at Astrakhan; departs Astrakhan on Caspian steamer.
Sept. 11	Arrives Petrovskoe (Makhachkala).
Sept. 12	Visits *aul* (mountain village) on outskirts of Petrovskoe.
Sept. 13	Travels to Temir Khan Shura (Buinaksk).
Sept. 22?	Departs Temir Khan Shura in company of Prince Jorjadze, spending night in Dzhengutai.
Sept. 23?	Dzhengutai to Gunib.
Sept. 24	In Gunib.
Sept. 25	Travels from Gunib to Gochob.
Sept. 26	Travels from Gochob to Tliarata, where he is hosted by the Naib.
Sept. 28	Travels from Tliarata to Bezhta.
Sept. 29	Spends day in Bezhta.

CHRONOLOGY OF KENNAN'S 1870 TRAVELS

Sept. 30	Travels Bezhta to Eniseli in Kakhetia, ascending along Bogos Ridge and passing Mount Nunikas-Tsikhe (3119 m) on Main Caucasus Ridge.
Oct. 1	First day at house of Prince Jorjadze in Eniseli.
Oct. 5	Leaves Eniseli for Tbilisi, spending night in Telavi.
Oct. 6?	Telavi to Tbilisi.
Oct. 10	Leaves Tbilisi for Vladikavkaz, taking Georgian Military Highway through the Darial gorge.
Oct. 13	Arrives Vladikavkaz.
Oct. 19	Departs Vladikavkaz.
Oct. 20	In Samashki.
Oct. 22	Departs Groznyi; arrives Vedeno.
Oct. 23	In Vedeno.
Oct. 24	Travels Vedeno to Karachoi, where spends night.
Oct. 25	Crosses the Andi Range via Kharami Pass (2177 m) above Lake Izalam (Kezenoiam) to *aul* of Andi.
Oct. 26	Travels Andi to Botlikh, over Rushukha Pass (1715 m).
Oct. 27	In Botlikh, takes day trip up river Andiiskoe Koisu.
Oct. 28	Travels Botlikh to Klokh (Tlokh), passing through Preobrazhenskii Fort just outside Botlikh; crosses the Khonkhodatel (Kvankhidatl) bridge.
Oct. 29	Travels Klokh to Khunzakh.
Oct. 30–31	In Khunzakh.
Nov. 1	Travels Khunzakh to Antzakhoul (Untsukul), passing through Tsatanikh.
Nov. 2	Travels Antzakhoul via Gimra to Temir Khan Shura.
Nov. 3	In Temir Khan Shura.
ca. Nov. 5–7	Leaves Temir Khan Shura for Vladikavkaz, probably via Khasvaiurt.
Nov. 19	Leaves Vladikavkaz for Poti, presumably retracing his route through the Darial gorge to Tbilisi and traveling through Kutais.
Nov. 26	Arrives Poti.
Nov. 28	Departs Poti on Black Sea steamer *Vesta*.
Nov. 29	At Ordu on Anatolian coast.
Nov. 30	At Samsun on Anatolian coast.
Dec. 2	Between Inebolu and Istanbul; arrives Istanbul.
Dec. 15	Arrives Vienna.

Dec. 17	Departs Vienna via Cologne, Brussels, and Ostend to London.
Dec. 24	Arrives London.
Dec. 27	Sails on *Siberia* from Liverpool.
Jan. 1871	Returns to Norwalk, Ohio.

THE CAUCASUS WRITINGS OF GEORGE KENNAN

[For each section of Kennan's writings, the source is indicated at the beginning in brackets. "Journal" (with page numbers) refers to the two-volume Caucasus journals, Kennan MSS, LC, Box 13.]

JOURNEY TO THE CAUCASUS

[Letter from New York, Kennan MSS, LC, Box 13, folder 1870–1878]

New York, June 10th, 1870

I RECEIVED MORRILL'S TELEGRAM YESTERDAY AFTERnoon just as I was about to engage passage for him. It wasn't exactly the fair thing for Ed to back out within 48 hours of the time for sailing when he had assured me positively that he would go and would be here Friday. A man ought to know whether he is going to Europe or not before he gets his passport and packs his trunk and I didn't dream for a moment that he would fail to go. However it don't [*sic*] make any difference to me. I've travelled alone before and am fully capable of taking care of myself. Company is nothing but a luxury which can easily be dispensed with.[1] Ed is foolish to give up as good a chance as this of seeing the world, but of course he knows his own business. He told me only a week ago that he had between $600 and $700 of his own in his pocket and

---

1. Ed Morrill was apparently Kennan's last attempt at a traveling partner. Earlier he had recruited John Hay, the writer who would go on to became an important statesman. To Kennan's chagrin, Hay backed out of the expedition when he became engaged to be married. Kennan, "An Island in the Sea of History," 1095.

that his Father had promised to let him have $400 more. I presume the last $400 has failed to come, but if I had made my arrangements to go abroad I would go if I didn't have more than enough to get to Liverpool and back.

I engaged first class passage yesterday afternoon in the steamer "Cambria" of the Anchor Line which sails tomorrow at twelve o'clock for Londonderry and Glasgow. We are forwarded to Liverpool on another steamer. I was fortunate enough to get one of the most desirable berths in the ship which had just been given up by another man on account of a death in his family. The Cambria is a fine ship and I have no doubt I shall have a pleasant passage. Putnam has agreed to publish my book, giving me 10 percent on retail sales. It will be out in September.[2] They were very complimentary—said they considered my three magazine articles among the best they had ever published. Putnam Jr. goes to London on the 20th and is going to arrange for an English edition of a few hundred copies if possible. Prospects for the sale of a couple of editions are fair. I concluded finally to carry most of my money in the shape of French exchange payable at sight to my order. This I can get cashed advantageously at St. Petersburg. What money I take will be in greenbacks and English notes and silver.

[Journal, 1–20]

Inversnaid Loch Lomond, Friday June 25th, 1870[3]

WE MADE THE FIRST LIGHT ON THE N.W. COAST OF Ireland about half past twelve Wednesday morning June 23rd. I went to bed about half past eleven and didn't get up till ten minutes after three. The sun had already risen, the sea was calm, and we were running along a precipitous rocky coast at a distance of perhaps three miles. The scenery was comparatively tame, but of course it seemed beautiful to us after

---

2. Kennan spent July in St. Petersburg completing the writing of *Tent Life in Siberia*.

3. Kennan spent five days in Scotland, sightseeing in Glasgow and Edinburgh, as well as making a side trip to Loch Lomond.

having been ten days at sea. Many of the passengers were already on deck and cries of "Look here!" and "Oh, just look there!" were heard from all directions as we swept past some particularly bold precipice or came in sight of some quaint wall-surrounded light house, or tumble-down stone terrace, which a vivid imagination could turn into a ruined castle. The rocky wall of the coast swept gradually backward and upward into a long range of high treeless hills, broken now and then by wide, sloping valleys which presented a curious and beautiful patchwork of cultivated fields, dotted here and there by smaller one-story stone houses with terraced roofs, whitewashed neatly and occasionally covered with climbing vines. The colors of the irregular patches on the hills and in the valleys were various shades of green, brown, and yellow ascending as the soil was newly plowed, covered with wheat or oats, potatoes or with wild mustard which mingled everywhere with the grain.

About five o'clock we passed a large island on the left crowned with a large lighthouse and an extensive white wall, and then rounding a long rocky point over which the surf was breaking furiously we entered the harbor of Londonderry. As we sailed up its west bank at a distance of only a hundred yards, the scenery was much finer than I had anticipated. Every bluff was guarded by a lighthouse of whitewashed stone surrounded by high walls and the channel was marked out by red iron buoys. The land sloped upward from the water's edge to a height of perhaps 800 feet in a very gradual ascent dotted with handsome stone villas, chequered with all sorts of geometrical figures in fields of oats, potatoes and yellow mustard & [. . .] by occasional dark green patches of bushes or clumps of trees. A pilot came off to us as soon as our approach was signalized from the high bluff at the entrance of the harbor and under his guidance we steamed on up the coast. About four miles from the heads we passed a very picturesque old castle founded on an immense rock, half of it still used and crowned with cannon and half ruined and covered with a dense vivid green sheet of ivy. Here we fired a gun as a salute to the old worlds and caught our first sight of Moville—a small village on the west coast where the Anchor Line steamers land passengers. A small steamer here came off to us and the Mr. Guckins (younger and older), the red haired Scotch lady and several others of our steamer acquaintances bid everybody goodbye and went ashore. Our parting with young Mr. Guckin—Sweet William as Dolph called him and "Sissy" according to the girls—was very affecting. Dolph would shake hands with him for about two minutes and then spit on his hands and go at it again and when he became temporarily exhausted by the violence of his exertions Marshall[4] and I would relieve him, and between us all Sweet William was shaken as thoroughly as a bottle of cough mixture before he finally made his escape.

As soon as we had transferred our passengers we steamed out to sea again with a fair wind and ran close along the north coast of Ireland till almost noon. Just as we approached the celebrated Giant's Causeway the steward's bell rang for dinner or rather lunch and we passengers looked at each other in consternation and perplexity. Should we lose our lunch and see the Causeway or lose the Causeway and get our lunch? Either was a hard alternative. The aesthetic gave way to the practical as it always does and we went below to lunch. I believe it is Goethe who says "take care of the Beautiful for the useful will take care of itself," but with all deference for such high authority I would say "take care of the useful (that is lunch) and let the beautiful (the Giant's Causeway) take care of itself." We gobbled down an indigestible lunch of hot biscuit, cheese, sardines and cucumbers as rapidly as possible and ran up on deck just in time to see the long series of precipitous basaltic cliffs known as the Causeway. The giant I believe is dead—at any rate we didn't see him. The causeway looks a little like the Palisades on the Hudson but it is considerably higher, flatter on top and is of a columnar formation. In many places it looked like gigantic organ pipes five or six hundred feet high standing side by side in a long wall. Some of the gorges between the bluffs of the Causeway are grand. From a height of about 500 feet there is a steep descent of debris scantily covered with grass and bushes and the whole beach is covered with immense picturesque masses of rock which have broken off and fallen from the cliffs above. Among these the sea must foam and thunder magnificently in a storm.

After passing the Causeway there was nothing particularly notice-

---

4. Kennan describes these acquaintances he made on the ship: J. H. Dolph was an animal painter and A. S. Marshall a young man from New Jersey who "was going to try to see Europe with even less money than I had . . . and agreed to go with me as far as St. Petersburg." MS Autobiography, 330.

able until we entered the Clyde. We passed Fair Head and the Island of Rathlin soon after noon, rounded the point of Cantive and entered the Firth of Clyde about noon. There is a conical rocky island in the middle of the Firth below Arran which would make a splendid pedestal for a gigantic monument or statue. A statue about 60 feet high of Walter Scott or of Burns could be seen for thirty or forty miles in any direction and would be a magnificent tribute to the genius of the men who have made Scotland famous. We began to see great numbers of steamers as we went up the Firth as well as many sailing vessels and pleasure yachts. The scenery as we came abreast of the island of Arran was very fine—unsurpassed by anything which I have ever seen in America. The background was made up of wild ragged mountain peaks on the Island and the foreground resembled the most beautiful slopes of the Hudson, indented with bays, and sprinkled everywhere with beautiful villas and white stone houses in patches of yellow and light and dark green.

After passing the Isle of Arran we entered the River Clyde proper and began to see the bold slopes and peaks of the Highlands in the north. All the foreground on the west and north side of the river resembled cultivated gardens and on the east we passed many old ruined castles. About seven o'clock we approached Greenock and heard the multitudinous hammering which announced the great ship-building region of the Clyde. Steamers with red pipes and black pipes whizzed past us continually at the rate of 15 miles an hour with loads of pleasure-seekers from Glasgow and Ayr. Great merchant ships passed us slowly and solemnly in tow of little black tugs, and as we came abreast of Greenock, we went into a perfect swarm of shipping of all kinds from the great black outlines of the iron man-of-war Black Prince down to the tiniest row boat. Here we stopped to wait for the tide to enable us to go up the river. Black Prince—marines in scarlet coats pacing along a platform hung over her side, long spars run out at her bows for boats, handkerchiefs waving from her port holes beside the muzzles of cannons, neatness of her rigging.

Greenock was a black, smoky, picturesque place with narrow streets and quaint buildings, flanked on both sides by ship yards full of iron steamers in the stocks and noisy with the sound of thousands of hammers, the hiss of escaping steam, and shrill whistles from innumerable steamers passing and repassing in the river. About half past seven the tug Flying Cloud made fast to our bows and the Flying Mist to our stern and we went on a flying trip up the river. Just above Greenock we saw for the first time the bold blue outlines of Ben Lomond—the celebrated peak of which I used to read in Scott's poems twelve years ago while sitting on the roof of the bathing house over the "back stoop" of our old home in Norwalk. I can still remember the old, coverless, mould-spotted volume, *Lady of the Lake,* which introduced me to the world of poetry as I sat cross-legged on that bathing house. The north bank of the river rising in a long gentle slope to a great ridge still presented a succession of beautiful pictures.

River in this vicinity very narrow. Bell-shaped buoys with crosses on them to mark channel. People strolling along banks. Dolph kisses his hand to all the ladies, gentlemen accompanying them look indignant. Tall chimneys of Glasgow in sight. Steamer touches bottom several times. At 9:00 PM, Wednesday, June 23rd we make fast to a long stone pier covered with a shed. Crowd in the street at the end of the pier watching us. Leon pelts men on the pier with lemons, aided and encouraged by Dolph and the minister. Intoxicating influence of land. Extravagant behavior of passengers. Custom house officers come aboard and make superficial examination of baggage. Marshall goes to engage cab and then he and I with Dolph, Leon and the Misses Beany and Pirnie,[5] take up our baggage and walk. Pile into a little cab with one horse, stow away our baggage on top and start through the streets, Dolph and Marshall waving their hats out of the windows and singing the Star Spangled Banner. Waverly Hotel. Waiter in white vest and dress coat. No rooms. Hotel on St. George's Square. Leon and ladies go in search of cigars. Billiard Saloon. "Most magnificent one this side of the Atlantic." Small balls and sharp ended cues. Poor playing.

Glasgow—very clean, well-paved streets. George's Square very fine place, ornamented with monument and statue to Scott. English barber shops. Dolph pays a sixpence for the privilege of shaving himself. No barbers chairs, no nothing! No office at hotels. Eat in coffee room. No registry books. Lady clerks. Glasgow Cathedral—fine old early Gothic structure. Ancient tombs with quaint inscriptions. Fine painted win-

---

5. All acquaintances he made on the boat.

dows. Gloomy crypts. Dolph sings the Star Spangled Banner over the tomb of some old Scottish Knight.

Steamer Thomas Wilson, *Baltic Sea, South of Gottland, July 3rd, 1870, Sunday* [6]

MARSHALL AND I, FINDING THAT OUR MONEY WAS running low, concluded to defer for the present all further examination of Edinburg [*sic*] and make our way as quickly as possible to St. Petersburg. We had only about 15 pounds left altogether and not being able to identify ourselves in Scotland could not avail ourselves of our drafts. We accordingly bought second class tickets to Hull by the North British railway and left Edinburg Tuesday night. There is nothing particularly noticeable about the scenery along the road south of Edinburg. For a short distance it is hilly and in the vicinity of Berwick Upon Tweed the road runs along the cliffs over the sea and presents some fine views. At Newcastle Upon Tyne we stopped twenty minutes and I got out for some refreshments. The depot was built very much in the style of the one at Cleveland except that it had three spans instead of one and was wider. The bridge over the Tyne is said to be a very fine piece of iron work but it was so dark that we could see little of the place. About three o'clock we reached York where we had to wait half an hour for the train to halt. It was already getting light and sparrows were beginning to sing in the green fields around the station. I am mistaken about waiting at York. It was at some junction, I forget its name, a short distance S.E. of York. I believe Milford Junction.

At 4:30, soon after sunrise, we entered the fine stone depot at Hull, walked up a long, deserted street in search of a hotel and finally by dint of long, continued banging at the door of the "Paragon" we roused a sleepy "Boots," got in and went to bed. The rooms were all named after distinguished men as "Wellington," "Nelson," etc. At half past eight we were called, had a fair breakfast of coffee, bread and butter and steak and set out in search of the steamer office. We were told to our dismay that the boat carried no second class passengers, that the first class fare was 5.3 pounds besides 6 a day for meals, and that she would not sail until the

---

6. July 3 was in fact Saturday.

next morning. I had strong misgivings that we couldn't rouse that amount between us but I didn't stop to find out, but went down to look at the steamer which lay among a throng of other vessels, mostly sloops and tub-shaped schooners at the west dock. She presented a scene of great activity and apparent confusion. Large gangs of men with huge steam winches and cranes were hoisting in railroad iron and boiler plates at three immense hatches. Carpenters and blacksmiths were sawing, hammering and filing in all parts of the ship and the decks were littered up with coils of rope and bits of rope yarn, chains, blocks of wood, water, railroad iron and all sorts of rubbish.

We went on board and tried to find the cabin but it was locked up and the steward gone. After watching them load iron a while we went back to the Paragon to talk over the situation. Upon examining our purses we found that we had not money enough left to pay for a first class passage to St. Petersburg. Here was a dilemma. We had money enough but it was in drafts and as we had no means of identifying ourselves we could not get it. Fortunately I had a letter of introduction from Mr. Palmer to a Mr. Ritso in London and in case of emergency I could go there and get my draft cashed. We finally concluded that if we could get steerage passage we would go in that way. Marshall goes to office to ascertain—makes arrangements for 2nd class £33 & 6, & 6d a day for provisions. Learns he must have passport vised[7] by Russian consul. Start in search of him. Wilberforce's monument "Place of Green Ginger"—Engine for High Street—Are told to go down one street and we will come to another with a high stone building on one corner with an arched front and after describing the situation of this street very minutely our informant tells us, "That ain't it." Then he describes another. That ain't it either. Finally he tells us to go straight h'on h'as far h'as h'ever we can and then turn to the left. That's it. Consul named Helmsing. Says he can't vise the passport till it has been vised by American consul. Start in search of the latter. Find him in Parliament [. . .]. He can't do anything more than write on it "produced at American consulate such and such a day" and affix the consular seal. For this he will charge us $2.00. We don't know whether this will answer or not. Go back to Russian consulate to find out. He gives us a blank to be filled up by the steamer owners Wilson and Sons certifying

7. To get a visa stamp.

that he knows us and is satisfied that we are what we represent ourselves. Back again to American consulate for vise. Consul takes us for sailors. Down again to steamer office. Wilson after some explanation good-naturedly signs the document. Knows we are Americans because we pronounce z "zee" instead of "zed." Back again for 3rd time to the Russian consulate. This time get the passport fixed and go to RR station to get my trunk and have it sent aboard. Trunk labelled "unclaimed baggage" and just about to be sent to York. Redeem it by paying tuppence. Find no steward on steamer and put baggage in wheel house. Watch loading of ship awhile and then go up town and take Scotch lunch in a bakery, price 11 pence. Two tarts, two round currant cakes and a cheese cake. More walking about city. Back again to steamer. Down town again for tea. A cup of tea and eight slices of bread for sixpence. Stroll around the piers and look at shipping. See them get in the Spanish steamer Zaire. Back to ship at dark. Wait for steward till 11:00 PM when it begins to rain. Take refuge in warm galley. Steward comes, lets us into cabin and we go to bed.

[Journal, 21–28 (pages 24–26 are the ship's log, mostly illegible, and have been omitted)]

On Deck, Gulf of Finland, July 5th, 1870

WAKE UP ON THURSDAY MORNING JUNE 30TH[8] AND find ourselves going out to sea. The Wilson is a brigantine rigged steamer of 1400 tons with a high deck from stern post to wheel house just forward of smoke stack, a low deck midship and a high forecastle. She steams about 9 knots in still water. Is very wide in proportion to length and has large capacity for cargo. Our cabin is just forward of and under the wheel house at the breast of the poop deck. It is elegantly filled up with rosewood and curly maple, marble mantle with a gilt mirror over it, velvet sofas and two tables. Has accommodations for about 25 passengers. She has 3 hatches, one long and one poop deck, one long one on main deck and a small one forward. Has one donkey engine, 2 winches and 3 steam cranes for hoisting in cargo, and carries six boats. She has on board 2500 tons of iron and a deck load consisting of 4 portable engines and furnaces and a huge boiler

8. Another discrepancy in date: June 30th was Wednesday.

weighing 22 tons. Cargo carried to Russia consist generally of iron and machinery then from there of linseed, hemp, flax and some grain. Only one passenger on board besides Marshall and I. He is an Englishman aged about 37 with blue eyes, light brown hair and whiskers and moustache. Wears striped flannel shirt, open black vest, tweed mixed pants with black stripe, blue coat with black binding, light colored stuff round topped hat with string tied to shirt buttons. Was terribly frightened the other night when it blew and he thought we were going down. Ship rolled heavily and the furnaces got adrift. Marshall and I dressed hastily and ran up on deck and found him there pale and agitated, holding on to the handle of the door at the head of the cabin gangway and looking as if he expected every minute would be his last. Furnaces were soon secured and ship which had been hove to again went on her course. Englishman sat up till 4 o'clock and then went to bed with his clothes on. When rallied next morning, in his timidity he declared that he wasn't hafraid. "It was honly hemotion which hI couldn't suppress." Today he says it was "biliousness." Biliousness has to cover a multitude of sins!

Northern coast of Denmark which we made on Friday PM, was low and sandy scantily inhabited. Passed two fleets of fishing smacks just at sunset. Great quantities of sail near Skan light. Counted 97 at one time. This whole route swarms with ships. Have not been out of sight of sails since leaving Hull. Sunday morning Marshall waked me with "get up and see Hamlet's castle!" "Hamlet who?" "Hamlet, Prince of Denmark. Get up!" I got up under protest and looked at it. It was the castle at Elsinore north of Copenhagen. Shivered around with a piece of hard bread in my hand for half an hour and then went to bed again determined to let Copenhagen go. Marshall got up again to look at it and called me but I ignored the summons. At 5 PM we passed Bornholm Island a large fine looking island well cultivated and thickly inhabited with a picturesque ruined castle of great extent on a high projecting bluff or islet. Imagined it to be an ancient habitation of the Vikings. Monday saw nothing particular. Ate, smoked and slept as usual with infinite relish. This morning we entered the Gulf of Finland and have been in sight of land all day though at a considerable distance. Passed Reock this PM. It looked like a pile of buildings on a high mound with a massive church a little to the eastward with a tall steeple. It is now 11:15 PM and we are nearly up to the Island of Hogland, a long strip of high land with a light house at each end. Marshall has gone to bed but the Englishman is still on deck and I shall stay up till we pass the island. Shall reach Cronstadt [=Kronshtadt] tomorrow.

[Journal, 29–37]

Hotel de Angleterre, St. Petersburg, Wednesday, July 6th, 1870[9]

I WOKE THIS MORNING ABOUT HALF PAST SEVEN and thrusting my head as far as I could out of the dead light I smelled the fresh earthy odor of the land and although I could see none on our side of the ship I knew that we must be close in to Cronstadt. It was rainy and misty when I went on deck and I could only see that we were running along between two green shores dotted here and there with churches, houses and light towers. After breakfast we caught sight of the two great forts which guard the entrance from the sea and behind them of a dense, leafless forest of shipping. Passing a light ship a few miles farther on, a pilot came off to us in a small boat and under his guidance we steamed swiftly in. The approaches to Cronstadt are very strongly fortified. The huge stone fort which we passed on our right has 50 casement guns and some in parapets and the moon-shaped fort on the other side has about 80 embrasures in 3 tiers. Besides these there are many other stone fortifications farther in and new ones are in process of construction on the left. Huge square pen filled with ships packed in like sardines in a box. Stop a few yards from a wooden wall inside which are steamers and ships. Custom house officers come off to us in small boats without number together with obsequious soldiers with bags full of huge tongs for sealing every thing up. Baggage tied and sealed with metallic seals pressed between the tongs.

Uniform of Russian officers long gray coat with cape gathered at back and white caps with little elliptical medal in front. Small steamers come alongside. Passports examined and stamped. In about an hour we

---

9. In both St. Petersburg and Moscow, Kennan stayed in hotels called *Hotel d'Angleterre*, something which suggests late nineteenth-century Russian aspirations to cosmopolitanism. The hotel in St. Petersburg is now part of the elegant Hotel Astoria, located next to St. Isaac Cathedral.

get on board one of the small steamers and take refuge from rain in a little cabin about 12 feet by 6 with sofas along sides. Little boat pitches about so as to suggest sea sickness. Finally start. Scrape [*sic*] acquaintance with Russian soldier who amuses me with story of how 36 Englishmen once piled into that little cabin and drank beer. Reach another pier at a little distance and are transferred to another steamer, the Vesta. Watch scenes in the pier till boat starts. Russian moozhiks[10] with long sheepskin coats, ragged unkempt beards, and long hair dirty, ragged, and miserable. Isvoscheks[11] in blue coats with skirt like a dress dragging on ground and inverted spittoons for hats. Isvoschecks' droshkies[12] look like toy wagons very small and low with four wheels about 18 inches in diameter and hind ones two feet. Russian officers in long gray cloaks with capes white and black, caps bound with scarlet and swords dragging along ground. Moozhiks kissing each other goodbye.

Room in Gorkovaya Street, Friday, July 8th, 1870

STEAMER "VESTA" SWIFT RIVER BOAT WITH LONG low cabin below aft, no skylight but side windows just above waters edge. Front part of boat railed off for moozhiks, who sit there on benches in the rain eating bread, drinking tea and smoking. Some of them look like picturesque old ruins. Charity boxes for the children of pilots. Start up river and are driven below by rain. Come up again as we approach city and see the great gilded dome of St. Isaacs.[13] Seems to me to be on wrong side of river. White and black numbered buoys mark out channel. Numerous sunken wrecks in river. Land on Vassilli Ostrof near Nikolaevskoi Most.[14] Go into custom house, large empty room with long

---

10. *muzhik:* peasant, man.

11. *izvozchik:* man who transports loads and passengers around by cart, a common sight in imperial Russian cities.

12. *drozhki:* a kind of carriage.

13. One of the largest domed cathedrals in Europe, St. Isaac Cathedral still dominates the skyline of central Petersburg. Its construction began in 1818, following plans by August Montferrand.

14. *Vasilevskii ostrov* (Vasilii Island) in the Neva River. Nicholas Bridge across the Neva, named for Emperor Nicholas I—now the Lieutenant Shmidt Bridge.

wide table running whole length. Baggage very superficially examined and satchels not looked at at all. Go out to engage carriage and are completely bewildered and mixed up by crowd of clamorous drivers who want us to take their respective vehicles. "Bahrin! Pazholtia! Sooda! Sidemsa Poiadem! Oo menya kraseevwe oodobnia kareta!"[15] Kraseevwe oodobnia kareta [the "nice-looking" carriage] consists of two forward and two hind axles and wheels connected by two long, bare poles—a sort of wooden isthmus which the traveler is supposed to straddle. Commissioner of Hotel de Angleterre, a man in gray overcoat and cap trimmed with golden cord, comes to the rescue and carries us off in triumph in a carriage overawing the moozhiks by talking to us in German which he supposed to be our native tongue. Admitted to the Hotel by a uniformed Swiss who greets us with a profound bow and a raising of the hat valued at one rouble.

Sunday Evening, July 10th, 1870 12:10 AM

I HAVE JUST RETURNED FROM THE SUMMER GARdens where there has been a grand illumination and goolania[16] for the benefit of the sufferers by a famine in Finland. We started out with Cumming[17] for guide about half past nine and even at that late hour it was so light that an illumination seemed to be entirely unnecessary. Walking along the quay of Vassilli Ostroff, we crossed at the Palace bridge and went up the Palace quay to the Letni Sad,[18] meeting everywhere crowds of tired pleasure seekers on their way back from the garden. Paying our 20 kopecks, we entered at a gate guarded by policemen into a fairy land of trees, grass, shrubbery, colored lanterns, brilliant costumes, music and Bengal lights. The trees and alleys everywhere were hung with great

---

15. Barin! Pozhaluista! Siuda! Sidemsia, poedem! U menia krasivaia udobnaia kareta!: "Sir! Please! Over here! Climb in and we'll go! I have a nice-looking, comfortable carriage!"

16. *gulian'e*: promenade.

17. A half-English, half-Russian friend who lived in a comfortable house on Vasilevskii Ostrov.

18. Summer garden.

festoons of prismatic colored lanterns, the walks were edged with millions of small bell-shaped colored lamps and crowded with people, bands of music, and choruses of singers were in full play at a dozen places at once. Bengal lights were burning, throwing weird green, red and blue glare through the forest and over the thronged paths, imitation fountains of colored lamps stood here and there at the corners and the whole garden was a fairy land of music, lights, motion, and picturesque costumes. Costumes—Hussars, riflemen, glittering helmets, Circassian uniforms, Turks, Persians, English, Americans, Bedlam of language. Ladies in white. Boys in fancy costumes. Houses for exhibition of lottery prizes at corners of principal alleys.

Restaurant illuminated with green lights hung under the eaves and around the windows. Crowds outside eating and drinking at little tables. Sign "American drinks—Raspberry, Lemon, Vanilla, Orange." Lake illuminated with rows of colored lanterns beautifully reflected in the water. Ship hung with lanterns in the center. Band plays Zheezn za tsara[19]— tremendous clapping of hands and shouting. Peasants drunk on grass. Two of them use another for a pillow. Fellows courting their girls around the trunks of trees. Central alley completely thronged. Chorus of Russian singers sing national songs and dance with tambourine. Mingled applause and hisses. Come out at half past eleven. Carriages of nobility outside. Pedlars. Boy offers us box of matches and calls on us to "sustain commerce." Man selling snuff by the pinch. Engage gondola-shaped boat and row down Neva by moonlight and daylight together. Shining spire of fortress against light sky of northern twilight. Moon over dome of Isaac's Church and on water. Meet many parties in boats. Peasants singing at a distance.

[Excerpt from MS Autobiography, Kennan MSS, LC, Box 88, 338, 358–61]

Toward the end of July, Marshall returned to western Europe. After his departure, I left the Hotel d'Angleterre and went to stay with Cum-

---

19. *Zhizn' za tsaria*: An 1836 opera by Mikhail Glinka, *A Life for the Tsar* is considered to be the beginning of Russian national opera. Presumably a promenade band would have been playing its popular overture.

ming. I devoted a part of every day to study, and accomplished, in the aggregate, a good deal of work. I wrote there the concluding chapters of *Tent Life in Siberia*, which I had not been able to finish at home, on account of the interruptions and distractions of the lecture field; and I took up, and virtually learned again, the Russia language. The knowledge that I had of it when I returned from Siberia was very imperfect and inadequate, and had been gained, almost wholly, by listening to the talk of Cossack and Kamchadal dog-drivers by the camp-fire. I had no aids to the study of Russian, and the best I could do was to make a vocabulary and grammar of my own by writing down in my notebook, in English letters, the words that I heard, and then framing rules for the inflections by a rude process of observation and induction. I did not even know the Russian alphabet, and it was weeks after my arrival in St. Petersburg before I could find a word in the dictionary, or give more than a guess at the proper way to spell it. I could use it colloquially, but that was all.

When I could recognize on a printed page the words that I had known for years by sound, I bought a Russian grammar. I opened it to the chapter relating to the declension of regular nouns. There were two or three pages of exceptions to the rule about to be set forth, and at the end of them the author announced that "with the above exceptions, all of the regular nouns in the Russian language may be declined in accordance with one or another of the following twenty eight paradigms." That ended Russian grammar for me. If there were twenty eight different declensions for regular nouns, there must be twice as many for the irregular. I decided that I would decline my Russian nouns in only one way: I would decline to have anything whatever to do with them in their grammatical aspect. Life was too short to be frittered away in learning terminations for seven cases in twenty eight different declensions. I have hardly looked into a Russian grammar from that day to this, and yet, I have gained a fairly adequate knowledge of the grammatical structure of Russian speech. I do not know a single rule, but I have studied good models until I have acquired an extensive vocabulary and some familiarity with the art of putting words together in grammatical form.

[Journal, 38–86]

Vweborg [=Vyborg], Finland, Aug. 21st, 1870[20]

WELL! I'VE GOT ONCE MORE INTO A STRANGE COUNtry and I feel about as helpless as if I had no tongue at all. The one I have is certainly of no use to me here. I left St. Petersburg this afternoon at ten minutes past five for a short excursion to Vweborg and the Falls of Imatra and I have succeeded in getting thus far on my way without much trouble. The drive from Hotel Kaiser to the station of the Finnish RR was a very long one, at least 4 miles, by way of the Palace Bridge and quay and the bridge next but one below it to the other side of the great Neva. The Finnish RR is a new one only completed to Vweborg within the past year but its stations are finely built and its cars the most luxurious I have seen in Russia. I came 2nd class—fare 2.40 roubles, and the accommodations were better by far than our first class. Seats put back to back, eight in a compartment, windows large of plate glass, upholstery gray. Backs of seats higher than ones head. Not many passengers. Priest and his wife who sat opposite me met friends at 2nd or 3rd station from Petersburg. Jolly crowd of old ladies. Ask me questions about stations which of course I can't answer and I tell 'em that I'm an American. Sensation! Manage to strike up conversation. In 2 or 3 more stations they all get out. Train stops only a minute and they all tumble out one after another head over heels. Old lady shouts to me as the train moves off and wants to know if that's the way they do in America!

Country along road very thinly inhabited and little cultivated. Alternate forests of pine and silver birch and swampy meadows. Moss in some of these meadows richly colored red, green and yellow so that ground looks as if covered with a Brussels carpet. Land generally low and no high hills at all. Occasional glimpses of the gulf. Curious stations or rather watch houses along RR. No door in front except a little square one right under the peak of the roof reached by a stairway parallel with the wall. Entrance to house from behind. Make acquaintance of young

---

20. A trip to Vyborg and Imatra Falls required no visa because Finland was at the time under Russian rule. The region was annexed by the Soviet Union at the beginning of World War II and remains part of the Russian Federation.

student from Vweborg Academy and get information about Vweborg and Imatra. Reach Vweborg and drive to Ehrenberg Hotel. Can't make anybody but porter understand anything. Ask for tea and they give me vodka. Drink the vodka out of spite and demand tea in all the languages I know. Dutch brings it. Woman comes in again and addresses the clerk very energetically with frequent repetition of the word Hannah. I hope Hannah will hurry up. At last boy appears with tea. Clerk tells him Hannah and he carries it out again. Hannah is a curious word. Wonder what it means. Give up finally in despair and prepare to go to bed but [the tea] at last comes. Curious currency here. Copper coin about as big as a cent is ten pennias. Silver coin as big as 3 cent piece—25 pennias. I must have an awful lot of pennias, about 4,657,284 more or less. I shall feel quite rich when I get my money all into Finnish currency. Can't see anything of the town from my window except gas lights and a big church where the bell is just striking ten. Bells strike ten times for ten o'clock here just as they do in an other country. Don't have to get the strokes translated into English before I can know how many there were. Good thing that. I'm off to bed. Wonder how Finnish fleas will go for a change.

Falls of Imatra, Finland, Aug. 22nd, 1870

GOT UP THIS MORNING ABOUT 8 O'CLOCK AND AFTER tea which I succeeded in asking for in Dutch, I took a walk around the town in search of curiosities. There is nothing of any interest in Vweborg except the old fortress which stands at the head of the bay. It is a huge castle built of stone and brick loopholed for cannons and musketry with a high massive tower on the top of which grass is now growing. There are ruins of quite an extensive courtyard back of the castle which appears to have been once surrounded by a wall and defended by a moat. The tower of the castle is much defaced and broken by shot and shell marks but when they were made I don't know. The building can't be very old for it is in a pretty good state of preservation. I saw only one other structure of the same date in the village and that was a large round tower about 30 feet in diameter and 30 in height loopholed for musketry and covered with a conical pointed sheet iron roof which is evidently a recent addition. It stands almost back of Ehrenberg Hotel, is now occupied I believe by the Government. Farther to the eastward is a small ornamental park in which stands a sort of conservatory surrounded by seats where on warm summer evenings there is probably music.

The situation of Vweborg is high and from the sea the view of the town is said to be picturesque. Returning to the hotel I found the dvornik[21] and, engaging him as interpreter, made arrangements for a vehicle to take me to Imatra—62 Verst.[22] They offered me a carriage but I thought I'd be economical and take the ordinary post telegas[23] which I presumed were no worse than those in Siberia previously. Was I disappointed! One equipage which they brought round for me was the worst looking concern that I've ever had to trust my body to yet. A two-wheeled cart just about as big as and very much like a hand express cart with no springs, the boards in the bottom all loose, a simple plank seat so low as to bring my knees almost on a level with my chin. One horse with a rough wooden collar, harness patched up with ropes, two clothes lines for reins, and a white-haired boy about twelve years old dressed in gray coarse coat and pants of coarse toweling and Yakoot[24] boots for driver. The horse looked as if it tasked his strength to the utmost to stand up but as soon as I got in we rattled away over the stony pavements at a very fair rate. People whom we met stared at me as if it was a new thing to see a tolerably dressed and apparently respectable man traveling in such a style. I did feel a little foolish and almost wished I had taken a carriage.

The scenery for the first stage was not remarkable for anything except pine forests, small lakes, hills and enormous red granite boulders. The scenery of Finland in general is decidedly gloomy, especially in such cold gray weather as we have had today. There is no light green foliage or grass to enliven the landscape. All is dark and solemn. The hills are covered with pines which look almost black in the distance and the only openings are small still dark lakes surrounded by huge mossy boulders. The abundance of these boulders is one of the most peculiar features of the country. I saw some today at least forty feet square—as big as a good-sized house lying in the midst of a dense forest and I couldn't but won-

---

21. *dvornik:* doorman.
22. An old Russian unit of distance, a verst is about two-thirds of a mile.
23. *telega:* a wagon.
24. Yakuts are one of the native peoples of Siberia. This probably refers to some fur boots Kennan saw there.

der how and when they came there. It was one of these boulders which was taken as a foundation for the statue of Peter the Great on Admiralty Square,[25] but there are incomparably finer ones ten or fifteen versts from Vweborg. In the first stage from that place there are some fine villas belonging, I presume, to Russian officers as tastefully built as any on the islands in the Neva. At the first post station I found a man who spoke a little Russian and got my large bills changed into 1 mark notes and silver and copper pennias. Had no difficulty in getting horses. As we went farther from the sea the rolling hills became higher and bolder and the

---

25. The famous *Bronze Horseman*, commissioned by Empress Catherine II.

The *"Bronze Horseman"—monument to Emperor Peter I*, St. Petersburg. Hermann Roskoschny, Russland: Land und Leute, 2 vols. (Leipzig: Gressner & Schramm, [1882-1884]), Vol. 2: 57.

scenery finer but it was still gloomy and dark in style. The jolting of the different 2-wheeled carts which I successively tried was almost intolerable notwithstanding the smoothness of the road and before noon I wished I had no more body than a cherub.

The last stage to Imatra I made in a sort of basket on wheels consisting of a wooden frame like a crockery crate, only not half so big, lined with coarse matting. It was a wretched-looking affair. The road everywhere lay through dense pine forests filled with boulders and over a succession of high hills. Noticed four or five varieties of evergreen trees, including most of those cultivated in America for ornament. Passed a number of Finnish villages. Small collections of rude, unpainted, weather-beaten log houses surrounded by fields of rye and potatoes only just in blossom. Finns almost all light-haired (I thought they were dark) and look as much like Germans as anything. They are very different from Russians. About 3 o'clock we began to hear the roar of the Imatra falls and caught our first sight of the Imatra river and in ten minutes stopped at the hotel which has been built on its bank over the fall. I'm tired and sleepy and can't write any more tonight.

Aug. 24th

THE FALL OF IMATRA IS ON THE RIVER VUOKSA which runs out of Lake Saima into Lake Ladoga. It is not properly a fall at all. It is only a succession of tremendous rapids falling through a narrow gorge about 600 feet in length. In these 600 feet there is a descent I should think of 50 and the river which is three or four times as large as the [. . .] is narrowed to a width of 50 feet between granite walls and tumbles down this descent in the finest rapids I think I have ever seen. They are not so extensive of course as those above Niagara, but the volume of water is greater in proportion to the width and it boils and roars through the narrow gorge at the rate of fourteen miles an hour sending spray 30 feet into the air, making a noise which can be heard four or five versts.

There is a hotel built just on the edge of the gorge above the rapids and pavilions commanding the finest views. The scenery in the vicinity is not especially remarkable. If the walls of the gorge were 500 or 400 feet high and there were mountains on both sides the falls of Imatra would indeed be grand, but as it is they are nothing more than fine rapids.

I spent the night in a house adjoining the hotel where rooms are filled up for visitors. I can't say I slept for the fleas murdered sleep but I managed to get through the night. There were gilt-edged pictures of eleven Russian saints over my bed, but they were all powerless against the fleas. The weather on the following morning was cold, gray, and rainy and, after going down to look once more at the falls and strolling up and down the river a ways, I ordered a horse and wagon and started for Vweborg. The vehicles were better than those which I had previously traveled and I made better time. Reached Vweborg in 5 hours. Had dinner there and started for St. Petersburg at 6:30. Made acquaintance of Russian artillery officer. He gave me some facts about Lake Saima. 200 feet above sea. Canal connecting them 24 locks. Finished 1856 and during the celebra-

The Falls at Imatra. Roskoschny, Russland, *Vol. 2: 121.*

tion the old castle at Vweborg burned the last time. Language generally used among higher class in Finland—Swedish, lower—Finnish. Back to St. Petersburg at 12 o'clock at night.

St. Petersburg, Hotel Kaiser, Aug. 27th

LEAVE IN TWO HOURS FOR MOSCOW. LETTERS YESterday from Nelson and Rush. Works in Russian language to buy—Lermontof, Pooshkin, Toorgenieff, Goncharof, Oblomof, Obecknovennia Historia, Tolstoi Lef Voina I Meer, Tolstoi Alexi, Kostomarof's Hist of Russia.[26]

Nizhni Novgorod, Sept. 6th[27]

TOOK BREAKFAST WITH VASSILI AT HOTEL BELLEvue a week ago. Son of Governor of a Province in Poland. Yesterday[28] started at 2:30 for Moscow. Second class cars like Finnish, only not so good. Fell asleep late in night and wake to find sun shining over me. Arrive at Moscow at 10:00 AM. First view of Moscow from station not impressive. Drive to Hotel de Angleterre. Major arrives Wednesday.

26. Mikhail Iur'evich Lermontov (1814–41), known for his stories and poems about the Caucasus, where he died in a duel; Russia's most famous poet, Aleksandr Sergeevich Pushkin (1799–1837), who also was forced to spend time in the Caucasus and wrote about it; Ivan Sergeevich Turgenev (1818–83); Ivan Aleksandrovich Goncharov (1812–91), who wrote the two novels listed here, *Oblomov* and *A Common History* (*Obyknovennaia istoriia*); Lev Nikolaevich Tolstoi (1828–1910), famous for *War and Peace* (*Voina i mir*) and also author of stories about the Caucasus, where he served briefly; Aleksei Konstantinovich Tolstoi (1817–75), author of novels about earlier Russian history; Nikolai Ivanovich Kostomarov (1817–85), prolific historian of early Russian and Ukrainian history. It is not clear which of Kostomarov's works Kennan may have acquired, since apparently his *Russkaia istoriia v zhizneopisanii ee vazhneishikh deiatelei* was published for the first time only a year or two after Kennan's visit.

27. Probably the date can be no later than September 5, if in fact Kennan was writing in Nizhnii, since he left the city on that day. He may well have caught up on his journal on the boat.

28. August 27. A good example here of Kennan's writing his journal well after the events.

Mostly servants all in white linen. Lunch chicken with chopped onions. Soup from shallots with fish pies. Organ playing constantly. Borstch, cold pig with horseradish and cream. Theater in evening. Leave next day for Nizhni. Zoological gardens with Gromska.[29] Have our photographs taken. Gromska homesick. Knows he shall cry when I leave.

Traveling companions to Nizhni: Russian merchant, two young fel-

---

29. Traveling companion he met along the way. Kennan seems to have done a bit of the standard sightseeing. His expense list (see Appendix) suggests he ascended the "Bell Tower of Ivan the Great" in the Kremlin, which commanded the best view of the city.

View of the Moscow Kremlin with Bell Tower of Ivan the Great. Roskoschny, Russland, *Vol. 1: 9.*

lows who speak French, and a woman. Uncomfortable night. Ringing 3 bells before train leaves a station. Nizhni. Drive two or three numbers before find place to stop. Temporary hotels. Room without bedding, soap, or towels. Fleas ferocious. Watermelon unloading from landing place. Immense quantities of merchandise along levees. Immense quantities of Central Asiatic cotton. Bags of dye stuffs. Hotel next door to me combines hotel and anatomical museum. Smoking forbidden in Nizhni. Pedlars in ragged coats, basket shoes, cloths wrapped around legs. Peddling grass, mushrooms strung on strings, bread baked in shape of baskets. Beggars, disreputable monks begging for churches. Bare-headed, long, ragged hair and hands, tin box locked with huge padlock around their necks, small, square board covered with black velvet in their hands. Sakvoyash[30] at their sides and a crooked stick. Beggars without legs, without arms, and with every possible distortion of body at every corner. Woman without legs with one distorted hand and humpbacked man driving around in little 4 wheeled carts with a lame horse singing and begging. Beerzhe.[31] Crowd around it. Skull caps and khalats of Tartars.[32] Tall cylindrical hats without trim, greasy ragged sheep skin coats, swathed legs and basket shoes of Russian peasants. Cutting hair and hunting for fleas in the streets.

Tartar Mosque—round building with a sort of balcony around the steeple where muezzin calls to prayers. Steeple small, round with a crescent on top. Attend prayers at noon. Assemble in 5 mins. About a hundred Tartars in white turbans, fur caps, striped red and yellow khalats. All wear over-slippers which they leave at door. Piles of them on window sill. Interior of mosque bare, cylindrical, with 3 arches on S.E. side

---

30. *sakvoiazh* (from French *sac de voyage*): traveling bag.
31. *birzha:* trading area.
32. *khalat:* robe. The term Tatar has been commonly used for the Mongols of the so-called Golden Horde, successor states to which had capitals at Kazan and Astrakhan on the Volga. Ronald Wixman explains how in the sixteenth to nineteenth centuries, "the term Tatar was used in a general linguistic sense to designate various Turkic peoples, [. . .] and sometimes in an ethno-racial sense to designate peoples that appeared 'oriental'." *Peoples of the USSR: An Ethnographic Handbook* (New York: M. E. Sharpe, 1988), 186. In this instance, Kennan is probably referring to Kazan Tatars.

through which can be seen 3 windows. Floors covered with green beige. Moolah stood and kneeled under the middle arch, facing Mecca and all the worshippers behind him in rows. First they all made a curious gesture to their ears as if somebody was going to box them and they were trying to protect themselves, then the Moolah said Allah il Allah or something that sounded like it and they all simultaneously bent half double as if they were about to begin a game of leap frog. Then they straightened up and their lips all moved as if they were silently praying or repeating verses from the Koran. "Allah il Allah,"[33] said the Moolah again and down they went on their hands and knees and pressed their foreheads to the floor, remaining in this posture about 30 seconds. Allah il Allah—heads upright but still on their knees with toes extended out behind, foot bottom side up. Allah il Allah—and all stood erect.

After a moment's silence, all kneeled again at the signal and held their hands before their faces as if there was something written on them and their lips moved silently as if they were reading it. More kneeling, pressing foreheads to the floor and getting up again. At last the priest turned around face to the worshippers and began a song in which there was very little melody but which sounded very wild and strange. I noticed particularly that the sounds of *l* and *m* were prolonged in a very curious way, especially the latter making a droning sound through the nose. At the end of the song there was another silent prayer kneeling and the service was over. It lasted about 15 minutes and not a word was said aloud by anyone except the "Allah il Allah" of the Moolah. I had never before been in a mosque, but it struck me as being very singular that there was no attempt at ornament in the whole building. Nothing but bare white walls, a floor covered with green beige and one window curtain of linen on the side toward Mecca before which the moolah kneeled. I noticed that the heels of all their boots were ornamented with green embroidery.

Things noticed in Nizhni and at fair.[34] Stone house in the center at the head of the boulevard—first floor occupied by traders in Siberian

---

33. The first "pillar" of Islam, the profession of faith, "Alla Ilaha Illa Allah": There is no God but Allah.

34. Fairs played an important role in Russia's national commerce until late in the nineteenth century. Located for several centuries in Makar'ev, the biggest fair on

precious stones, Circassian and Central Asiatic goods of all kinds. Persian carpets and khalats, kinjals,[35] silver belts, slippers, etc. System of bargaining. Band plays in the open space at the head of the boulevard in the evening. Curious crowd assembles of Persians, Tartars, Chinese, Russian, English and a large deputation from the demi monde. Persian dress—a very tall conical hat of Astrakhan lamb's wool without trim, a khalat of maroon colored cloth open in front showing a shirt of blue silk fastened about the waist with a silver belt. The sleeves of the khalat are so long as to hang below the knees but are scalloped and embroidered at the wrists, cut open with a long slash from the armpit to the wrists to show the under-sleeves of the blue silk shirt. The ends of the khalat sleeves are either allowed to hang down below the hands or are thrown back over the shoulders. Pantaloons are very wide and loose, of dark blue cloth and on the feet are slippers with turned-up toes.

The complexion of the Persians[36] is very dark, as dark as that of American mulattoes, hair black, sometimes tinged with red, eyes black, nose a little aquiline, features generally thin, strongly marked and wild looking. Their finger and toe nails are stained red with henna. The Tartar costumes are various. Generally a cylindrical but low hat of gray lamb's wool, larger at the top than the bottom and under that a small gold-embroidered skull cap. Kaftans of all colors, fitting tightly like a dress over the upper part of the body, gathered in pleats about the waist and hanging like a dress below the knees. Sometimes they are made of cotton cloth striped up and down with red, yellow and white, and have a very fantastic appearance. Pants tucked in high boots or, in the poorer classes, legs swathed in bandages[37] below the knee crossgartered with

---

the Volga was moved in 1817 to Nizhnii Novgorod when burgeoning trade with Asia swelled it beyond the capacity of the Makar'ev Monastery. Anne Lincoln Fitzpatrick, *The Great Russian Fair: Nizhnii Novgorod, 1840–90* (New York: St. Martin's Press, 1990), I, 15–17, 23–24.

35. *kinzhal:* Caucasian dagger.

36. The Volga was Russia's major trade artery, Astrakhan an important transit point for trade with Persia. Persian merchants typically accompanied their goods to the Nizhnii Novgorod Fair. See Fitzpatrick, *The Great Russian Fair,* 80–81.

37. Kennan is referring to wrapping of the calves and feet in lieu of socks, which the Russians call *portianka.*

hempen cords and feet covered with basket shoes stuffed with hay. Some of the poorer Tartars are nothing but rags from head to foot. It would seem impossible that garments could ever in the natural way become so dilapidated. They look as if a lifetime had been devoted to tearing them, repatching them with cloth of all colors and then tearing them again.

Russian costumes are also various. Head covering with the poorer classes is generally a hat shaped like a truncated cone with a brim an inch wide, a sheep skin coat with the tanned side out, buttoned under

Engraving of Tatars. Roskoschny, Russland, *Vol. 1: 224.*

the left arm and black with grease, gathered about the waist and hanging in thick folds to the knees, pants of linsey woolsey tucked in boots or legs from knees down, bandaged and feet covered with basket shoes. Variation No. 1, spittoon-shaped hat and kaftan of coarse gray cloth with skirts dragging the ground. Frayed out and hanging in tatters. Variation No. 2, black caps, red cotton skirts hanging to the knee and gathered about the waist with a belt, dark blue cotton pants very loose and full tucked carelessly in high boots. This is the natural costume of Russian Moozhiks. Variation No. 3, Black cap with glazed visor, red skirt, covered to the waist with a long double breasted vest—shirt tails hanging down from under the vest before and behind. This is the Russian pedlar and fruit vendor's costume. Var. No. 4 Broadcloth cap common pattern, long vest buttoning to throat, no appearance of shirt at all, common cloth pants, good looking kaftan of dark cloth and polished boots. This is the dress of the ordinary Russian merchant.

Women are all dressed very much alike. Calico dress girded tightly about the body above the breasts and below, giving them the appearance of being double waisted, men's boots and gaily colored cotton handkerchiefs tied over their heads. Noticeable things about the fair grounds. Fur row. Tartars whipping out furs. Piles 20 feet square of fur skins—squirrel skins, sables, martens, astrakhan lambs skins, gray, white and blacks. Chinese row. Fanciful pagoda-shaped buildings with turned up corners and plaster figures of Chinamen. Piles of tea sewn up in raw hides and marked with Chinese characters. Retail row across the canal. Hundreds of little board shanties and booths filled with notions, fruits of all types, and nuts. Independent pedlars with their whole stock on a bread board carried by a strap around their necks. Brass jewelry scarfs and cotton handkerchiefs most abundant. Handkerchiefs with railroad maps of Russia on them. Shops for 2nd hand clothes, dresses, and garments of all sorts hanging up outside. Street always crowded with the worst-looking characters in the whole fair. Restaurants, 2 theatres, and the usual side shows.

Volga River below Teloosta [?], Sept. 6th, 1870

LEFT NIZHNI YESTERDAY MORNING AT 11 O'CLOCK. Drive to RR station to get ticket. Meet church procession. Gendarmes on horseback, bare-headed priests in robes of silver and golden brocade, carrying golden crosses and one with a silver bowl filled with water in which he slipped a brush of twigs and sprinkled the crowd and the sidewalks. Deacons carrying banners hung crosswise on long poles, enormous garnet-studded Bibles with golden clasps and pictures of saints four or five feet square in heavy gilded frames. Deacons and priests chanting prayers, great bare headed crowd following on foot. Barbaric splendor of the procession. Don't know reason for it unless town had been so contaminated by the presence of so many foreigners that it was necessary to purify it by sprinkling it with holy water.[38] Although it was Sunday, trade was going on in the fair as usual. Drive from hotel to prestan of Kavkaz[39]

38. The procession Kennan encountered would have been for the eleventh week of Pentecost. Processions of the cross, in which icons were carried, were in fact a normal part of Orthodox ritual.

39. *pristan'*: dock. *Kavkaz*: Caucasus.

Steamer "Colorado" in front of Nizhnii Novgorod Kremlin. S. Monastyrskii, Illiustrirovannyi sputnik po Volge v 3-kh chastiakh *(Kazan, 1884), Pt. 2: 21.*

and Mercury steamers. Shipping in the Oka and Volga all decked with red, white, and blue flags. Steamer Tsezarovna Maria—crowd of Tartars and moozhiks already on board with great many Persians.[40] Go on hurricane deck and watch landing. Young officer going to Caucasus 3 richly dressed young ladies at landing to see him off, 2 probably sisters and one sweetheart. Family servant on old gray-bearded moozhik in sheepskin coat comes running up in haste, face all perspiration, to bid his young master goodbye. Good honest and faithful expression of his face, evidently considers himself one of the family and looks with pride upon the young officer as one of his own children. Officer kisses him goodbye twice, long and affectionately.

Another family scene. Good-looking young man from upper class of peasants, well dressed and apparently intelligent, going away to seek his fortune. Whole family there. Father in black kaftan and cap, long brown moustache and beard. Mother in calico, hair parted neatly and smoothly and half-covered with cotton handkerchief, eyes red with weeping. Grandmother old and feeble, leaning on a stick, tears running silently down her withered cheeks. One sister. All stand looking at the young man as if they never expected to see him again, saying nothing, but crying bitterly, even the father, who tries his best to be composed. Young man himself evidently much affected, dares not trust himself to speak and keeps his face immobile as a statue while his eyes are full of tears. Finally tries to whistle but fails entirely and the nervous working of his fingers and the rising and falling of the lump in his throat show that

40. Kennan sailed on one of the "American-type" steamboats of the Caucasus and Mercury Line. The *Princess Maria,* built in 1867 and some 220 feeet long, was still in service in 1884. A competitor, the A. A. Zeveke Steamship Line, also featured the shallow-draft American-type boats, several of them named for American rivers. For that line's *Colorado,* in front of the Nizhnii Novgorod Kremlin, see illustration, page 77. See S. Monastyrskii, *Illiustrirovannyi sputnik po Volge v 3-kh chastiakh s kartoi Volgi: Istoriko-statisticheskii ocherk i spravochnyi ukazatel'* (Kazan, 1884), pt. 3, first pag.: 43, and second pag.: 8–13, 20–21, which provides schedules for the various Volga lines. The distance from Nizhnii Novgorod to Astrakhan was 2165 versts, covered downstream in 1884 by the Caucasus and Mercury Line boats in somewhat under five days. In 1884 the departure time was still 11 A.M. from Nizhnii Novgorod, and there were three weekly departures, one on Sunday.

he can hardly keep from crying. Beside the gangway stands a swarthy, thin-featured Persian in tall lamb's wool hat, khalat and silver belt, who looks first at the weeping family and then at the young man with a disagreeable, cynical smile like an oriental Mephistopheles. He evidently cannot understand such family affection and considers it foolish. Last bell rings.

General kissing, hat touching and bidding goodbye. Plank drawn in. Peasant family watch the face of their departing son and brother with a devouring intensity, which is almost painful to witness, eyes streaming with tears. Persians now on board with hands full of loaves of bread, watermelons, bottles of preserves, tea and sugar which they have been purchasing for the journey. Steamer moves off. Beautiful views of the two monasteries below Nizhni. White crenellated walls, slender towers and gilded domes half way up the steep precipitous bluff rising out of masses of dark green foliage and overtopped by the hill 3 or 400 feet in height. Picturesqueness of the right bank. Left bank low grassy and shrubby. Stop at several small villages. High bluffs crowned with clusters of log houses, white churches with silver domes. Valleys opening back into interior shaggy with hazel bushes. Broad sloping beach of yellow sand under the bluffs on which stand a few houses reached from the villages above by steep paths.

Picturesque appearance of village on the heights and of groups of peasants in varicolored holiday attire, sitting on the grass at the edge of the bluff watching arrival of steamers. Goats half way up bluff. Peasant women with waists of dresses directly under armpits cut against neck and bordered around throat with blue. Moozhiks all in red shirts and blue pants. Pass river Kerzhentza. Legends of the river—concealed treasures, hermits, etc.[41] See guide book.[42] Village of Leeskova [=Lyskovo] on right bank. Great haunt of the Cossacks of Stenka Rasin.[43] From

---

41. The River Kerzhenets was the location of an important settlement of religious dissenters (Old Believers).

42. It is not clear what guide book he may have had. Presumably not a Baedeker, which was not yet available for Russia and would be published in English only many decades after Kennan's trip.

43. Stenka Razin led the Cossack rebellion along the Volga in 1670–71.

Makar'ev Monastery. Photo © Daniel C. Waugh.

this village are sent yearly 700 vessels with goods, principally grain, to the value of 2 millions of roubles. Gorod[44] and monastery of Makarief on the left bank. Curious, deserted, but oriental appearance of monastery. High, white crenellated walls fixed with loopholes and long slits with round half-ruined towers at the corners. Trees against the walls, half a dozen silver domes over them, low arched entrances, group of peasants around the tower nearest the river watching steamer.

    Nizhni Novgorod fair originally here at Makarief Monastery, now deserted and half in ruins, town sunk into insignificance. Beautiful appearance of river toward evening. Yellow, orange, and red tints of sunset. Vast expanse of still glassy water like lake, high bluffs, green and shaggy with bushes on right sweeping away to the eastward in a succession of bold promontories, bluer and more aerial as they are more distant, till they are lost to sight 30 miles away. Long swells raised by steamer catch reflection of sunset on one side and moon rise on the other and look like alternate waves of deep orange and silver in long regular rows. Air warm and balmy. Richness of color on water as sun sinks. River soon flooded with silver by moon, villages on bluffs hardly to be noticed except

    44. *gorod:* town, city.

for white walls and glittering domes of churches. Fishing stations on left, sort of half under ground and half above ground, lodkas[45] on beach. Fishermen somewhere on broad river but invisible, singing in chorus of peculiar Russian melancholy songs.

On deck above Samara, Sept. 7th

ON THE RIGHT 200 FEET DISTANT IS A RIDGE 500 feet high, rising abruptly from water and from the ridge project massive buttresses between which are steep ravines all densely timbered. Buttresses break off in places in rocky outcropping edges which resembles ruins. Foliage beginning to take on russet hues of autumn. Occasionally, deep wild ravines break through the whole ridge—generally, however only separate buttresses. River a mile in width, smooth as glass, on left low land rising in a long sweep to rolling hills timbered with pines—variegated here and there with yellow wheat fields and dotted with hay stacks. Green domes of a church and a few grass-thatched houses. Far in distance in high hills, domes of Samara. Have just heard that Gen. MacMahon[46] has surrendered with all his forces and that Napoleon is a prisoner.

Below Saratoff, Wednesday, Sept. 8th

NOTHING VERY PARTICULAR TO WRITE ABOUT TODAY. Banks of river since leaving Samara have been generally lower on both sides and right bank almost bare of vegetation. Scenery not remarkable. Rafts 300 or 400 feet long with fire and one or two houses on them floating down river. Lonely floating settlements. Steamers towing 8 or 10 Volga transports. Long with flush deck fore and aft, one mast. High sterned and bowed sloops, square at both ends and covered with wood carving. Barges piled up to height of 20 or 30 feet with Central Asiatic cotton and dye stuff—a peculiar sort of reddish root.

---

45. *lodka:* boat.

46. Field Marshal Marie Edmé Patrice Maurice, comte de MacMahon, headed the army of Napoleon III, who had declared war on Prussia on July 19. The Franco-Prussian War would continue until January, with besieged Paris reduced to eating rats.

Central Asiatic cotton said to be not so clean as American. At Samara I hired a droshky and drove around the town. Guide book said that the droshkys in Samara were bad but cheap. On the contrary, I found them good but dear. My isvostchik wanted a rouble for half an hour's drive. Samara from the river presented rather a picturesque appearance. Situated on a hill rising from water in rather long slope. Camp of white tents above town. Slope of levee covered with piles of wood and a whole village of little booths as big as hen coops for sale of fruits, notions, and market stuff. Village dirty and full of bad smells. Steamer stops an hour. Women at all these prestans bring wood on board and tow boats, men being engaged in the fields.

Description of steamer. Draws 8 1/2 feet water, about 100 or 125 feet long. In the Bow is a small hatchway leading to forecastle. Immediately back of that is the 1st cabin below deck, with a saloon above it, the roof of which makes a sort of forward hurricane deck with railing and seats. Back of this are the wheel houses, over which is the bridge and pilot house and under which is a sky light through which can be seen the machinery. Capt's cabin, machinist's room and office are forward of wheel houses. Bridge is connected with forward hurricane deck by narrow railed bridge. Back of the wheel houses are galleys, etc. and then the whole deck to the very stern is covered with a corrugated sheet iron roof, protected on the sides by canvas curtains, furnished with longitudinal rows of seats and occupied by 3rd class passengers. Near stern is a small house covering gangway to 2nd cabin. 2nd cabin is a large room about 40 feet square with two or three large tables in the center and cots or sofas in a row all around the sides. It looks precisely like a ward in a hospital. You bring your own bedding and pillows, take up a sofa somewhere and sleep without undressing. There are about 20 passengers in the 2nd cabin and we all live, sleep and eat together in the same room.

Meals you order when you want them and somebody is eating or drinking tea all day long. The 3rd class passengers camp out on the upper decks and a motley looking crowd they are. There are a great many Persians on board and I never tire of watching them smoking their enormous nargilehs,[47] talking in their strange gibberish, or saying their prayers on the bridge. With one of them, a merchant from Astrakhan,

---

47. Hookahs, water pipes.

I have struck up an acquaintance. He has written his name in my notebook in Russian and Persian (not Arabic)[48] and has promised to give me his picture.

Persian saying his prayers on the bridge at sunset. Tall, thin black man in high pointed lamb's wool hat, yellowish *khalat* of some cotton stuff and white cotton pants coming down only halfway from his knees to his ankles and leaving his legs bare. Thin, dark features, scanty black beard, shaven head. Black eyes, slightly aquiline nose, gloomy expression of face. Comes on bridge, looks around at sun and at his compass to determine direction of Mecca, spreads down his overcoat on deck, shuffles off his slippers, lays down his compass and a coarse comb and begins his prayers—going through the same motions which I have already described. He bows his forehead when he kneels to the comb and compass. What the comb is for I don't know. Strange appearance which this particular Persian presents as he stands on the bridge in the red light of the setting sun, his thin cotton pants flapping in the wind around his bare black legs and feet, his hands raised before his face, his lips silently moving, his dark, stern features, wearing an expression of intense earnestness. Sometimes steamer goes around a bend while he is praying and first thing he knows he is saying his prayers toward Pekin and not at all toward Mecca.

2 Persians last night were praying together on the same carpet, one put his comb and compass on the deck at the edge of carpet. The other noticed it in the middle of his prayer and they began to dispute as to whether it was orthodox to pray unless the comb and compass were on the carpet. After quarreling a little while about this trifle with a great many significant gestures, they finally went on with their prayers but in the mean time the steamer had turned around so that they were almost [with their] backs to Mecca. Scenery on the right bank of river tonight is very grim again. High columnar cliffs like the Palisades looking white and chalky in the pale moonlight. Narrow strip of beach and prestan at bottom. Passed German colony this PM.[49] Everybody has gone to bed and it's time I went.

48. Was Kennan perhaps not aware that Persian is written in the Arabic script?

49. German colonies on the lower Volga date from the time of Empress Catherine II (1762–96). The German autonomous region of the Soviet era was disbanded by Stalin on the eve of World War II and its inhabitants shipped off to Central Asia.

Below Astrakhan, Sept. 10th, 1870

BELOW TSARITZEN,[50] THE SHORES OF THE VOLGA become lower and lower and there is little in the scenery to describe. Last night about 11 o'clock we came to Chornaya Yar [=Chernyi Iar], a place famous for its watermelons and so far as I know for nothing else.[51] They began at once to bring wood on board and throw it down on the deck with a noise which made sleep utterly impossible. Besides that the fleas kept me awake. As soon as the steamer stopped, one after another of the 2nd class passengers got up and dressed themselves and started out after watermelons. One after another they returned each with a melon as big as his head and some with two or three. Every man as he entered the cabin was greeted with shouts of laughter and questions as to how much he paid for his melons. Prices varied from three kopecks to five. In a few minutes the cabin table was covered with a pile of melons and surrounded by half a dozen passengers who found it impossible to sleep and who concluded to pass away as much of the night as possible in eating melons and telling stories.

I bought a melon for 5 kopecks but it proved to be a green one and I was compelled to accept a part of one of the passenger's. We sat there telling stories and eating melons until two o'clock, when the steamer finally started once more and we went to bed. Today one of our watermelon party, the one whose parting with his family at Nizhni I particularly noticed, was taken with cholera and I'm afraid the poor fellow died. He looked as if he was dying when we left the steamer at Astrakhan. Besides this I learned that the inhabitants of that place were dying of cholera at the rate of 100 a day and of course I didn't eat any more watermelons. Fruit along the lower Volga is very cheap. Melons 3 to 5 kopecks, white grapes 10 kopecks a pound, and pears and apples almost for nothing. Approaching Astrakhan banks low and sandy, look almost as if it was a perfect Sahara back from river. Boats loaded with hay—appear like roofs of houses, loaded upon narrow canoes. Get first sight of cathedral of Astrakhan at 1 PM.

---

50. In the Soviet period, Tsaritsyn was renamed Stalingrad and later Volgograd.

51. Indeed, S. Monastyrskii, *Illiustrirovannyi sputnik*, 295, notes its huge melons but also the fact that there were two fairs, with the largest turnover of any in the province.

Richness of Russian language in oaths and abusive expressions. Kirgis,[52] Tartars, Persians and all the numerous nationalities who have dealings with Russia as soon as they get very angry with their own language and begin abusing their antagonist in Russian.

Caspian Sea—Ocean Steamer, Sept. 11th, 1870

LAND AT ASTRAKHAN. KREMLIN[53] WALL LIKE THAT in Moscow, enormous high cathedral square with H towers at corners. Kalmuck Tartars[54] on landing—very dark complexions, broad faces, high cheekbones, dressed in dirty blue linsey woolsey shirt and pants, feet generally bare, hat fur like Circassian hats only fatter and broader. Find upon landing that steamer leaves for Petrovskoe [=Makhachkala] at 6 PM. Go across with Kavkazets[55] to visit Kalmuck Tartar kibitka tent

52. It was common to refer to Kazakh and Kyrgyz people collectively as "Kirghiz."
53. *kremlin:* fortress.
54. Kalmyks: descendants of Mongols who settled in the lower reaches of the Volga basin. See Wixman, *Peoples of the USSR,* 90.
55. *Kavkazets:* literally, "Caucasian." Kennan evidently made a traveling acquaintance who went by this name.

Kalmyk yurts near Astrakhan. Roskoschny, Russland, *Vol. 1: 260.*

a little like the Korak[56] tent only smaller. Frame of poles in this shape [*sketch*], covering of thick voilock or felt, walled around bottom. Fire on ground in centre hole in roof for escape of smoke. Wooden bowls, iron kettle and domestic utensils all dirty lying in disorder around inner circumference. One bench for bed opposite door piled with furs and dirty quilts. Women dress much like men, hair parted in middle and hanging in two long braids down back, look like Korak women only darker and faces broader. Return with artillery officer and visit Kremlin and cathedral. City horribly dirty and great ponds of water everywhere in street. Don't wonder that they have cholera. Said to be dying at rate of 100 a day there. Sail for Petrovskoe at 6:30. Dispute between 2 Persians.

Priest refuses to give his blessing to a Persian about to sail and the latter gets angry, begins in Persian and ends in Russian. Magnificent sunset, water smooth as glass and all one scarlet and orange glow. In the east full moon. Dark outlines of house against red sunset and barkas[57] with high, triangular, bigger sails. Break fisherman's net. Magnificent moonlight night. Supper on deck of our barge. [. . .] Armenian. Songs, stories. Kavkazets gets very merry. Go to bed at 11 o'clock.

When we awoke on the following morning after leaving Astrakhan we were fairly out of the mouth of the Volga and could see land only in one or two places. About ten o'clock we were transferred to the sea steamer, a long, narrow iron schooner with a high poop deck under which was the second cabin just back of the engine and boilers. The weather throughout the day was very pleasant, but toward evening the breeze from the Asiatic deserts freshened up and by dark it was blowing a stiff breeze. The air was so bad and it was so hot in our cabin that nobody tried to sleep there. Kavkazets stretched himself out among Persians and Tartars on the hatchway amidships and the two young officers and I lay on the poop deck aft and gazed at the stars and the moon till we fell asleep. I can't say that I slept very well. The wind kept blowing my blan-

---

56. The Koryaks are a native people among whom Kennan lived on Kamchatka while surveying for the telegraph line. The yurt that he goes on to describe here is typical of yurts one still finds today.

57. Long boat.

ket off, the ashes they emptied overboard every now and then sifted in my face, and toward morning the ship began to pitch and roll in a very uncomfortable manner. Kavkazets and the young officer with spectacles were both very sick & didn't attempt to get up. "Peter the Great" & I however got up & drank tea but I began to feel symptoms of sea sickness again & had to lie down in the cabin. The steamer rolled and pitched tremendously although the sea was not at all high. About ten o'clock the wind went down, but the ship continued to roll and we passed a miserable day. About noon I caught sight of the high, bold mountains and bluffs of Daghestan and at two o'clock we sailed into the little harbor of Petrovskoe.

Town scattered over a gentle slope rising from the water's edge, backed by a long, precipitous ridge 1000 or 2000 feet in height. Harbor artificial—simply five or six acres of water walled in with massive rocks blasted from the mountains back entrance 100 or 150 yards in width—on the right as you enter stands the lighthouse—a tall tower of whitewashed stone rising out of a large white house. Farther to the right an extensive brown stone-walled fort with low round towers at the corners, near it the white tents of a camp. Government steamer & 2 or 3 barkas in harbor, go ashore in lodka and take room in low one-story hotel. Variety of costumes. Tartar in one shirt fastened about waist with broad woven belt, skull caps, everybody armed with pistols and Kinjals—Mountain Tartars and Chechenses in beshmet[58] and Khalats with enormous fur caps, long Kinjals, shashkas,[59] brass-barreled pistols 15 inches long with round knobs for handles stuck in belts behind. Principal street, narrow rows of one-story houses covered with earth and clay, some roofed with boards, almost all with a projecting gable and window. Sidewalks blocked up by stone steps of houses. Everybody walks in middle of street. Long lines of Tartar on carts loaded with flour passing constantly through the street with a hideous creaking of wheels. Ask Tartar why he doesn't grease his axles. He replies, "Did you ever see a robber go into someone else's house to steal? He goes carefully and noiselessly on tip toe while the honest man walks in with firm loud steps,

---

58. *beshmet:* quilted jacket.
59. *shashka:* sabre.

careless whether anybody hears him or not. So with our creaking wagons. We let them creak so that everybody who hears them will know that a Tartar is coming—an honest man—and that there is nothing to fear." Tartar carts are very small and ride mounted on two wheels with very small axles and huge double conical hubs. Their oxen fastened to wagon by yoke consisting of a frame as this [*sketch*]. Whole equipage extremely rude.

ACROSS THE MAIN CAUCASUS RIDGE, WITH PRINCE JORJADZE

[The following description of the Caucasus, written after Kennan's return, is inserted here to introduce the continuation of his description of Petrovskoe. Excerpted from pages 170–75 of "The Mountains and Mountaineers of the Eastern Caucasus (1874)"]

IF I WERE ASKED TO COMPARE THE CAUCASUS, FOR the purposes of illustration, with some better-known range of mountains, I should say that it resembles a little in relative geographical position the Sierra-Nevadas of California. But of course [. . .] and the general facts which can be affirmed of the Caucasian range as a whole are not very numerous. You can say that it is 700 miles long, that it is from 8,000–18,000 feet high, that with its spurs and secondary lateral ranges it is from 75 to 150 miles wide, that it has steppes on the north and fertile valleys on the south; and that is about all you can say of it.

The province of Daghestan is a rather long and slender triangle lying wholly on the north side of the Caucasian range, having for its apex the peninsula of Apsheron, on the coast of the Caspian; for its base, one of the spurs of the Caucasus known as the ridge of Ande; and for its sides, the Nogai steppe on the north, and the main ridge itself on the south. The greatest length of this triangle from east to west is about

A Dagestani landscape. Photo © Chris Allingham.

275 miles, its width at its base something like 120, and its superficial area about one-third that of the State of New York. This comprises the so-called Eastern Caucasus. Its Turkish name, Daghestan (the land of mountains), is accurately descriptive of its character; for, although not the highest, it is one of the most broken and rugged portions of the whole Caucasian range. From side to side, and from end to end, it is nothing but mountains, precipices, gorges, and profound ravines.

I hardly know how to convey, without a great deal of wearisome explanation, an adequate idea of the physical configuration of this region. Near the northwestern corner of Daghestan there rises out of the main Caucasian range a sharp snowy peak nearly 14,000 feet in height known as Mount Barbale. At this mountain the central ridge of the Caucasus separates, as it goes eastward, into two parallel branches or arms, the southern arm being known as the main range, which slopes directly into the valley of Georgia; the other as the snowy range which lies wholly in Daghestan.[1]

As regards height, they are at first nearly equal, but the main branch runs entirely through to the Caspian without getting much lower; while the snowy range falls gradually, as it goes eastward, to 4,000 or 5,000 feet, and is finally lost among the spurs of its longer rival. Between these two mountain branches there is a great elevated valley or trough and in this trough rise three of the largest rivers in Daghestan—the Andieski Koisu,[2] the Avarski Koisu, and the Samour. Running at first in easterly and westerly directions through this elevated valley, the two Koisus finally force the snowy range in two great gorges, and, flowing northward through Daghestan, unite and empty at last into the Caspian, after a fall of not less than 5,000 feet from the level of the trough in which they have their rise.

It seems at first sight incredible that running water in any conceivable lapse of time should be able to disintegrate and carry away such immense quantities of rock as have been disintegrated and carried away from Daghestan; that it should carve out such mountains as the peak of Goonib, such profound valleys as the gorge of Bognadala; that it should cut a mountain plateau into a perfect network of tremendous galleries which look as if an army of Titans had been digging parallels and carrying on siege operations against the granite ramparts of the great range itself.

The physical geography of the Daghestan watershed may be summed up as follows: the backbone of the country is the main Caucasian ridge, averaging about 10,000 feet in height, reaching in two or three places 13,000. The principal rivers rise between this ridge and the equally high snowy range, pierce the latter and flow through enormously deep and

---

1. It is possible that Kennan's sources for the interior geography of the Caucasus were not fully accurate. His "Mount Barbale" may be Mount Dikosmta (4285 m), which is not actually on the Main Caucasus Ridge but from which a ridge stretches east that becomes the Andi Range separating Dagestan from Chechnya. The main glaciated peak within Dagestan is Mount Addala (4151 m; 13,619 ft) in the middle of the Bogos Range separating the Andiiskoe Koisu and Avarskoe Koisu. This latter range is probably his "snowy range," although later he also uses the term for the Nukatl Range.

2. *koisu:* a Turkic word meaning "sheep river." Minorsky, *A History of Sharvan*, 85.

*The Main Caucasus Range, as seen from Mt. Elbrus.
Photo © Daniel C. Waugh.*

narrow valleys in a northward direction to the Nogai steppes, where they turn abruptly to the eastward, and empty into the Caspian.

The characteristic features of this watershed are, first, its flat-topped ridges and truncated cone-shaped mountains, seamed with strata of sandstone and calcareous rock, and, second, the profoundly deep valleys, ravines, and gorges through which all its streams flow. It is almost impossible to exaggerate the depth, narrowness, and gloominess of these valleys. They are rarely more than 300 or 400 feet wide at the bottom, and are shut in by walls which rise steeply, sometimes perpendicularly, to heights of 1,500, 2,000 and 3,000 feet, broken occasionally into terraces by thick strata of limestone. These ravines render travel across the country extremely difficult. The getting out of one and the entrance into another frequently involve five or six hours of hard climbing in tortuous zigzags; and, as a general rule, the distance of a cannon-shot across two or three of these ravines is a good day's work, as they can be entered and left only at certain favorable points.

There are no forests in the country except in the trough between the main range and the snowy range, and a few small trees in some of the valleys. Even firewood is extremely scarce, and timber for Russian houses has to be rafted down the Volga and across the Caspian to Petrovskoe. There are no lakes anywhere except one small one at a height of 6,100 feet on the ridge of Ande.

The climate varies, according to location and altitude, from the climate of New York City to that of Siberia. On the steppes north of Daghestan spring begins in March, in some of the deep, sheltered valleys, in February; and on the mountain plateaus, up to a height of 5,000 or 6,000 feet, in May. The line of perpetual snow on the main Caucasian range is a little above 10,000 feet; on the snowy range it falls somewhat lower. A few small glaciers descend from the higher peaks of the main range on the northern side, but none that can be compared in point of magnitude with those of the Central Caucasus between mounts Kazbek and Elbrooz.[3]

[Letter home from Petrovskoe (=Makhachkala),
Kennan MSS, LC, Box 13, folder 1870–1878]

Petrovskoe, Sept. 12th, 1870

MAGNIFICENT WHITE CAUCASIAN GRAPES IN CLUSters a foot long cost only one cent a pound and for 50 cents each you may have all you can carry away in a wheelbarrow. Watermelons as big as a pail cost two cents each and apples, peaches and pears are to be had almost for nothing. For the last two days, ever since we left Saratof on the Volga I've been living principally on fruit. It seems as if I could never get enough of these splendid grapes—I've eaten about half a dozen pounds since morning. Russian faces and dress have almost entirely disappeared and in their places are the enormous fur caps, long khalats,

---

3. Mount Elbrus (5642 m; 18,510 ft) is the highest peak in the Caucasus—and in Europe. Mount Kazbek (5033 m; 16,512 ft) lies along the Georgian Military Highway south of Vladikavkaz.

daggers and pistols of the swarthy Daghestan mountaineers and the black stupid faces of the Kalmuck Tartars.

The language I no longer understand, the geography of the country with the outlandish Tartar and Chechense names is entirely unknown to me, and I feel as much at a loss as if I had been set down suddenly in the middle of China or in Central Africa. I find that my Russian companions are going to Vladi Kavkaz[4] by the direct road along the foot of the great Caucasian range and thus they leave the wildest part of Daghestan on the left. I have decided therefore not to accompany them but to plunge into the mountains by myself and follow the crest of the range westward to the Dariel Pass.[5]

So far as I can learn no foreign traveler has ever explored the interior of Daghestan and its scenery is said to be grand beyond description. I don't know how I shall get along with the Mountain Chechenses but somehow or other I presume I shall get through. A man don't know what he can do until he tries and my experience has been that difficulties and obstacles which seem insurmountable at a distance vanish as you approach them. I have not the slightest idea how I'm going to travel in the mountains. Horseback, in a cart or on foot, or where I shall stay. I have full faith in my own resources and I know there isn't any danger.

I go tomorrow to Timour Khan Shoura [=Buinaksk], formerly the residence of the great Caucasian hero Shamyl and from there to a place called Goonip [=Gunib] somewhere on the slope of the great range about a hundred versts south of here. Beyond that point I have made no plans. I shall go wherever I find it possible to go and hope to turn up in ten days or so at Vladi Kavkaz, a Russian town near the Dariel Pass on the north slope of the mountains. From there a diligence runs daily to Tiflis. Petrovskoe where I now am is a small town of 4 or 500 inhabitants situated on the Caspian Sea north of Derbent in the province of Daghestan.

---

4. Vladikavkaz was renamed Orzhonikidze in the Soviet era and is still designated under that name on many maps. It guards the northern end of the military highway to Tbilisi.

5. The Darial Pass, cutting through the Main Caucasus Ridge, is the route of the Georgian Military Highway between Tbilisi and Vladikavkaz. Kennan's limited understanding of the geography is evident here, since there is no way he could have followed the crest of the Caucasus Range to the pass.

The country back of the town looks very much like Kamchatka, high and mountainous, but in this land of mountains it is only called "hilly." In England such mountains as those immediately back of the village would be considered grand and would be visited by tourists and celebrated by travelers and poets. The population of Petrovskoe is extremely varied and picturesque and seems to be made up principally of Kalmuck Tartars, Persians and all sorts of Daghestan mountaineers.

Persians and Tartars I became somewhat familiar with on the Volga but these Chechenses and Daghestanese are a new people. I have been out on the streets watching them all the afternoon. Imagine a man of middle height, strongly built with dark eyes and a complexion as swarthy as a Sioux Indian. He is dressed as follows [see illustration, page 96]. In the first place he has on a fur hat of curly Astrakhan lamb's wool shaped like a muff, about a foot in height and fourteen inches in thickness. His body is covered with a khalat—a coat of some dark cloth fitting tightly as far down as the waist and hanging from there to the knee in thick folds like a dress. Across his breast from shoulder to shoulder is a row of little cloth pouches about six inches deep in which are stuck fifteen or twenty silver tubes containing rifle cartridges. The tops of these silver tubes project about an inch out of the cloth pouches and are of course very ornamental. Around the man's waist is a belt of golden cloth studded with silver knobs. From this belt in front hangs a long kinjal or Circassian dagger with a pure solid silver sheath or one made of leather silver mounted. Behind in the belt are stuck two long-barreled pistols also silver mounted with round knobs for handles.

In addition to these weapons many are also armed with "shashki" or Circassian sabres and quaint flint-locked rifles all more or less ornamented with silver. Pantaloons are of the usual pattern but wide around the ankle and the feet are covered with peculiarly covered leather boots with turned up toes. Imagine this swarthy keen-eyed individual in his enormous fur hat, breast glittering with silver cartridge tubes, golden belt stuck full of daggers and curiously shaped pistols and you will have an idea of a Chechenetz or Daghestan mountaineer.

Since my Russian left for Vladi Kavkaz at three o'clock I have engaged transportation to Timour Khan Shoura, got letters of introduction to Russian officers at that place who will give me all necessary advice and assistance, have visited an "aoul" or settlement of the Daghe-

A Dagestani mountaineer. Markov, Ocherki: *423.*

stan mountaineers in the mountains back of here about 2000 feet above the sea, returned by moonlight and have picked up more curious information in six hours than I've gathered in all the time I've been in Russia. Verily this is a curious country. The aoul is the strangest-looking settlement that I have ever seen yet, and looks more like a lot of eagles' nests plastered against the face of an enormous precipice than it does like a collection of human habitations. We came down a horrible zigzag road with two horses from a height of twelve or fifteen hundred feet with no light but that of the moon to guide us and I wonder that we did not break our necks. I say we—I've already made some acquaintances and, strange to say, they are Jews. A man makes all sorts of friends in traveling in this way round the world. One of my companions on the Volga steamer was a Persian and now here in Daghestan I am befriended by Jews! They are good fellows at any rate.

One Tartar friend whom we visited in the mountain "aoul" set before us in an immense flat iron dish about three feet across and an inch deep twenty or thirty pounds of the most magnificent white grapes I ever saw and I sat there cross-legged on the clay floor of his house and ate grapes until I could hardly get up. It is astonishing to see what quantities they raise here. In some places they are selling at the rate of three pounds for a cent! And delicious wine—the pure juice of the grape—can be bought for about ten cents a bottle.

[Journal, 87–94]

Timour Khan Shoura, Sept. 14th

TO CONTINUE MY DESCRIPTION OF PETROFSK. AT the end of the principal street is the market, consisting of four or five rows of low sheds, open in front with narrow passages between them. Here are sold all sorts of produce—wheat, maize, potatoes, cabbages, and enormous quantities of fruit. Grapes are most noticeable. Immense piles of splendid white grapes in every stall which can be bought for 2 kopecks a pound. Watermelons about a kopeck apiece. Pears, apples, & cherries almost for nothing. Market affords an excellent opportunity to study costumes. Cossacks in black trimmed with red short brass handles. Roman sword hanging vertically on left thigh, red shoulder straps with K^6 and a number on them. Officers dressed from head to foot in white-linen which sets off to advantage their dark sunburnt features and black hair and whiskers. Persians in more or less ragged beshmets & Khalats, small skull caps, heads shaved everywhere except just over ears where two long locks are allowed to grow. On their feet, slippers with high heels and

---

6. *K* for *Kavkazskaia Armiia* (Caucasian Army).

turned-up toes only half long enough for their bare feet so that the heel of the slipper comes right under the instep of the foot. Almost all have mustaches and this week's growth of black beard on their cheeks.

Next mountain Tartars . . . By the way, I don't know why they call these Daghestan mountaineers Tartars—they are not at all like the Tartars of Kazan or the Kalmucks of Astrakhan. They wear beshmets and Khalats like everybody else in the Caucasus, a hat of white or black curly lamb's wool which sometimes looks as if it [is] even their own hair, boots or shoes with pointed toes and always carry long Kinjals with ebony or ivory handles hung to their belt in front at an angle of 45 degrees so that the point projects beyond their left thigh just above the knee and the hilt comes to the waist on the right side. Many in addition carry a long-barreled brass or silver-mounted pistol stuck bottom side up in their belt behind. In full

Urban market in the Caucasus. Photo from Kennan archive. Courtesy of Library of Congress.

dress they wear the huge muff-shaped hat and the cartridge tubes across their breasts. Weapons are their delight and all the money they can earn above what suffices to supply their daily wants is spent for splendid silver-mounted pistols & kinjals. Next, Persian women in long white veils with two round holes for eyes. Russian women in flowery calico, girded under the arms as usual. Next Tartar porters in nothing but a little skull cap and one long coarse white cotton shirt, gathered about the waist with a wide thick belt of woven flax or hemp in which is stuck an iron hook with a long leather tassel, heads shaved and feet and legs bare. These are all the costumes which I can remember that are particularly noticeable.

"Hotel Daghestan," where we stopped, had as far as I could see only 2 rooms for travellers. One of these we took. It had, however, a billiard table and the first game of billiards I ever played in my life I played here. Our room had two bed steads but as usual no bedding, no looking glass, no soap, no towels, no nothing. Russian custom of helping a man wash himself by pouring water on his hands. Russians frequently take successive mouthfuls of water, spit it out upon their hands and wash their hands and faces in that way. Dinner however was good, especially the dessert of peaches, musk melons, and white grapes. After dinner Stryker, who is a Jew although I would never know it, took me to see some Jewish friends of his in a store on the corner near market. Fair stock of European dry goods and bijouterie. Evening billiards. Stryker and the young Russian officer discuss all sorts of things—especially Jews—till one o'clock. Fleas as usual. Yesterday morning Stryker, Leshef and I took a bath in the Caspian off the wooden pier. Women sat on the shore looking on with the greatest composure. Water of the Caspian intensely salt and bitter; warm however and easy to swim in. Billiards till noon. Stryker engages tarantass[7] and troika to carry him and the young officers to Grozna [=Groznyi] for 15 Rs. At 3 PM we have a farewell bottle of beer together, sing Kingdom Coming together once more, and they set out. I go to visit the Jews and get a letter of introduction which they promised me to Timour Khan Shoura. Drink tea there and two of them invite me to accompany them to a mountain aoul and Tartar village about 3 versts from Petrovskoe. It was situated on the slope of the high, precipitous ridge which I have previously mentioned. On the way there

7. *tarantas* springless carriage.

they told me many curious things about the Persians and Tartars at Petrovskoe.

First was a description of the Persian festival which they call "Saksee" of which I had never before heard.[8] It occurs once a year or rather once every 13 months coming every year a month later and lasts 30 days. It begins with daily services in all the Persian mosques,[9] in the course of which the moolah reads the history of some event or other in Persian history. One of the Jews said it was an account of a war between the Turks and a Persian queen named Sortia, while another said that it was an account of a war between two sects of Mohammedans in Persia and of the killing of the leader of one of these sects.[10] At any rate the moolah reads this history and the worshippers begin crying, howling, and beating their breasts in grief. These demonstrations frequently continue for three hours at a time every day. Toward the close of the month begins the serious fast of the Saksee. On the 28th day the crying, howling, and beating of breasts becomes indescribably animated. The Persians all gather together in a yard of one of the houses, form a circle and begin dancing around, shouting "Sak-see Bak-see, Sak-see Bak-see" beating their breasts at every syllable and working themselves up to a terrible state of excitement. The shouts of Saksee Baksee, Ali, Ali, Go Ali, saksee baksee become louder and louder and at last they all draw their Kinjals and begin cutting and slashing themselves over the head and breast which are naked (they have nothing on but drawers) shouting Saksee as before. The blood runs down their naked bodies in streams and it frequently happens that they kill themselves in

---

8. Reference to the penitential festival of the Ashura, most important of the Shia year, celebrated 10 Muharram during the month of mourning. See Bennigsen and Lemercier-Quelquejay, *Islam in the Soviet Union*, 179.

9. Most Dagestanis are Sunni Muslims of the Shafei rite, but the Azeris and Tats are Shias. See Alexandre Bennigsen and S. Enders Wimbush, *Muslims of the Soviet Empire: A Guide* (London: C. Hurst & Co., 1985), 148. Kennan is referring to the Shia mosques.

10. Husain, son of Ali, grandson of the Prophet, killed at Karbala while leading a revolt against the Umaiyad caliph in A.D. 680. "Shia religious energy is absorbed to a great extent in the remembrance of the martyrdom of Husain in particular and of the imams in general, all of whom are supposed to have been murdered by the Sunnis." Francis Robinson, in *Atlas of the Islamic World since 1500* (New York: Facts on File, 1982), 23, 47.

their frenzy. From this yard they go to another where stands a horse and this horse they rub with the blood from their own bodies. One of my informants said that they sometimes form two parties and slash each other with Kinjals. This murderous performance at any rate lasts 3 days, alternated with reading, howling and crying in the mosques. The self torture takes place everywhere in the open streets. I have never read any account of this custom. The Jews say it is a terrible thing to witness. Custom of sprinkling newly born infants with salt observed by mountain Tartars. They say it makes them hardy, brave and enduring.

Caucasian animal *burvolok* resembles a buffalo somewhat but has a longer more pointed head, horns straight or nearly as turned outward and backward, body dark brown with profusion of long light brown hairs about the shoulders. Larger and heavier than an ox. Loves to lie in mud puddles and wallow.

Clicking language of Tartar mountaineers.[11]

Frequent murders between Derbent and Baku. Disarming of people in consequence. Persian murders mountaineer. Relatives of latter appeal to justice of peace for revenge. Latter demands witnesses and mountaineers go to place where their relative was murdered, cut down a neighboring tree, gather up the bloody dust and bringing them to the justice say "Here are our witnesses."

[Kennan, "Mountains and Mountaineers," excerpted from pages 176–77, 182]

There are two widely-spread errors with reference to the Caucasian mountaineers which it may be well to notice,—first, that they are all, or nearly all, Circassians; and, second, that the Circassians, properly so-called, were the most determined antagonists of Russia in the Caucasian war. Both these popular opinions are wide of the truth, although they have apparently misled as well-informed travellers as Capt. Burton, and more recently Sir Arthur Cunynghame.[12]

The mountaineers of the Caucasus are not all Circassians any more than the inhabitants of Constantinople are all Greeks. The true Circassians form a comparatively small portion of the mountain pop-

---

11. The Northeast Caucasian languages are characterized by consonant clusters pronounced with tense stops that produce clicking-like sounds.

12. On Burton and Cunynghame, see Introduction, note 46.

Shamil's fortified home at Gunib. Painting by Zankowskii. Markov, Ocherki: *503.*

ulation, and are settled only in that part of the range which borders the Black Sea. They have been taken as representatives of the whole race of Caucasian highlanders simply because from their location they happened to become better known to Europeans than the equally powerful Lesghians[13] of Daghestan or the far fiercer Chechenses of Ichkeria.[14]

13. In pointing out the error in calling all mountaineers "Circassians," Kennan makes the error of calling all Dagestanis "Lezgins." The Lezgins live in the south of Dagestan and make up about 10 percent of the republic's population (Bennigsen and Wimbush, *Muslims of the Soviet Empire,* 165). It was common practice in the last century to lump all Dagestan's inhabitants under the misappelation "Lezgins" (Minorsky, *A History of Sharvan,* 80).

14. Ichkeria is the region on the north slope of the mountains between the lowlands of Chechnya and Dagestan. Kennan passed through it on his return to Dagestan.

In the second place, the Circassians were not, as a matter of history, any more determined in their resistance to the Russian conquest than the mountaineers of Daghestan. The last organized resistance to Russia in the Caucasus was not made by Circassians. It was the heroic attempt of Shamyl and 300 Lesghians to hold the peak of Goonib in Central Daghestan against 28,000 Russian Cossacks under Prince Baratinski.[15] The defeat of Shamyl in Daghestan was the Waterloo of the Caucasian highlanders, not the last battle on the coast of the Black Sea [. . .]

Strange are the articulations of the mountaineers—I cannot make these clicks, although I tried faithfully to learn them. None of these mountain languages have ever been written, nor can they be.[16] The only medium of written communication in Daghestan is the Arabic, which is understood by most of the Mahometan moolahs, or priests. The Viceroy of the Caucasus has committed to Gen. Oosler and Col. Geetchinkov, two Russian philologists, the task of studying and classifying these languages. They have already published vocabularies and grammars of four or five of them, and Gen. Oosler is now at Timour Khan Shoura collecting materials for more. They had found, they told me, strange archaic forms of numerous Aryan and Semitic languages, various dialects of Tatar and Mongol origin, and a few which had no discoverable connection with any known tongue.[17]

15. Aleksandr Ivanovich Bariatinskii (1815–79), a field commander and from 1856 Commander-in-Chief and Viceroy of the Caucasus, who orchestrated the final defeat of Shamil.

16. An oversimplification, albeit one that appears frequently in other sources. Classical Arabic was used extensively by intellectual and political leaders (Wixman, *Language Aspects*, 104), but there are early examples of Avar being written in the Georgian alphabet (AN SSSR, *Istoriia Dagestana*, 1:229). Shirin Akiner notes that the Arabic script was used to write Avar from the seventeenth century on and "many eigh-teenth and nineteenth century Avar poets and scholars used both languages." *Islamic Peoples of the Soviet Union* (London: Kegan Paul, 1983), 134.

17. Uslar was the first to show conclusively that the Caucasus languages deserved to be classed as a distinct family, in contradiction to earlier linguists who had assumed Georgian to be Indo-European and the other Caucasian languages Altaic. See A. A. Magometov, "P. K. Uslar—kavkazoved," in P. K. Uslar, *Etnografiia Kavkaza*, 1064.

[Journal, 95–102]

Timour Khan Shoura, Sept. 16th

TO CONTINUE ACCOUNT OF OUR TRIP TO MOUNTAIN "aoul"—wide level plain stretching away to northward. High, almost precipitous bluff in front with even, level top and rude natural terraces. Tartar aoul on the right—houses perched up on these terraces like eagles nests at heights of 800 and 1000 ft. Turn to left and begin to ascend bluff by horrible road of long zigzags, running a good deal of way in a bed of a mountain stream. Saklas[18] scattered here and there everywhere in confusion on the terraces, some built half in the side of hill and half out. Some built against side of a terrace so that you can drive right off the road onto the roofs. Hard to tell which is road and which roofs. Saklas all rectangular, generally square or rather cubical. Frame of timbers and poles mottled with small withes of some flexible bush. This woven frame is then covered with one layer after another of

---

18. *saklia:* Caucasian dwelling.

Dagestani aul (mountain village). Markov, Ocherki: *415.*

clay mixed with straw, allowed to dry separately until wall is a foot thick. Roof perfectly flat of poles covered with clay, frequently grown up with grass. Whole sakla seen from above looks like a brown paper box. Frequently on south side, long piazza going whole length of house, roof of which is supported by round poles. Among saklas, haystacks and mottled enclosures for chickens. No barns. Saklas often built on sloping side of hill in an excavation so that only half is outside, thus [*sketch*]. This roof covered with grass and undistinguishable from ground so that coming downhill you may walk off on roof and over edge before you know it. Windows small glass.

Sept. 17th

AFTER CLIMBING UP ABOUT 1000 FEET, WE FOUND ourselves in the aoul among barking dogs and at last, after hailing and questioning several boys, we succeeded in finding the Tartar of whom we were in search. He came down from his sakla by a steep almost inaccessible path with a lantern and guided us up. His house was low, square with hard earthen floor, earthen fire place and chimney. Opposite door were piled up six feet high feather beds, comforter and pillows. Tartars always have lots of bedding. Against right wall hung rifle in leather case with hair on, a couple of silver-mounted, long-barreled, knob-handled pistols, and 3 or 4 immense copper and polished iron platters about 2 1/2 feet in diameter and an inch deep, elaborately chased and engraved with scroll work.

On the other wall was a shelf upon which stood the domestic utensils—wooden bowls gilded in Russian style, large, metallic pitchers holding four or five gallons, shaped like those of which we all picture in Bible dictionaries [*sketch of a jug shaped like an amphora*], earthen pitchers also of antique shape, with spouts, silver-mounted drinking horns holding a couple of quarts or so, and various smaller articles. Against this wall hung also a couple of Persian mirrors so uneven as to make a man's face polyangular and distribute his features irregularly all over his body. Under the shelf was spread down a wide sheet of thick felt—voilok—upon which we proceeded to squat in eastern style. There were no chairs or tables in the house. Along a pole hung from the ceiling were suspended ten or fifteen haunches of mutton, very fat, in process of curing, the smell of which filled the room. As soon as we had rested ourselves, our Tartar host set before us on one of the big iron platters about 20 lbs. of magnificent white and black grapes upon which, in defiance of the cholera, we proceeded to eat.

The Tartar's wife was much taken with my Jewish friend's little boy who was with us, and brought him a present of half a dozen eggs. We had brought a bottle of Caucasian wine with us and proceeded to drink it but the Tartar couldn't join us as spirituous liquor is forbidden by the Koran.[19] After eating about 3 lbs. of grapes each, and drinking up all our wine, we started back for Petrovskoe. Tartar guided us down steep path to road with lantern, carrying the little boy, and we drove down a better but zigzag road to the plain. Fine view. Moon just rising out of a bank of clouds over the Caspian. Appearance of a second moon under the great plain stretching away to northward, hazy blue and indistinct lights of Petrovskoe in the distance, roofs of saklas under our feet and extending out from side of road. Haystacks and sometimes cliffs on one side and precipice on the other. Road cut out of side of hill. On way home, Jews tell me about Armenian marriages said to take place at midnight. Man and wife can have no connection till after 3 days and are sealed with seal of church.

On the day after the departure of Kavkazets and the two young Russian officers for Vladi Kavkaz, I succeeded in getting transportation to Timour Khan Shoura and set out in a rickety old telega or tarantass with a Russian merchant. The morning was very hot and the Russian had skillfully disposed himself on the shady side so that I lay in the full blaze of the sun. Our road turned away to the westward around the bend of the bluff, which I had visited the previous night toward a pass in the mountains back of it. Petrovskoe lies at the very extremity of the foothills of the Caucasus range and north of it there is nothing but one

---

19. Men in Dagestan today consume large amounts of alcohol. Even in the latter half of the last century there was plenty of drinking, to judge by statistics stating that in 1867 in Dagestan six murders were committed under the influence of alcohol and another twenty-three drunken attacks resulted in nonfatal injury. See Kavkazskoe gorskoe upravlenie, *Sbornik svedenii o kavkazskikh gortsakh*, vol. 1 (Moscow: ADIR, 1992; reprint of original published in Tbilisi, 1868), 72.

immense plain or steppe stretching away beyond the limits of sight. In about an hour we found ourselves among low but picturesque mountains covered with low shrubbery with great outcropping masses and ridges of sandstone rock. Turning again to the southward, we entered a narrow pass and began ascending the ridge in a series of long zigzags. Road cut out of mountain side with cliffs on one side and precipices on the other, guarded by a low stone wall with narrow openings at short intervals. Some view over the Caspian Sea and the great plain to the north ward. Plain almost as blue as sea but hazier in the distance. Occasional haystacks and cultivated fields looking about as big as a pocket handkerchief. Gleam of water from a small distant lake. Green winding ribbons of fresher foliage marking course of streams. Zigzags of road so long that we had to go a mile to make 100 feet upwards.

On the road above an aoul in the ravine, we stopped to water our horses and eat a watermelon with which my Russian friend had provided himself. Mountains all around us except in the north where we had a view of the Caspian—blue as indigo—and the great hazy steppe stretching away to the northward. Zigzags higher and higher until at last we come out on the summit. Magnificent view to the southward. Long wide valley with low mountains on each side and about 60 versts distant a great range of high blue mountains which my Russian friend pointed out as the mountains of Shamyl. Their tops were hidden in clouds. Came down the south slope at a fast trot. Road excellent. My Russian friend enquires about America. He had heard of Pres. Lincoln, the Great Eastern,[20] and the Siamese Twins, all of which he connected in some mysterious way with America. Every Russian whom I meet almost enquires about the marriage relation in America and whether it is possible to get divorces or not and the facility with which divorces can be obtained in U.S. appears to meet their unqualified approval from which I infer that married life in Russia is not always a state of filialty. My Shoura friend was also interested in wills and the laws by which property descends from father to son and, failing a son, to other mem-

---

20. Largest steamship in the world in the second half of the nineteenth century (Microsoft Encarta '97 CD-ROM Encyclopedia). I was asked in a Dagestan aul in 1996 how Reagan was doing as president!

View of Temir Khan Shura. Markov, Ocherki: *587.*

bers of family. He kept supposing all sorts of impossible cases and then wanting to know what the law for such cases was in America. [. . .][21]

[Kennan MSS, LC, Box 64, envelope "Part of First Caucasus Article"]

Petrovskoe seemed to me to differ very little from other Russian towns of its class, but Timour Khan Shoura must, I thought, present something distinctively Caucasian and oriental—something that should

---

21. I have omitted a few lines here which provide cryptic notes elaborated on in the next selection.

embody in material form the mystery and strangeness of the East and the adventurous romance of the Middle Ages. But I was greatly disappointed. I caught occasional glimpses of a high stone wall, foliage, clustered houses and a pointed church dome, but it was not until we came up out of a shallow ravine within pistol shot of the place and stopped for a moment on the crest of the hill to rest our horses that I was able to group my fragmentary impressions into a complete and definite mental picture. Before us at a distance of two or three hundred yards lay a compact little town of perhaps 400 stuccoed or adobe houses, thickly interspersed with clumps and rows of slender dark green Lombardy poplars and grouped without much apparent symmetry of arrangement around a large red Byzantine church.

The houses, with the exception of a few government buildings, were one-storey adobe cottages thatched with reeds and grass; the streets were unpaved and dusty and had no sidewalks; and there was not a trace of color anywhere except the green of the trees, the dull red of the old church, and an occasional patch of bright scarlet or yellow where the painted tin roof of a Russian government building caught the sloping rays of the afternoon sun. The town was very unlike a Russian town, and yet it did not answer at all to the anticipations which I had formed of a Caucasian stronghold. With the exception of a gray stone wall partly thrown down and in many places outgrown by the settlement which it had once encircled, and the ruins of a square, loop-holed watch-tower on a bluff over the ravine which we had just crossed, there was not a suggestion in the whole picture either of war, or of the Middle Ages, or the wild, semi-barbaric life of the Caucasus which had been so often described to me.

After five minutes rest, my driver, who in the meantime had been making a survey of his rickety telega, patting his horses and adjusting their harnesses, sprang to his feet, gathered up his reins, uttered a peculiar wild cry which acted upon the horses like a shock of electricity, and away we dashed at a headlong gallop toward the town gate. A Russian driver always enters a village or town as if he were bringing the good news from Aix to Ghent. The horses seem to have a tacit understanding with their driver that they are not to be urged out of a walk or a slow dog-trot until they are within two hundred yards of their destination but that they are then to do their "level best." They may saunter along the road all day in as languid and spiritless a manner as they please, but

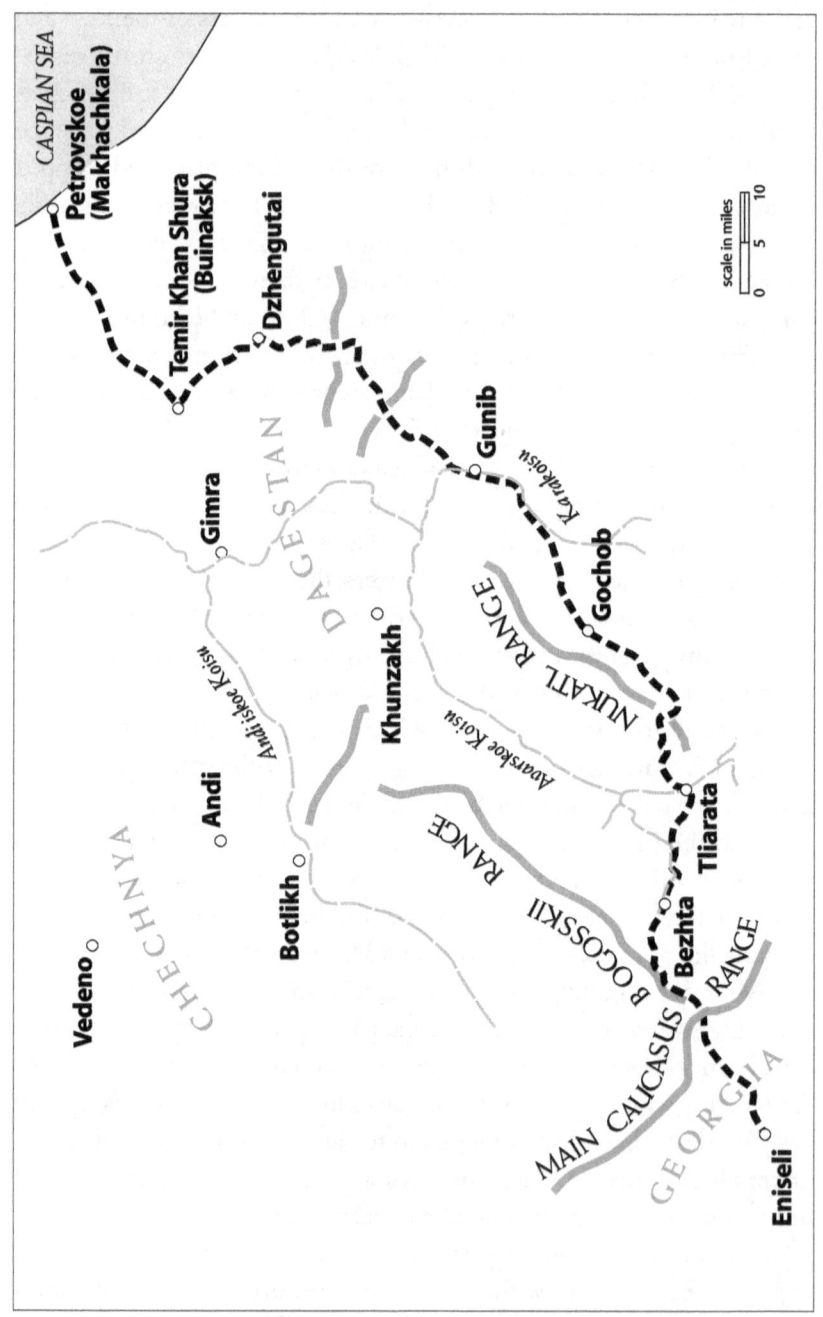

Map 3. Kennan's route from Temir Khan Shura to Eniseli.

they must be prepared to go into the village at night as if they were heading a charge of the Light Brigade. The very dogs fled from us in dismay as we thundered through the gate into the market place of Timour Khan Shoura. My driver stopped his horses in the middle of the dusty, straw-littered, hoof-trampled square and, turning half around in his seat inquired with the hyperbolic courtesy of the Russian muzhik who hopes that his flattery will be the measure of your generosity, where my "High Nobility" would deign to pass the night.

"Is there a hotel here?" I asked.

"There is, your High Nobility, but it's full, or was when I left here yesterday."

"Full! How so?"

"His Excellency the Grand Duke Michael[22] is here inspecting the post and his people have taken all the rooms, but I will drive you there if you order it."

"There's no use in going there if the hotel is full," I replied.

"Then where shall I take your High Nobility?" he asked again.

I looked vaguely around me. One-story adobe houses whose low doors and small square windows opened directly upon the street and whose sloping, thatched roofs of rotten straw were overgrown with faded grass and dead weeds stood around three sides of the bare, dusty market place, and two or three rows of gray, weather-beaten booths whose broad, sloping counters were piled with heaps of melons and grapes and open sacks of millet, rye flour and maize occupied the fourth side. It had been market day in the settlement and had I arrived five or six hours earlier I should have found the square crowded with two-wheeled buffalo carts and thronged with soldiers, traders, Tatars and picturesque, heavily armed horsemen from the hills; but it was now late and nearly all had gone. A faint, impalpable dust which pervaded the hot motionless air like a soft, golden mist was the only remaining sign of the day's bustle and activity.

A cart canopied with an arched tilt of bright colored calico and drawn by two lazy, writhing East Indian buffalos, moved slowly across the market place toward the village gate with the shrill, continuous creak which is characteristic of Tatar vehicles and a hooded falcon in one of the booths,

---

22. Grand Duke Mikhail Nikolaevich, brother of Tsar Alexander II, was Viceroy of the Caucasus from 1862 to 1882.

roused to a frenzy of excitement by the sound, filled the air with fierce discordant screams and the furious flapping of wings. Two or three bareheaded women, with antique water jars of red earthenware upon their shoulders crossed the square on their way homeward from the river. A tall, shaven-headed Persian with dark saturnine features came out of one of the houses with a copper pitcher in his hand, squatted down upon his heels in the dust and cleansed himself for the evening prayer by taking a mouthful of water, spitting it out in a thin jet upon his lean, henna-stained hands and rubbing it over his swarthy face and blue, hairless head. The swarthy Persian finished his perfunctory ablutions and after a prolonged stare at my telega disappeared; the creaking of the buffalo cart gradually died away and we were left alone in the deserted square.

"Has your High Nobility no friends in Timour Khan Shoura?" enquired my driver. I shook my head.

I knew that the natives of the country in journeying from village to village stopped at night with hospitable friends or acquaintances, but where a vagabond American who had no friends or acquaintances was to stop I hadn't the vaguest idea.

"Where are you going yourself?" I asked the driver.

"Oh, I'll find a place. We have koonaks[23] everywhere. You might go to the postayali dvor," he suggested tentatively. "You could stay there three days." I had not the faintest idea what a postayali dvor was, and the limitation of one's possible stay there to three days indicated that it was some sort of Caucasian home for the friendless; but in my perplexity I caught eagerly at the suggestion and told my driver to take me to the postayali dvor. That institution was evidently a Vagabond's retreat of some kind and I was too hungry and tired to make any unnecessary inquiries as to the nature of the accommodations that it afforded.

[Journal, 103–9]

My room in the Zayezhny Dvor,[24] a sort of post station house, was large and bare containing a table, a few chairs and a couple of bedsteads—no bedding, no washing conveniences, and no mirror as usual. Timour Khan

---

23. *kunak:* friend in another aul with whom one stays.

24. The *postoialyi dvor* and *zaezzhyi dvor* were places where travelers could get fresh horses, a simple meal, and a room.

Shoura is a large village rather than a "gorod" as the Russians call it and contains perhaps 8000 inhabitants. It is situated on a high bluff which breaks off abruptly on the N.W. to a small stream. The site of the village is uneven. On the N.W. is a high bluff terminating in a mass of sandstone rock on which stands an old ruined tower of stone overlooking the town and the valley on the N.W. and all the approaches to it. On this high bluff stand all the government buildings, powder cellars, magazines, and the Governor's residence. Just south of this elevation is the Government park, two or three acres in extent, planted all around with rows of tall slender poplars and laid out in shady walks with seats, a bowling alley and at the south entrance of the garden is the club building where there is a dancing hall and a restaurant.

A band of music plays in the garden every evening and the whole public assembles to promenade the walks, gossip, listen to the music and play nine pins. South of the garden lies the town on a gentle slope, at the summit of which stands the church, a large old building differing somewhat from Russian churches in general. It stands in the middle of an open square around the sides of which are the principal stores of the place. They are emphatically variety stores. They contain a very good assortment of European dry goods, knicknacks, and jewelry but not much that is peculiarly Caucasian. One can buy in them almost anything—jewelry, stationery, drygoods, boots and shoes, crockery, vases and bijouteries—in fact every article which an interior Daghestan town needs. From this open square the streets descend in a gradual slope to the east and north. Streets narrow, no sidewalks, have to paddle through mud in middle of street. Houses low, one story of brown clay mixed with straw and sometimes white washed, windows small glass panes. Roof also clay—generally peaked. Bazaar—large open square: pigs, geese, ducks and chickens strolling around in mud. Round sides, rows of low board shanties open in front like sheds with low broad counters piled with grapes, potatoes, cabbages, piles of watermelon, peaches, pears, apples, bags of millet, maize, rye.

Counters frequently covered with white awning. Inside stand Persians, heads shaven except just over the ears, skull caps, beshmets, cherkaskas,[25] short slippers with turned up toes. In one place you will see a

---

25. *cherkeska:* ubiquitous flaring jacket with cartridge holders across the breast worn by Caucasian men.

Persian barber shaving the head of another Persian or staining his nails with henna. Falcons in several booths screaming and flapping their wings. Shoemakers stalls—shoes and slippers hanging in rows over counter, mostly short with high heels and sharp pointed turned up toes. Half a dozen Persians disputing about something so loudly that their voices can be heard all over square. Old Persian with magnificent beard squatting over ditch with curious teapot-shaped earthen pitcher, performing ablutions required by Koran. Russian Cossacks in black coats, white pants, red shoulder straps with number on them.

Dag mountaineers come in with ox carts covered with awning, thus [*sketch*]. Inside, mountain women with hair cut short and hanging down over forehead and with two long heavy curled locks over cheeks. Stalls of cap makers. First day or so spend in walking around these streets, present letter of introduction to brother of Jewish friend and am invited by him to lunch. Make acquaintance there of German named Gazr [=Gasser]. Return to house to find a Lutheran priest in my room. Old, fat grey-haired man. Begins to apologise in French. He is German by birth and speaks Russian with perceptible foreign accent. Grand Duke Michael reviews troops. Ten regiments of Caucasian troops pass this principal street. Grand Duke in carriage followed by body guard of richly dressed gortse.[26] [. . .] patron[?] Asiatic band consisting of trumpet and drum. [. . .] Regiment in white Kaftans and big white muff hats, white bashliks[27] bordered with crimson. Weapons—rifle in leather case, sabre silver and gold-mounted, silver and gold-mounted kinjals and pistols. After this white regiment came another, also mounted, dressed in black, singing a wild Daghestan mountain song. On 3rd day after my arrival, make acquaintance of Tatarin called Gretingkov—was taken prisoner when only 9 years old by Russians in battle and sent to Kief to be educated. Speaks Russian, French, German and Italian, besides Persian, Arabic and various mountain languages. He is Lezgin by birth. Tells me

---

26. *gortsy:* mountaineers. Refers to people who live in the highlands of the Caucasus. According to Richard Pipes, the term "has no ethnic significance; it is merely a general term used to describe the numerous small groups inhabiting the valleys and slopes of the Caucasian range" (*Formation of the Soviet Union*, 16).

27. *bashlik:* a folding hood.

many curious things about mountaineers. Tribe in mountains who eat raw meat, have no religion but fetichism and instead of burying their dead, stand them up in corner of room in some house which is occupied by family and leave them there to decay. When bones fall down is considered dead, but not until then. Bones are then buried. Inhabitants of Petrovskoe and all the region north of Gunib are mostly genuine Tartars of Mongolian descent.[28] Lezgins said to be descended from Crusaders who stopped in Daghestan on their way homeward from the Holy Land. Proofs of this are numbrous—first the Lezgins when first known wore steel helmets with capes of chain armor and shirts of mail, spikes on knees. Names sometimes resemble names of Crusaders. Nearly all blondes or with brown hair and eyes—very few brunettes. Features tolerably regular and expressive.[29]

Lezgin languages very peculiar clicks, four distinct sounds of kh, ts, more or less prolonged, has 46 letters—alphabet invented by Gretingkov and Gen Oosler who is compiling a comparative grammar of all the Daghestan languages.[30] Two villages only a few versts apart frequently speak entire different languages. There is one village in southern Daghestan which has only 28 smokes [= households] which speaks a peculiar language of their own not found in any other part of the Caucasus. Peculiarities of some of the mountain languages. In one there are no active verbs. It is impossible for instance to say I did or you do— you must use passive form it was done by me or it is done by you.

Peculiar custom among some of the mountaineers when they receive

---

28. Referring to Turkic peoples who live primarily in Dagestan's flatlands. These include the Kumyks, who make up about 11 percent of the total population, and the Nogai people—they number less than 2 percent of the total population. For more on demographics, see Bennigsen and Wimbush, *Muslims of the Soviet Empire*, 173.

29. There is no evidence to support the legend of the Crusaders having passed through Dagestan. Since Kennan lumps all the non-Turkic Dagestani people together and calls them "Lezgins," it is not clear exactly to which mountaineers he is referring. Only one thing is sure—*Lezgins* they were not! Kennan did not visit southern Dagestan, so he was never in Lezgin territory.

30. Uslar devised an alphabet for Avar that is based on Cyrillic, with the addition of modified characters to express the thirteen sounds unique to Avar.

a guest they bring to him after supper a young girl—a virgin—with her he can spend the night, but no serious connection is permitted. Resembles the American custom of bundling.[31]

["Mountains and Mountaineers," 182–83]

The political organizations of the Daghestan mountaineers previous to the Russian conquest were of two kinds—hereditary khanates and "free communities." The khans were the descendants of the old Arab conquerors, and were six in number. They governed about 125,000 of the population, mostly in the northern part of the province. The free communities numbered forty-three, and embraced 275,000 souls or more, settled principally along the north slope of the snowy range, and in the valleys between it and the main range. These free communities were nothing but republics in their most primitive form, ruled by assemblies and sometimes having a presiding officer, all elected by popular vote. There were only two ranks, freemen and slaves; the slaves being mostly Georgians and Persians, captured by the mountaineers in their raids through the valleys, on the south side of the range.

[Journal, 110–17]

Goonib, Sept. 24th, 1870[32]

ON THE 3RD OR 4TH DAY AFTER MY ARRIVAL IN Shoura, as I was buying some trifling article in a store opposite the church, a Russian officer came up to me and enquired if he might be permitted to enquire if I were an artist. I replied that I was not but that I loved the beautiful in nature and came to Daghestan to see it. We make acquaintance. He enquires where I learned Russian. I tell him in Siberia. He proceeds to relate to me the narration of the landing of a party of Ameri-

---

31. This custom is also described by John F. Baddeley in *The Rugged Flanks of the Caucasus* (London: Oxford University Press, 1940), 13.

32. Several days have elapsed; the chronology and route for the part of the trip between Temir Khan Shura and Gunib is not entirely clear. They stopped in Dzhengutai and spent the night there. Probably they departed from Temir Khan Shura on September 22 and arrived in Gunib on the 23rd.

cans at the fork of a river near Behringe Straits—how they built themselves a little underground house, how cold it was and how finally two other Americans came after them and brought them to a settlement. Of course he was very much astonished to learn that I was one of those two Americans. He tells me that I am first American who has ever visited Daghestan. He was a correspondent I afterward learned of the Moscofski Vaidemost[33] and after my departure he sent whole biography of me to that paper for publication. He was very much amused at the idea of Gasser and I talking Russian together. A German and an American talking Russian in Daghestan!

I learn that there have been three English travellers in Daghestan. First Cameron, who was consul I believe at Tiflis. He crossed the Caucasus range from Goonib into Kakhetia. Second Marshall, who travelled on the north slope of the range but did not cross. Third, a man called "Ronson" as the Russians here pronounce it, probably Bronson or Ranson. He was in Goonib about two weeks ago and wanted to cross into Kakhetia by the same road which I am about to follow. Alone however he did not like to attempt it and after waiting here several days for Prince Jorjadze he finally started for Vladi Kavkaz by way of Botlikh, Veden and Grozne.

Prince Jorjadze and the Ispravnik[34] have just been relating to me some of the customs of the gortse, which I must write down at once before I forget them. First, among the Lezgins the father has unlimited power over his family. If his son commits some great sin such as incest or even omits to pray for two or three days, the father has a perfect right to kill him without being answerable to any one for so doing. The brother has the same power over the sister. Blood revenge prevails and the duty of avenging the murder of a relative descends from father to son.

Curious custom with regard to divorce. A man among the Lezgins has a right to have four wives at once but no more. If after a month or

---

33. *Moskovskie vedomosti* was a conservative daily, one of the two most important political papers of the day. See Louise McReynolds, *The News under Russia's Old Regime: The Development of a Mass-Circulation Press* (Princeton: Princeton University Press, 1991), 25, 102.

34. Kennan's first meeting with Prince Jorjadze is described in a later section (Journal, 118–19). *Ispravnik:* district police superintendent.

six months or a year one of these wives does not suit him he has a right to divorce her without being obliged to give any reason for so doing or being answerable to any one. The young Lezgin who told me this said that his own father had at different times 11 wives. In case after a divorce the husband makes peace with his former wife and desires to live with her again, he is permitted to do so only under certain conditions. She in the first place must be married again to another man, must live with him one day and must be again divorced. Then and not until then has the first husband a right to be remarried to his former wife. The Ispravnik even said that in the Zakatala okroog[35]—the wife must sleep with husband number 2 in an upper room and husband number 1 must lie in room below with earth falling down on him.

Among the mountain Mohammedans every man is required to pray 5 times a day. Among the Tovihetti[?][36] and several of the wilder mountain tribes, when a woman is about to give birth to a child, she is conducted to a particular house at some distance from village or in suburbs and is left there alone without any assistance whatever and there her child is born. In this house she must live alone for a whole month. Food is brought to her at stated intervals but aside from this she has no communication with any one.[37] Many of the wilder mountain tribes are very inhuman. There are villages where a Russian has never been seen and where a whole community has lived in isolation for years.

Many of the names of mountain villages are almost purely French and Italian—going to show that the mountaineers are mixed at least with Crusaders. Persians are all Shiite Mohammedans and Lezgins and gortsi Sooniti. Placing a comb on the carpet and bowing forehead to it during prayers prevails only among the Shiites. A stone may be substituted. If one man in consequence of a dispute kills another, he is obliged

---

35. *Zakatala okrug:* Zakataly District, located south of the Main Caucasus Ridge in the Alazan R. valley of Georgia. The town of Zakataly lies to the southeast of Prince Jorjadze's estate at Eniseli.

36. Probably here he means the Tushetians. See Wixman, *Peoples of the USSR*, 200.

37. No one I asked in Dagestan had heard of this custom, but a similar practice endures in the Kalash communities of northern Pakistan, as I learned at the Third International Hindu Kush Cultural Conference in Chitral in August 1995.

to pay a fine and is sometimes driven from the village. The relatives of the murdered man have a right to demand blood for blood and kill the murderer at sight. Custom with regard to theft: if a man is robbed of a horse and finds the track of that horse leading to another village, he has a right to go to that village, show the local inhabitants the tracks, and take the best horse he can find in the settlement without regard to whom it may belong. The owner cannot remonstrate or demand the return of his horse until he produces the stolen animal.

Custom of marrying young sons: among some of the mountain tribes, it is customary for a father to marry his son aged 7 or 8 years to a girl aged 18 or 19—until the son reaches maturity the father lives with his son's wife as if she were his own. When the son is of age—he becomes of age at 15, I believe—he lives with his wife so that her children belong half to the father and half to the son. The son in like manner marries his son—or rather his father's son by his own wife—to another girl and lives with her until the boy becomes of age just as his father had done previously. This must create a terrible confusion of relationships.

Wandering minstrel dervishes. There is a class of poor mendicants in Daghestan who gain a livelihood by wandering round from village to village singing songs which may be called religious songs. For instance one of these minstrels with a bag hung round his neck comes to a house and begins singing. He reminds his hearers that there is a place called Hell where the wicked will be tortured, dwells upon the nature of the torments which will there be inflicted, and the necessity of living a holy life, he then describes the pleasures of paradise, the honors[?] etc. and exhorts his hearers to so live that when they die they will go to heaven and not be tormented forever in hell. At the conclusion of the minstrel's song his hearers give him money, food, etc. and he goes on. The songs of the Lezgins are mostly war songs of the battles, victories and exploits of their ancestors. I heard one played by the band here tonight and several in Joongootai [=Dzhengutai]. They are all rather quick as to time, staccato, have a peculiar wild melody which is almost indescribable, and seem to be pervaded by a spirit of exultation.[38] The stories and fables of

---

38. It is not clear from this comment about the singing in Dzhengutai whether Kennan visited the village near Temir Khan Shura more than once. He wrote down some of the music in the back of his notebook on pages 169–70, one example of which

the mountaineers are Arabic in character and resemble the stories of the 1001 nights—probably introduced by the Mohammedans.

["Mountains and Mountaineers," excerpted from pages 180–81]

The mountaineers of Central and Southern Daghestan support themselves chiefly by keeping large flocks of sheep and goats, which they pasture upon the mountains. They also cultivate, in the valleys where they can, a little wheat, corn, millet or rye, and sometimes cut the sloping side of a ravine into terraces and cultivate that. Arable land is very scarce and valuable. Good soil is worth the price of the kid, sheep, or cow that covers it lying down. It was undoubtedly this scarcity of tillable land that led the mountaineers to begin those plundering raids into the valley of Georgia, which finally became such a terrible scourge to the people of that beautiful but unfortunate country. For more than a thousand years the Lezgins of Daghestan were a veritable sword of Damocles suspended from the snowy heights of the Caucasus over the fertile valleys on the south side of the range. Compare a mountaineer's dagger with one of his wretched ploughs, and you will at once see the direction which his genius has taken and the means by which he has obtained a livelihood.

[Journal, 118–19]

To return to Timour Khan Shoura.[39] In the course of three or four days I made several acquaintances including the brothers Roodnef Khetegrafhen, an artist from St. Petersburg traveling through Daghestan in search of the picturesque, and Russian Doctor previously mentioned who corresponds for Moskofski Vaidemost. Gretingkov had a photograph of Lincoln and was quite familiar with American history. On the 10th, the Grand Duke returned from Deshlagar and received a regiment of

---

is reproduced below (page 126), following his detailed later account of being entertained at Dzhengutai while there with the prince after they were already on the road to Gunib.

39. Kennan gets to writing up how he came to meet the prince only several days after they had been on the road and thus probably at least a week after the events he describes.

Cossacks on the plain south of the village. Shoura makes pretensions to being a walled town. It has several arched gates as the Derbent gate, the Avarski gate, etc. The brothers Roodnyef give me some particulars with regard to mountain scenery. Gimri sports enormous precipices, road cut out in face of rocks in zigzags—in air line about a mile and a quarter from top to bottom. By road 13 miles. At Shoura I found myself in rather an unpleasant situation.

    I didn't know how to get horses, where to hire an interpreter or in what way to travel. I had about concluded to go with the young St. Petersburg artist by way of Gimri, Goonib, Veden, Grozna and Vladi Kavkaz when late in the evening Doctor Kosternerefski came rushing into the photographer's house where I was sitting, saying that he had just heard of an excellent opportunity for me to cross the mountains into Kakhetia—Prince Jorjadze was to leave next day for Zakatala across the great Caucasian range and I could go with him. Undecided what to do—go with artist or with Jorjadze. Sat there talking the matter over when Gasser sent for me. Took supper with him and Polish Catholic priest. Concluded to go with Jorjadze. Early next morning called on Jorjadze and his brother—house near Zayezhny Dom. Reception room ornamented in Persian style with red and green frescos. Half a dozen mountaineers standing round in their picturesque costumes. Knaz[40] Jorjadze—Georgian by birth—in Persian Kaftan with long sleeves and calico beshmet.

    ["An Island in the Sea of History" (1913), excerpted from page 1104]

I introduced myself as an American traveler, explained my plans, and requested permission to join his party. The prince, a fine-looking, gray-haired man 55 or 60 years of age, began at first to make objections, on the ground that I had had no mountain experience and was unaccustomed to the fatigue and hardship that such a journey would involve. When, however, I had given him a hasty account of my explorations in Kamchatka and northeastern Siberia, he yielded, rather ungraciously, and said: "Get yourself some heavy riding boots, a boorka,[41] and a pair

---

    40. *kniaz'*: prince.

    41. The *burka* is a heavy sheepskin cape worn by men all over the Caucasus. In addition to being warm enough to sleep under on cold mountain nights, the burka is a prized possession and amusing legends praising burkas abound, citing their useful-

Frith Maier in a burka. Photo © Chris Allingham.

of saddle-bags, and be prepared to leave here tomorrow afternoon at half past one."

[Journal, 120–22]

[. . .] Go with Gasser to Seratchef to get atkreete leest.[42] Seratchef very accommodating, gives me atkreete leest for 2 horses in all parts of Daghestan Oblast. Return to Knaz Jorjadze, who promises to send horses to hotel after me when his brother is ready to start. Begin packing up. Run all over town after an outfit of saddle bags, boorka, bashlik, big boots, etc. Am obliged to abandon half my baggage. Am finally fixed out complete. Miserable accommodations in Hotel de Goonib—bare room 1 RS

---

ness for glissading down snowy slopes (Baddeley, *Rugged Flanks of the Caucasus*, 34, 258), and even in stopping a knife fight (Chenciner, *Daghestan*, 181).

42. *otkrytyi list:* a kind of permit allowing its bearer to procure fresh horses at post stations.

a day with fleas thrown in. Those detestable insects tormented me so that I slept the last two nights on a small square table with my feet on the window sill. So many fleas on my blanket that I couldn't use that and I could only lie down in my overcoat with nothing under me and nothing over me. Fleas were worse in the hotel than in the Zayezhny dom where I first stopped.

Tartar grave stones shaped thus [*sketch*] and in night look like men in long grey cloaks, round knob at top frequently painted in red and green stripes, inscriptions in Arabic. Tartar quass[43] which I tasted on way to Shoura, detestable stuff full of flies, white, sour, made out of whey. Left Shoura from house of Knaz Jorjadze at 3 PM for Goonib. Large escort of 25 men in their picturesque costumes went filing in a long line through the Avarski gate. High mountain ridge behind us with a few white clouds along its side illuminated with dazzling brilliancy by afternoon sun. In front another high range, its summits hidden in clouds and its lower slopes in deep shadow, dark green almost black with an occasional gleam of a mountain torrent or white foam of cascade or waterfall. Cross low mountain range by a good road and see before us, in a broad cultivated valley covered with patch work of corn, rye, maize etc; the aoul of Joongootai.

[They spent the night at Dzhengutai, where they were entertained. Kennan described the performance in detail in one of his lectures (one assumes with a certain amount of literary license). Kennan MSS, LC, Box 64, handwritten lecture notes, 46–63. Compare the published account in "An Island in the Sea of History," 1107.]

The clapping of hands and the roll of the kettle-drums almost drowned the shriek of the tormented fife, while now and then both were lost in the banging of pistols which were fired into the air by the dancing mountaineer and the excited bystanders for the purpose of enlivening the proceedings. In two or three minutes a woman glided out of the ring, her partner touched his hat and also retired and another couple took their places, the clapping of hands and pistol firing going on as before.

Presently one of the mountaineers came in with a grin of satisfaction on his face, bringing a small three-legged milking stool, and a round club, like a rolling pin about two feet long and an inch and a half in

---

43. *kvass:* fermented bread drink.

diameter, split half way down so as to divide it into four sections. The milking-stool was placed upon the floor in the middle of the room, the club laid across it and the mountaineer retired. I asked Prince Jorjadze what these preparations portended, but he declared that it was something new to him, while all the satisfaction we could get out of our own interpreter was that we'd see.

I determined that I would see and took a front seat for that purpose, but it was a hasty action which I soon had occasion to regret. After a few moments of quiet whispering among the women, one of them advanced to the milking stool, took up the club and began to sing what seemed to be an address to the man, improvising with the greatest facility both words and music. Presently she stepped up to the group of fierce-looking mountaineers, raised the club, and struck one of them a light blow upon the shoulder, as if she were conferring upon him the accolade of knighthood.

The man shrugged his shoulders, but seated himself submissively upon the milking stool, paying no attention to a faint laugh which ran around among his comrades.

The woman stood silently in the middle of the room until he had seated himself and then resumed her song, addressing her remarks however to the particular man whom she had seated instead of to the group of men as at first. At the end of every stanza the whole audience joined in with a jolly chorus of "Hi Hi Hi An-nan-nan-ni," the singer striking her unfortunate victim three or four resounding blows across the shoulders with the club, and resuming her song as the chorus died away. This alternate singing and flogging interrupted by frequent "Hi Hi Hi"s continued for three or four minutes, the young woman smiling with satisfaction as she called attention with the club to the strong points of her musical address, while the mountaineer took his punishment with stoical indifference.

I looked enquiringly at Prince Jorjadze to see what he thought of this extraordinary performance and whether he foresaw as clearly as I did what we were coming to. He was laughing heartily at the ridiculous appearance presented by a fierce-looking mountaineer who was armed to the teeth with pistols and knives but who sat submissively on a milking stool while a woman beat him over the back with a rolling pin.

The women one after another called out, pounded and sang improvised addresses to the men, and the men in turn selected victims from among the women, while the chorus, instead of explaining the performance as a Greek chorus would have done, contented itself with shouting Hi Hi Hi in a deep bass voice as a sort of idiotic interlude between the verses.

In a few moments I saw three or four girls in one corner whispering, laughing and pointing at us, and I knew that it indicated trouble. I had a strong presentiment that the next victim would be either Prince Jorjadze or myself, and I was just considering the practicability of making my escape through an open window in the rear when one of the girls stepped forward and touched the Prince on the shoulder. He had not seemed to realize until that moment that he was in any particular danger but he yielded gracefully to the force of circumstances and took his seat on the milking stool. The performance went on precisely as before except that the Prince, on account of his high rank, was allowed to take his punishment by proxy.

One of the mountaineers volunteered in the most disinterested and self-sacrificing manner to act as a substitute and the young woman, while singing an address to Prince Jorjadze, bestowed her blows upon the man who heroically squatted down beside him on the floor. As soon as I saw that substitutes would be permitted I felt very much relieved, never doubting in my own mind that a sovereign American citizen would be entitled to quite as many privileges and exemptions as a petty Caucasian prince. But I was very much disappointed. My turn came next—and not a substitute offered himself.

Everybody laughed and I saw that there was no hope. Mentally regretting that I had not taken the precaution to put on a few more clothes, I took my seat on the three-legged stool, consoling myself with the reflection that I was probably the first foreigner who had ever enjoyed this peculiar experience.

With a few preliminary flourishes of the club intended evidently to strike terror to my soul, the young woman began to sing as follows, the words being translated to me by our interpreter.

This young man has come from a far-off land to see our Daghestan (Chorus: Hi Hi Hi An-nan-nan-nan-ni! Hi Hi!)
To observe our ways and our social customs and our mode of life (chorus)
And to write them down, and perhaps to print them in that far-off land. (chorus)

We must therefore show to this traveler how we always treat our friends. (whack! Whack! Chorus)

When a traveler comes and desires to join us in our social games (chorus)

We receive him gladly and we try to treat him with all due respect. (Whack! Whack!)

In this manner the girl continued to sing for some time, striking me two or three times over the shoulders at the end of every verse—and the verses unnecessarily short and unreasonably close together. Prince Jorjadze joined in the chorus of "Hi Hi Hi" with great spirit. At last the girl closed by striking me three or four farewell blows and handing me the club. A ridiculous appearance I must have presented, in a blue flannel shirt, a short English shooting jacket and top boots, standing over a lady richly dressed in Persian silks and laces, pounding her over the back with a club and singing "Hi Hi Hi An-nan-ni" . . . I did not attempt to carry the farce through. Overcome with laughter, I handed the club to a muscular-looking mountaineer and asked him to sing my song and avenge my injuries.

[Journal, 169]

Song sung by Lesghian girls at Joongootai. Three or four voices sang the first four notes and then prolonged the fifth until the rest of the choir had finished the strain when they broke in again with An-nan-ni—thus.

[...]

[One can imagine this was the way Jorjadze and his party
were greeted as they moved on from Dzhengutai toward Gunib.
"An Island in the Sea of History," excerpted from page 1105]

A large party of mountaineers, richly dressed and glittering with silver-mounted weapons and cartridge tubes, came galloping out of the stone gate, lashing their horses, shouting, whooping, yelling and firing at us incessantly as they dashed furiously down upon our escort. The distance between us narrowed to 50 feet, 30 feet, 10 feet, until the living thunderbolt of men and horses seemed actually to strike us. Then suddenly up went the hand of the leader, back went the trained horses upon their haunches as the sabers of their riders flashed in the air, and the whole attacking force in mid-career halted, slid a yard or two, and stopped within 6 feet of Prince Jorjadze's saddle-peak. For an instant the horsemen, with uplifted sabers, faced us in a superb battle tableau; then, with a great cry of Asalaam alaikoum! (Peace be with you) they sheathed their weapons, dismounted and advanced on foot to greet Prince Djordjaze.

[Journal, 122]

Beyond, another range of mountains half hidden in clouds. Village irregularly built, houses of clay and stone, high stone tower of mosque from which a couple of moolahs look down curiously upon our cavalcade as it trots through the narrow, crooked streets and between crowds of ragged, wild-looking mountaineers with kinjals and pistols in their belts and black and white papakhas.[44]

[He leaves no description of Gunib, even though it was the
famous site of Shamil's last battle. After Gunib, Kennan was not always
careful to name places, but a note at the end of the first book of the
journal clarifies the route. Journal, 172]

---

44. *papakha:* lamb's wool hat.

Dagestani aul. Markov, Ocherki: *421*.

First aoul where we camped after leaving Goonib was Ochaw [=Gochob] in the Karakhaki ooschele and obshestvo;[45] 2nd Tlarata Bokhro dalaki obshestvo; 3rd Bezhuta. Aoul before Ochaw was Tloroshe [=Tliarosh].

---

45. *Karakhaki ushchele:* Karakhaki Gorge. The modern name for the river is Karalazurger. *Obshchestvo:* society; here "community."

ACROSS THE MAIN CAUCASUS RIDGE

[Journal, 122–28]

Camp Grassy Side Hill. 4 hours from Goonib.[46]

LEFT GOONIB THIS MORNING AT 8 O'CLOCK. FORtunately I had an excellent horse—a powerful dark bay—I enjoyed my ride more than any part of trip since Petrovskoe. Descended by about 20 long zigzags to the bed of the river which runs past Goonib and a half an hour or so entered a wild ravine. Road runs along right—western side. On opposite side alternate cliffs of sandstone rock and grassy slopes at a height of 800 or 1000 feet in gigantic projecting buttresses. On western sides also high overhanging sandstone cliffs under which runs road with a precipice of 100 or 200 feet at its edge. In some places, gorge so narrow that it seems almost dark at bottom. Road winds around in a serpentine course up and down, around buttresses, into ravines, across rude bridges built up in places with rocks, thus [*sketch*]. Finally come out of this ravine and ride up on the mountain side where there is aoul.

Women with huge silver earrings, circular about 4 inches in diameter. Yard full of bee hives. Opposite where we are camped mountain rises steeply to height of 1500 feet seamed with strata of sandstone which break off in precipices.

Resting Place by river side above aoul. Threshing out grain with a sort of sled, rough on under side with a stone on it. Sled drawn by two oxen. In aoul below here there was a girl sitting on sled. Plough of this shape [*sketch*[47]] made of wood and pointed with iron—scratches up ground to a depth of only 3 or 4 inches. Woman dressed in one dirty linsey woolsey shirt and blue wide gun barrel pants, shoes large with sharp, turned-up toes. Met 3 or 4 returning from field work just now,

---

46. Kennan probably began this section on his lunch break and completed it when they arrived in the next aul (Gochob) for the night. He notes at the bottom of pages 124–25: "written in mountain aoul where we stop for night."

47. For a drawing of a scratch plow of very similar shape, see *Narody Kavkaza*, vol. 1, M. O. Kosven et al., eds. (Moscow, 1960), 442; see also the photograph on page 273.

some with huge pitchers of clay and metal on their backs, others bending double with huge bundles of hay, dark complexions, hair tied up over forehead in dirty handkerchief. Road for last 20 versts runs along river between two ranges of high mountains. Scenery grand but bare. Road runs for last 10 versts along south side of mountains 800 or 1000 feet above creeks.

From where we stopped to lunch we kept going up and up till at last we crossed the ridge at a height of at least 6000 feet and caught first sight of great snowy range rising in sharp white peaks at a distance of 20 miles but seeming to be less than 5.[48] Magnificent view from this point. Deep valley of which bottom could not be seen, cultivated fields 2000 feet below our feet, grand bare mountains all around and snowy range appearing above nearer green mountains. Road a mere bridle path cut out of mountain side. Begin to descend. Last descent had a grade of at least 1500 ft in 100, road zigzag a mere shelf with precipices above and below, horse began to slip on splinters of slate near the corner of a zigzag and I thought I was going over edge. Horse however very surefooted and I gave him the rein. As soon as I attempted to guide him he would shake his head furiously as much as to say "I know these mountain paths better than you do." His judgment with regard to best place to step was really remarkable.

At last we reached what I thought was the bottom but far from it. Pass through an aoul. These aouls quite different from Tartar aouls. 3-story stone forts with loop holes and very small windows, occasionally with square towers at corners. Built always high up on some inaccessible precipice. Houses generally ranged in terraces with passages 3 or 4 feet wide between them. After village another terrible zigzag descent down which we were all compelled to walk and lead our horses. Reach river[49] and begin ascending it. Mountains on both sides like all Daghestani mountains which I have seen, high, steep and grassy, cut horizontally or diagonally with seams of sandstone rock from 10 to 200 feet in width, which crop out of the steep, grassy slopes in perpendicular

---

48. Kennan is referring here to the peaks of the Nukatl Range between the Avarskoe Koisu and Karakoisu.

49. The Karalizurger, which he refers to above as the Karakhaki, a tributary of the Karakoisu.

precipices and tremendous buttresses. On these buttresses are built generally the mountain aouls.

    Houses rise one above the other like seats in a theatre so that each one commands a view of the whole country for 30 or 40 miles. Each house has an open balcony in 2nd or 3rd story. Resemble very much old feudal castles of middle ages. Some are at least 3,000 feet above river, so high that they are swept by ordinary summer clouds—cumuli. Old ruined loopholed towers. Situation of these aouls very picturesque on the edge of these enormous buttresses. Cross river to left bank at last, make another very steep zigzag ascent 3 or 4 miles long to this aoul which is situated about 2000 feet above river on an enormous rocky buttress inaccessible except

Dagestani aul. Markov, Ocherki: *425*.

by this path.⁵⁰ Commands magnificent view of the ravine. Boodoon⁵¹ just calling to prayers as we enter from roof of mosque and sound of his voice echoes from cliffs and is heard all over settlement. Take up our quarters at house of Lezgin merchant known to Prince. Upper room reserved for guests balcony with opening 8 or 10 feet wide closed in bad weather with curtain, wide divan at end opposite door which opens upon roof of lower story. On this roof haystacks. Around balcony room hang long silver-banded rifles, kinjals and pistols. Divan covered with Persian carpets. Adjoining room very dark, used as sleeping room in cold weather and here I am writing in a sort of shelf at side. Family lives in lower story.

Scholars learning in mosque bring complimentary letter to Prince written in Arabic, with expectation that he will give them money. This is one of their *obuichai*.⁵² Communication between many of these settlements entirely cut off in winter by snow. Left side of mountain range over river cultivated in terraces cut by ravines down which run streams in cascades. Stone structures and basins built over springs. Supper—1ˢᵗ. American pancakes 8 inches in diameter and honey—best thing I've tasted in Daghestan. 2ⁿᵈ: boiled mutton. 3ʳᵈ: shanks of lean mutton boiled with some kind of seasoning and boiled eggs. Pink beards of many mountaineers. Dirty sheep skin shoubas. No uniform costume here at all. Conjectures as to weather—clouds up soon after dark—we fear more snow. Whole ravine now filled with clouds so that looking from balcony of aoul one would think himself floating in a white misty sea or "up in a balloon." Everybody has gone to bed and I must go. Hospitality of mountaineers—If stranger arrives in village the

---

50. This aul was Gochob, which the modern map shows to be on the north side, down in the valley. It may in his time have been located on a precipice on the south side of the river. The road today forks about 4 kilometers east of Gochob, one branch crossing to the south side of the river and climbing well above the valley to a promontory.

51. The assistant to a *kadi*, or Islamic judge, the *budun* was responsible for reading prayers in the mosque and calling the faithful to prayer (Kavkazskoe gorskoe upravlenie, *Sbornik svedenii o kavkazskikh gortsakh*, 1:78). In that latter capacity Kennan also refers to him as a muezzin.

52. *obychai:* customs, traditions.

Starshine[53] cries out in the streets, "who will entertain the stranger?" and somebody takes him in.

[Kennan MSS, LC, Box 64, notes for lecture and article]

During the evening that we spent in the aoul of Ochau [=Gochob], while we were lying on the divan after supper, smoking and talking about the American Indians, in whom Prince Jorjadze was greatly interested, the curtain which concealed the doorway was pushed aside and a ragged boy about 15 years of age with a large white turban on his head entered the room and, bowing profoundly to Prince Jorjadze, read from a piece of paper which he held in his hand an address from the schoolboys of the village. He was a scholar, living and studying Arabic in the village mosque. There are of course no regular schools in these wild regions of the Eastern Caucasus, and those boys who desire to get a little education in Arabic so as to be able to read the Koran leave their homes and keep house together for themselves in the mosque, where they are taught by the moolah or village priest.[54] Every Thursday night they go the rounds of the village singing songs under the windows of the houses and taking up a collection of flour, meat and corn for their subsistence during the week. Whenever a traveler passes through the village they send to him flowers and complimentary address with the hope of getting a little money to provide themselves with a few luxuries. The address which the ragged boy, with a curious sing-song intonation read to Prince J. was:

From the scholars of the Ochau mosque to the greatest of the great, the wisest of the wise, the most generous of the generous, the bravest of the brave, Prince J—May peace be with thee and may the light of thy sun never be extinguished till the awful day of judgment. Amen. When we heard the joy-giving news of thy coming and the light of thy resplendent countenance illu-

---

53. *starshina:* village elder.

54. In 1996 in Untsukul, we visited a boarding school that opened a couple of years ago. The students, all boys ages six to sixteen, study only Arabic and religious subjects. Their curriculum also includes wrestling, a sport in which Dagestan has produced several Russian national champions.

minated the eastern horizon of prosperity, the members of our body rejoiced together over the glad tidings and the radiance of the sun of happiness drove away from our hearts the dark clouds of melancholy. To thee oh Prince the aim of all students is well known and thy immeasurable generosity loudly famed throughout the whole world convinces us that our embassy will not return from thy threshold with empty hands.

And with another profound bow the boy stopped and stood before us in silence looking with a wistful expression at the remains of our supper. Prince J gave him a small amount of money and with many thanks he retired.

[Having spent the night at Gochob, the next morning the party sets off to cross the Nukatl Pass. Journal, 129–32]

Village between mountains, Sept. 27th[55]

LEFT GOTSCHOB ABOUT 7:30. HERDS OF GOATS AND sheep far up on mountain side, man watching them. Little low stone houses for shelter of herdsmen. Our Khazine[56] accompanies us to summit of snowy mountain. [We] turn away to right from mouth of ravine and follow small mountain torrent up. Soon reach snow and about half way up, perpetual snow lying in hollows and ravines. No road at all but no dangerous places. Grows colder and colder as we ascend. Fine morning, only cumulous clouds. Tremendous black rocky peaks on left scantily sprinkled with snow, inaccessible, with clouds breaking and curling swiftly around their summits. Piles of stones to mark out roads in storms and fog. Reach summit at last—very cold and strong wind in our faces.[57] Magnificent wild view. Deep ravine of which bottom cannot be seen. Group of enormous snowy peaks on left—so steep that snow can hardly lie on them—apparently no outlet from this ravine, road seems like wind-

---

55. Probably Tliarata, which was the next overnight stop.
56. *khoziain*: host.
57. From the top of the Nukatl Ridge, Kennan would have had a good view of Mount Addala (4151; 13,619 ft), highest summit in the Bogos Range (the "2nd snowy range"), and then dropped down into the Avarskoe Koisu valley.

ing thread far below. Descend on foot. Roaring of mountain torrents falling like silver ribbons down mountain sides. Stop to lunch by side of stream just above an aoul. High hills on left, green with just the tops of the 4 snowy peaks rising above them. Formation of country changes entirely on this side of range—ledges of sandstone rock no longer seen. Slates and shales appear. Below village timber begins—first timber of consequence I have seen in Daghestan. Rest for lunch half an hour and then enter another tremendous valley with mountains on each side rising to height of 3000 or 4000 feet covered half way up with timber and topped with snow. Road runs along stream in bottom of valley 2nd snowy range appears at end of valley. Scenery resembles very much scenery of California. Entirely different from that on north side of first range. Equally wild, picturesque and beautiful, but not so bare and sterile. Bottom of valley covered with trees and bushes giving grateful shade from hot rays of sun—wild barberries, hollyhocks, American blueberries also. Timber slides down sides of mountains.[58] Cascades. Good road under shady trees. Lose sight of group of high mountains. Ravine narrows between rocky precipices nearing no room for passage between them and stream. Road ascends steeply side of mountain on right side of stream.[59] Soon reaches height of 600, 800, or 1000 feet, and runs along mountain side round bluffs and into ravines, giving magnificent views of timbered mountains on other side, snowy range at end, torrent tumbling in white cascades at bottom. Road pretty good of its kind—mere foot path 18 inches wide with precipices 600 and 800 feet falling from its very edge. Stop again to rest on sloping plateau. Dog runs away up mountain side. Circassian leaves his shashka on grass. Descend again to bed of torrent. Ruined stone towers on projecting rocky bluffs over stream guarding road.

Arrive at this village[60] about 7:30 very tired and with back ache.

58. Kennan is describing the way they harvest timber from the hillsides, sliding it over the frozen snow in winter, as it was explained to me.

59. Judging from the modern map, after descending from the Nukatl Pass to the aul Kardib, Kennan then would have climbed across the ridge to its northwest, and descended to the valley of the Ukhtil'or, a tributary of the Dzhurmut, which in turn flows into the Avarskoe Koisu.

60. Tliarata.

Village situated in a deep narrow side ravine at junction of 2 streams. Houses built on both sides of ravine, one above another on rocks. Ride to house of Naib at upper end of village. Man comes out to meet us with flaming pine knot. Already quite dark. Naib very large man with close-shaven head and henna-stained beard.

["Unwritten Literature of the Caucasian Mountaineers" (1878), 440–41]

The etiquette of salutation in the Caucasus is extremely elaborate and ceremonious. It does not by any means satisfy all the requirements of perfect courtesy to ask a mountaineer how he is, or how his health is, or how he does. You must inquire minutely into the details of his domestic economy, manifest the liveliest interest in the growth of his crops and the welfare of his sheep, and even express a cordial hope that his house is in a good state of repair and his horses and cattle properly protected from any possible inclemency of weather. Furthermore, you must always adapt your greeting to time, place and circumstances, and be prepared to improvise a new, graceful and appropriate salutation to meet any extraordinary exigence. In the morning a mountaineer greets another with "May your morning be bright!" to which the prompt rejoinder is, "And may a sunny day never pass you by!"

A guest he welcomes with "May your coming bring joy!" and the guest replies, "May a blessing rest on your house!" To one about to travel the appropriate greeting is, "May God make straight your road!" to one returning from a journey, "May health and strength come back with rest!" to a newly-married couple, "May you have sons like the father and daughters like the mother!" and to one who has lost a friend, "May God give you what he did not live to enjoy!" Among other salutations in frequent use are, "May God make you glad!" "May your sheep be multiplied!" "May you blossom like a garden!" "May your hearth-fire never be put out!" and "May God give you the good that you expect not!"

The curses of the Caucasus are as bitter and vindictive as its greetings are courteous and kind-hearted. I have heard it said by the Persians and Tatars who live along the Lower Volga that there is no language to swear in like the Russian; and I must admit that they illustrated and proved their assertion when occasion offered in the most fluent and incontrovertible manner; but I am convinced, after having heard the curses of experts in all parts of the East, that for variety, ingenuity and force, the profanity of the Caucasian mountaineers is unsurpassed. They are by no means satisfied with damning their adversary's soul after the vulgar manner of the Anglo-Saxon, but invoke the direst calamities upon his body also; as, for example: "May the flesh be stripped from your face!" "May your heart take fire!" "May your name be written on a stone!" (i.e. a tombstone), "May the shadow of an owl fall on your house!" (this, owing probably to the rarity of its occurrence, is regarded as a fatal omen); "May your hearth-fire be put out!" "May you be struck with a hot bullet!" "May your mother's milk come with shame!" "May you be laid on a ladder!" (alluding to the Caucasian custom of using a ladder as a bier); "May a black day come upon your house!" "May the earth swallow you!" "May you stand before God with a blackened face!" "Break through into hell!" (i.e. through the bridge of Al Sirat); "May you be drowned in blood!"

[Journal, 133–34]

All day today the prince has been hearing complaints and deciding disputes among the mountaineers. The case that attracted most attention was that of a man whose horse was stolen a long time ago and which he recently found. Adat.[61] If a man loses a horse and years afterward finds him in possession of another man, he at once claims his property. He gives the man 20 kopecks, a piece of cotton cloth, and a paper stating that the horse is his and that he has taken him. The second man at once goes to the 3rd from whom he bought the horse and claims a return of the purchase money. The 3rd man cannot refuse; he returns the money taken. The 20 kopecks, the cloth, and the paper pass through the hands of perhaps 15 or 20 men who have successively bought and sold the horse, the purchase money being in every case returned. At last the paper reaches the man who originally found or stole the horse; he returns the money which he got for him, and the case is ended. Another adat. If a man loses a horse and has a suspicion that a second man has stolen it he accuses him of it, and the second man must bring witnesses who are willing to swear that he has not stolen it and that his character is good. By a word he must justify himself from suspicion—if he cannot do this, he must pay for the horse.

61. Customary law.

[Kennan's interest in customary law will also be seen in some of the following selections. A comparison of the material above with what he wrote about customary law after his return, without specifying exactly where he had witnessed the involvement of the prince, provides insights into the way he elaborated on his notes. "Mountains and Mountaineers," 183–85]

Prince Jorjadze and I stopped one day in an aoul where a large number of mountaineers collected in the house which we occupied to stare at the newcomers; and then a man entered, wrapped in a large, white cotton cloth which resembled a sheet. He seemed to be in search of somebody, and in a moment he stepped up to another mountaineer, and began in a very excited and vehement manner to talk to him. I could not, of course, understand what was said; but the other mountaineers all crowded around, and, after a few moments of excited debate, the man who had been thus rudely accosted, left the house. He was gone perhaps twenty minutes. He returned, bringing in his hand forty rubles in paper money, which he gave to the man who had first addressed him, and took in exchange the large white cloth in which the latter had been wrapped up, together with a small silver coin worth, perhaps, twenty cents.

The whole transaction was perfectly incomprehensible. Upon inquiry it appeared that six months previous to this time a certain man had lost a horse. At the end of four or five months he heard of his lost horse as being in the possession of a mountaineer in a neighboring valley. He wrapped himself up in a white cloth, took his weapons and a small silver coin, and, accompanied by witnesses, went to the mountaineer to demand the return of his property. The white cotton cloth was a burial shroud, the silver coin was to pay a priest for reading prayers over a grave, and upon the result of the negotiation depended the question whose shroud and whose grave they should be, his or the other man's. The shroud and the money were intended to be significant of his determination to have his rights at all hazards. If his adversary returned the horse peaceably, well and good; if not, he would fight for it; and he showed that he had fully considered the consequences by coming in a burial shroud, and bringing with him money to pay the expenses of his own funeral.

It was either a horse or a grave for somebody. In this instance the horse was peaceably returned, and the owner transferred the shroud and the silver coin to the other man, who wrapped himself up, took his weapons, and started in search of the mountaineer who had sold the animal to him. He wanted a return of the money which he had paid. In this way the shroud and the coin had been through six or eight different hands when I saw them, and were still on their way back to the man who had originally found the horse or stolen him. He would have to refund the amount which he had received for the animal when he sold him, and then, if he were not guilty of theft, the whole question would be dropped, the shroud and the silver coin remaining in the hands of the last man.

This is one of the so-called "adats" or customary laws of the Daghestan mountaineers, and it prevails over all the southern part of the province. The laws of the Daghestan "free communities" are of two kinds—first, the *shariat,* or written law of the Koran; and, second, the *adat,* or unwritten law of custom or precedent. The first was introduced by the Arabs with the Mahometan religion in the eighth century, and the last has existed from time immemorial. All questions concerning religion, family relations, wills, and inheritance are decided by the Koran; while all criminal cases, including infractions of public regulations, are tried by adat, or the law of custom. Every aoul elects by popular vote a certain number of jurymen whose duty it is to try all cases in accordance with the general law of the Koran or the customary law of that village. These jurymen assemble at stated times, either in the open street or upon the square in front of the mosque, to listen to complaints. The trial of every case begins with the statement of the plaintiff or person having a direct interest, is followed by the statement of the defendant, then by the examination of witnesses or the oaths of compurgators, and is finally decided by a majority of the jurymen.

The witnesses are sworn and examined as with us; but not every man is legally competent to be a witness. Relatives of the plaintiff having a direct interest in the case are not permitted to testify; neither are persons having a pending lawsuit with the defendant, nor debtors of the defendant until they have paid their debts; nor persons having blood revenge against him; nor persons who have made a vow never to take an oath. Women are admitted as witnesses only in one free community, in the Darginski Okroog; and there the husband or brother takes the oath instead of the woman herself. Every witness swears that he will tell the truth, either by the name of God or by the legality of his marriage. The last oath is the oldest, and is considered the most sacred. If a man perjure himself, and the fact of his perjury be proved, he is compelled to separate at once from his wife. If he has more than one wife, he is required to state beforehand by which of his marriages he wishes to swear, so that the proper wife can be divorced. Besides the testimony of witnesses, which may be called direct proof, the law admits, in many cases, indirect or negative proof; or, in other words, allows an accusation to be brought against a man by suspicion. In this case the defendant can only clear himself by taking the oath of purgation, with a certain number of compurgators, part of whom he selects himself, and part of whom are chosen from his relatives by the accuser. The number of these compurgators varies from twelve to seventy, according to the nature of the accusation.

If a single one of them refuses to swear that he believes the defendant to be innocent, he is considered guilty. Sometimes the plaintiff himself takes the oath, also supported by compurgators, part of whom are chosen by the defendant and part by himself. If they unanimously swear that they believe the defendant to be guilty, guilty he is. The option of taking the oath himself or requiring it of the defendant rests wholly with the plaintiff; but accusation by suspicion is permitted only in the absence of direct proof. The number of persons who can be successively accused of the same crime varies from one to seven.

The adats, or customary laws, differ as widely as the people who observe them. The free communities of Daghestan, in the first place, are very differently situated—they are made up of diverse elements, and are at different stages of culture and development. Cases for which there were no adats have been decided according to the best judgement of the jurymen, thus establishing new precedents; and the result of all these causes is a remarkable dissimilarity in the adats[62] of different parts of the country. Almost every settlement has its own laws, differing more or less from those of its neighbors.

---

62. Esadze claims that in Dagestan "adat" often depended on the arbitrary judgment of those in power (*Istoricheskaia zapiska ob upravlenii Kavkazom*, 2:106).

ACROSS THE MAIN CAUCASUS RIDGE

[Journal 134–68, 170–71]

Balcony of Naib's house, same place, Sept. 28th, 1870[63]

MEN ARE SADDLING HORSES FOR A start. after dinner yesterday we took a nap and after that my young Lezgian friend organized a dance in one of the houses of the village. Before this we looked over several saklas. Saklas generally two or three stories high built of undressed stones of all sizes plastered together with clay. They stand on rocks on the precipitous sides of a ravine so that while the roof comes right against the mountain on one side, it falls 30 or 40 feet to ground on the other. Out from the 2nd or 3rd story is built a large open balcony with a roof over it and a railing round it. First story for cattle, 2nd for sheep, 3rd for family. Doors on side thus [*sketch*]. Kitchen of a Lezgin house is a square room 12 or 15 feet across entered by a very low door. It has generally only one window, and that is a mere loop hole without glass or any substitute for it, which can be

---

63. Tliarata, where Kennan stayed, is today the most significant settlement in this part of the Avarskoe Koisu watershed. On page 172 of his journal, he describes

Dagestani sakla—on the balcony of a mountain home. Markov, Ocherki: *430.*

closed with a wooden door or shutter. Of course the room is very dark. On one side against the wall is a place for a fire on a low clay hearth, over which is a wide-mouthed chimney coming down to within about 4 feet of floor. Floor of earth covered with home made carpets, skins, or pieces of felt. Fire place provided with sort of andirons to support kettles etc.

Prince's room, Bezhuta [=Bezhta], Sept. 29th, 1870[64]

ON OPPOSITE SIDE OF ROOM ARE TWO LONG SHELVES running whole length of room upon which are ranged in order earthen pots [in] antique shapes, wooden bowls, copper pitchers, plates, knives, spoons, etc. Room always more or less smoky, especially if there be any wind. Occasionally there are one or two cupboards in the room, but no chairs or tables. The sleeping rooms are not essentially different. They have fire place and carpets and instead of shelves on one side are piled beds and bedding to height of 4 or 5 feet. Sometimes there are rude bedsteads or a sort of a raised platform on which bedding is spread at night. Rooms all very dark, loopholes for musketry—pegs driven in wall for hanging up weapons. Houses in all these settlements stuck against precipitous sides of ravines without any reference to each other or to streets—passages between them narrow muddy and dark, overhung by balconies. Walls of rooms in houses are of course plastered with mud and sometimes painted in gaudy colors in Persian style. Roofs of all are easily accessible and children play on them.

At noon on the day of our arrival at Naib's,[65] all population went down into bed of stream at bottom of ravine to wash and pray. Long

---

the Naib's domain as "1500 smokes or from 6000 to 7000 people," which would be consistent with its location and continuing prominence.

64. Kennan's account is confused by his spelling, "Bezhuta." This was actually Bezhta, the ancient center of the western Avarskoe Koisu, on the way up to the Main Caucasus Ridge. Some maps show another aul, Bezhuda, lying at the base of the Nukatl peaks, but north of the obvious route over the Nukatl Pass from Gochob which would have brought him to Tliarata at the end of a long day of travel. Here he is not describing the prince's room in Bezhta but is continuing his description of a typical room in Tliarata.

65. Probably the day after their arrival, which was in the evening.

line of men squatting by water far up and down ravine washing themselves. Dressed in blue nankeen pants, beshmets of some ragged stuff, dirty and greasy, long white sheep skin cloaks with sleeves wide at shoulder but tapering gradually to wrist like long tails with no opening at bottom for hands. Sleeves not made to put arms in. Caps of white and black sheepskin with very long, wavy hair hanging over forehead to eyes and over ears. Looks like man's own hair as if sheep's wool grew out of his head instead of hair. Long kinjals hanging to belt, on feet very thick, heavy woolen stockings and short Persian slippers. Kinjals and slippers they take off when they pray. After washing, all the men scattered along the stream up and down the ravine, spread down their sheep skin coats on the grass, took off slippers and all their weapons, turned faces to Mecca and began to pray in usual style. Long line of men bending half double with hands on knees looked as if about to begin a game of leap frog.

Lezgins all talk with great many gesticulations. After dinner yesterday[66] we took a nap and after that my young Lezgin friend organized a dance in one of the houses of the village. House in which it was held was situated about half way up side of ravine, door to 2nd story in side about 20 feet from ground reached by short horizontal bridge. Room smoky from fire of pine splinters against wall on one side. In one corner were squatted 2 or 3 women in blue nankeen shirts, veils tied over heads concealing all hair and the throat, drawers of blue nankeen with red and yellow stripes about 2 inches from bottom, shoes of thick woolen, very large and striped and of this shape [*sketch of shoe with upward curving pointed toe*]. In the other corner were the musicians in usual southern Daghestani costumes. Instruments a fiddle of this shape [*sketch*] like a wooden bread bowl with a long handle and sheep skin stretched over it—4 strings, peg at bottom. It is held like a bass viola, peg resting on ground and whole instrument turning from side to side as man fingers and plays with bow of this shape [*sketch*][67]. Tone very good. Other instrument huge tamborine about 2 feet and a half in diameter. This is held

---

66. Probably here he means day before yesterday (i.e., September 27).

67. For a similar bow, see *Narody Kavkaza*, 1:340. The fiddle depicted there has a similar shaped bowl to that drawn by Kennan, but the one he draws has a shorter neck and more elaborate head for the string pegs.

in left hand before the face and played by striking it with open fingers of right hand and of left alternately. Very sonorous.

We seated ourselves on a bench beside fire, a dozen men or so squatted around sides of room and music began. The "motif," as the Russians say, was very monotonous: one simple strain played over and over again in rapid time. Presently, man sprang into open space before fire, which was covered with a piece of felt, stretched out one arm, placed other on his hip and began to dance a sort of double shuffle moving his feet with the greatest rapidity, walking rapidly around in a circle and whirling swiftly like a top on one toe. All spectators clapped their hands in time to music. After dancing about half a minute, this man retired and another took his place, going through substantially the same performance. They thus danced alternately about 5 mins and then touched their hats to each other and resumed their cross-legged position on the floor. Afterward the violinist played a wild melancholy protyanooti[68] song which reminded me of the songs of the Kamchadals. Dancing continued about an hour and a half. I sang for them Kingdom Coming which is a universal favorite all over the world among Koraks and Choukchis, Russians, Caucasian Jews, Lezgins, Georgians and all. They told me they would never forget me or these American songs. Sang also Yankee Doodle in remembrance of Dolper.

While this dance was going on, preparations were being made for the grand dance of the evening. A huge fire was built in the yard of the Naib's house and about 8 o'clock a man came to tell us that all was ready. A young Lezgin with silver sabre and kinjal lighted a pine torch and guided me across the bridge and through the narrow, crooked streets to the Naib's house. We took seats on the long, wide balcony and the performance began. Round the fire on the grass were sitting cross-legged about a hundred and twenty-five men in sheepskin shoobas and caps, all armed with kinjals and many with pistols. Musical instruments: 2 tamborines, a violin and a nazora[69] or Daghestani fife. High mountains on one side showing only a stripe of dark, starry heavens above, stone saklas rising in tiers on the other. Above balcony, groups of women and children on roofs. Gleam of white snowy peak opposite mouth of ravine.

68. *protianutyi*: drawn-out.
69. Actually *zurna*.

Black crags lighted up by red firelight, wild appearance of the circle of cross-legged mountaineers, roaring of mountain torrent. Dancing begins to music of nazora and tamborine. Men dance alternately in twos. Now and then man tosses fire brand to somebody in outside circle. Not much excitement, no singing or crying out. Dance nothing but a Caucasian variation of the universal jig. After half an hour it became monotonous and tiresome and the want of women made it less interesting than it would otherwise have been. At 11 PM it closed.

I will write down here a few facts which I learned in that village. All Daghestan is governed by Naibs. A Naib is an officer appointed by the Gov't who receives 600 RS a year and who has authority over a certain district embracing perhaps 5 or 6 villages and from 1000 to 1500 smokes.[70] The Naib in whose house we stopped governed 1500 smokes or from 6000 to 7000 people. The Naib is assisted by a sort of local assembly consisting of one or more deputies from every village or community according to the number of its smokes. These deputies are chosen or elected from among the oldest, most respected and trusted inhabitants of each village. All complaints and disputes as to land, property, etc. are investigated by the Naib before this assembly which has the power to settle them, to impose fines, etc. If plaintiffs or defendants are not satisfied with the decision of the assembly, they can appeal to the courts at Goonib and Timour Khan Shoura and finally to the Gov. of the province. The Gov't endeavors as far as possible to accommodate its policy to the prejudices and customs of the mountaineers, and when Daghestan was conquered, the Emperor [tsar] directed that all things should be left as they were under Shamyl.

Among the Daghestani mountaineers there are now three kinds of law. The Shariat, or written law, according to the Koran. The Adat, or unwritten law of custom or usage. And finally, the laws of the Russians. During the rule of Shamyl, the Shariat was the ruling law, religion was the sole thought and business of every man and all things else were subordinated to it. Muridism recognized no duties but religious duties, prohibited all pleasures and turned the whole population into devoted fanatics. Dances were prohibited as well as music. Smoking was punished in the most barbarous manner. The nose of the offender was pierced and a piece of tobacco suspended to it. His face was then blacked, a dog

---

70. That is, hearths or households, the basic census unit.

tied on his back and he was paraded through the whole village. Women were never allowed to appear in the presence of men unveiled and so strict was the observance of religious duties that a father killed his own son for omitting for three days to pray. Men fought against the Russians with the most devoted heroism, believing firmly that if they died fighting the Giours they would go at once to Paradise. They believed also that God had immutably fixed the date of every man's death and they went into battle with the conviction that if the predetermined day of their death had come, nothing could save them and that if it had not come, nothing could kill them. This fatalism of course made every man a hero, and Gretingkov told me that he had seen a single Daghestan mountaineer with no weapon but a kinjal throw himself upon a whole Russian battalion and receive their fire without being in the least daunted. Muridism fell, however, with Shamyl, and the Shariat lost in a measure its force. The Adat then became the ruling law and the Russian Gov't even now respects it as far as possible.

2 brothers renowned for villainy of all kinds. There were three of them but one killed another and then married his wife. They committed so many crimes that the village finally requested their exile and while we were there, a petition to that effect was presented to Prince Jorjadze. A community in Daghestan has a right to demand in this way the forcible removal of any of its members whose presence is prejudicial to the public welfare. The offenders must find themselves another place and bring the written agreement of another village or community to receive them.

Customs of shaking, or rather pressing, hands upon meeting prevailed in Daghestan long before time of its conquest by Russians. Georgians only bow. Graves of distinguished warriors at Gotschob—Little shrines of stone containing stone tablet with Arabic inscription, pile of broken quartz on top, the whole surmounted by tall pole and ball. We left Naib's village about 8 o'clock yesterday morning,[71] crossed the stream by an Asiatic bridge[72] which trembled under our feet, and went up river to mouth of transverse ravine which we ascended. Ravine clothed in

---

71. September 28.

72. By this he probably means a cantilever bridge made of logs, brush, and rocks. At Kvankhidatl later he described a "frail swinging bridge" (a suspension one made with ropes?) and at Tlokh an "American bridge," having a girder frame which he sketched.

foliage, pine, spruce, birch, poplar, oak, beech, quantities of wild barberry bushes full of red fruit. Begin a tremendous climb of about 4000 feet over a big bare mountain, road runs up in steep zigzags. Magnificent view of the great snowy Caucasus range apparently only 4 or 5 miles away, with huge green foothills rolling up to it, and deep valleys 30 or 40 miles away filled with dark purple mist. Reach summit and cross. On other side a tremendous valley of which bottom could not be seen but smoke ascending from it. Cultivated fields 3000 feet below. One side of valley shaggy with forests, other side bare and dotted with countless herds of black and white sheep and goats, which look like ants or moving specks. Shouts of herdsmen and barking of dog come up faintly from below. In the distance the snowy range stretching away to eastward with deep valleys and huge foothills purple with distance. Finest view in Daghestan.

Residence of Prince Jorjadze—Innesay [=Eniseli] Kakhetia, October 2nd, 1870[73]

DESCEND A TOLERABLY STEEP SPOOSKA[74] AND STOP for lunch on the side hill near a little stream. After lunch Prince Jorjadze and I start out on foot while men are saddling horses. Descend still farther into wooded valley. Women at work getting wheat into barns. Ride through valley a short distance and come out upon tolerably large stream which we follow up to Bezhuta.[75] Bezhuta is a village of 250 or 300 houses situated among the foothills of the great range in a valley on both sides of a small stream. Houses here have more wood about them than Lezgin houses in general and are, if possible, more irregular in construction. They are generally 2 or 3 stories in height and upper story is frequently built entirely of boards and set on the stone foundation like wooden boxes thus [*sketch*] with a projecting balcony. House nearly opposite ours on other side of creek had 3 stories. First was used as stable for cattle, second, which was all open in front, as a barn filled with hay, 3rd as residence of family with balcony, while roof was temporarily covered with

73. Although in the narrative Kennan is on the way to Bezhta, he is writing only several days later.
74. *spusk:* descent.
75. Bezhta today matches this description. The large stream is the Khzanor.

shocks of wheat stacked up as if it had grown on the roof. Many houses are built in this way [*sketch of "stacked boxes" of houses*] with Story No. 1 used as a threshing floor for wheat, 2 as a sort of a barn to store it in case of wet weather, 3 as stables and 4 as family residence. There are all sorts of variations, however, from this plan and it is almost impossible to give a general idea of the appearance of such a settlement.

As we entered, we saw women at work on the roofs in a great many places threshing out wheat. Sled about 4 feet long made of a thick plank turned up at end. On under side are made small square holes in rows thus [*sketch*], and in every hole is wedged a small, rugged, sharp-cornered piece of quartz rock. To this sled are then harnessed a pair of bourvol[76] or oxen, somebody stands on the sled or a big stone is put on it, and it is dragged around over the grain. Gradually the kernels are separated from the straw, which is constantly turned over by the women with forks until finally it is all threshed out and the wheat remains on the floor and the straw is stacked up. Some small pieces of straw of course remain with the grain and from these it is separated by repeated sifting.

Women in vicinity of Bezhuta wear a somewhat better, more picturesque costume than those on the other side of first snowy range. Head covered with handkerchiefs covering hair and hanging like long veils behind. Over these a crescent-shaped piece of cloth covered with pieces of silver coins. Body covered with long loose shirt of blue nankeen hanging nearly to ankles and tied about waist with heavy sash. Drawers loose, not gathered about ankles. Shirt and drawers both ornamented with two or three broad stripes of red or yellow round the bottom 2 or 3 inches from edge. Shoes of woolen yarn tastefully knitted in colors with toes turned over like skates.[77] Over the breast hangs a rectangular piece of cloth—a sort of tab about a foot long and ten inches wide completely covered with silver coins of all kinds, Persian and Caucasian. Women coarse-featured, dark-complexioned and not at all handsome. Evidently degraded and brutalized by hard work. Haven't seen a good-looking woman since leaving Joongootai.

We took up our quarters at Bezhuta in a house which seemed to be

---

76. For his description of the burvol, see Journal, 94, above.

77. Called *chariki*, these beautiful, tightly knitted shoes are traditional year-round footware of the Bezhta region.

untenanted. Large dark kitchen opening upon ground behind and upon long wide balcony in front. At one end of balcony was door opening into small room made of boards containing a table, a portable camp bedstead and a sort of rude wooden setter. Door very wide and no means of closing it. Carpet hung over it at night. No windows. Cracks between boards an inch or two wide through which cold wind blows. Two Russian officers, both Georgians stationed at Bezhuta, call to pay respects to Prince and in half an hour or so after our arrival the latter begins hearing complaints. Conversation carried on in Georgian so that I don't understand a word. So cold that I have to wear my overcoat all the time. After tea and supper of black bread, salted Lezgin cheese,[78] red wine, soup of boiled mutton filled with little shards of fat, and boiled trout—we retire for night.

Day in Bezhuta—At first appearance of dawn the boodoon or muezzin half sings, half intones the first call to prayers—"Allah il Allah bey, Al lah il Al lah bey" drawling out every syllable to a great length and closing at least an octave below the pitch with which he started in a sort of moan. Dismal sort of sound. By sunrise the village is astir. The women are first to get up and the air is filled with the lowing of cattle as they are driven out of the settlement to pasture. One after another women pass by through the narrow dirty streets with children strapped into long narrow baskets and slung horizontally across their backs by a wide strap. Some have long ropes hanging in festoons from their sash behind to be used in tying up the immense bundles of hay or straw which they will bring back from the fields where they are going to work. All have silver coins on breasts and heads. Many are busily engaged in knitting as they go to work. An idle woman in Daghestan would be a curiosity. I have never yet seen one who was not occupied with something. They drive cattle to pasture, milk cows, feed horses, reap grain, bring it on their backs, make fires, keep house in order, take care of children, knit woolen shoes and stockings, make their own clothes and their husbands' and keep them in repair, bring water on their backs from streams in huge earthen or copper pitchers, in fact do almost everything that is to be done.

The only work that I have ever seen the men do was to plough, sow grain, and assist in threshing. As soon as the women have all gone afield and the sun gets up a little so as to warm the atmosphere, the men in

---

78. *brinza:* this ubiquitous Caucasian cheese keeps for several years in brine.

dirty sheepskin shoubas and caps begin to congregate under the balcony and on the balcony of the mosque and sit there in idleness for hours. The children make their appearance on the flat roofs of the saklas or in the streets and with joyous cries and laughter engage in various diversions such as running races, pitching heavy stones, pelting each other with mud, throwing cats by the tail against the stone walls of the houses, etc. They are dressed generally in imitation of their parents. There was one bright cunning little fellow about 6 years old who particularly attracted my attention. He had nothing on but a coarse woolen skirt coming below his knees and a dirty white sheepskin cap. His hair was shaved all over his head except just above the ears where it hung in two long thin locks. His bare legs were plastered with black mud, as well as his hands, and he was engaged in throwing mud balls at one of his comrades on the roof. He had a very bright intelligent face and I have no doubt that if he could be taken to American now and educated he would make an able useful man. The more I see of wild people the more I am inclined to believe that it is education which makes the man. There is no reason to doubt that the innate capability of these wild Lesghian mountaineers is equal to that of the average Englishman or American and the only difference between them arises out of the circumstances in which they are respectively placed. One has advantages, education, culture, and the other has not. One grows up an intelligent, thinking reasoning human being and the other a mere wild animal.

From 8 o'clock till noon the men sit around the mosque and smoke and talk and the children play in the streets and on the roofs. At 12 o'clock the boodoon, a grey bearded old man in a greasy sheepskin shouba takes his stand on the balcony of the mosque, turns his face toward Mecca and in a loud voice drawls out Allah il Allah bey—there is no God but God and Mohammed is his prophet. In the course of five minutes the men of the village begin to assemble at the mosque, shuffle off their Persian slippers, and enter through the low dark door to pray. Comparatively a small proportion of the inhabitants of a village say their prayers in the mosque. I don't believe that for morning prayers they can muster a corporal's guard. Toward sunset, the women begin to return from the fields bending double under immense loads of hay and wheat which they carry on their backs. Soon afterward the cattle are driven in by hundreds lowing and fighting through the streets. The men gather in still larger numbers on the pile of timber under the piazza of the mosque and around the bridge leading across the creek. A fight between a couple of bulls draws a much larger crowd in a much shorter time than the call of the boodoon to prayers. As soon as it grows dark the village becomes quiet. The men and children go home and, except for the firelight in a few of the houses, there is no sign of life in the settlement and the roaring of the mountain streams is the only sound to be heard. Once more late in the evening the boodoon shouts out the call to prayers and soon afterward the last light is extinguished and the whole village is dark and silent.

Same place [=Eniseli], Oct. 3rd

FOR SUPPER AT BEZHUTA WE HAD TROUT, ROUND thin bread pancakes about 10 inches in diameter, salty white Lezgin cheese newly taken out of brine, Siberian youkala[79] soup and boiled mutton and fried lumps of lean mutton. No vegetables. The mosque at Bezhuta, as is usually the case in Daghestan villages, was not particularly noticeable. It was simply a large square stone building with the back end under ground, a flat roof, a broad, elevated piazza in front and one low door in the middle. There were no windows visible. The last night of our stop in Bezhuta, a child died in the adjoining house and we could hear the wailing song which the women kept up over its body and the sobs of the mourners. I would have liked to get a translation of the words which the women sang.

The following are some of the customs of the Lezgins which I learned at Bezhuta from the two Russian officers and the prince. First, with regard to support of moolahs and boodoons—A tenth part of all the grain grown in a settlement is reserved for religious and charitable purposes. Of this tenth, one third is given for support of moolah (who, by the way, is chosen by people), one third for support of boodoon and scholars learning Arabic in the mosque, and one third to the poor. Besides this there occurs once or twice a year a sort of grand donation party for benefit of poor. Every [. . .] brings what it can spare in the way of food and it is divided among the poor.

2nd: in case of a drought, the women of the settlement all march in a body around the village singing Allah il Allah and offer up on the sum-

79. *iukola:* a kind of dried fish.

mit of every hill a sheep. Men assemble at some designated place with moolah, every man picks up a stone, moolah says a prayer over every stone separately, puts them in a basket and leaves them in water of stream or on banks. In case of pestilence or contagious disease among men women or cattle, an arch is dug through some projecting bluff, the moolah stands on top with water over which prayers have been said, and sprinkles it over the people and animals as they pass in procession through the arch. The disease, they believe, cannot pass through but must remain behind.

Lezgins are very particular what they eat. If Christian kills or cuts up an animal, it is unclean and they will not eat it. If they shoot a deer in the mountains and the deer dies from the bullet before they can cut its throat, its flesh is also unclean. They will not eat it. If Christian shoots a deer and Mohammedan cuts its throat before it dies, it is considered clean. The village where there are only 28 families and where a language is spoken unlike all others in Caucasus is called Innookh.[80] It was to the right of our road across mountains. The Lezgins are accustomed to leave the face of a handsome child unwashed. I saw one at Bezhuta. When asked why they do so, they reply that if the child's face was clean it would have an evil influence over every one who looked at it—would make them sick. I conclude out of regard for health of inhabitants to leave my face dirty! When man divorces his wife he cannot marry again for three months. This probably is intended to give him a proper appreciation of women's society. Illegitimate intercourse between sexes punished by stoning to death. Prince says there was such a case in 1865 in his district. The day that I spent at Bezhuta was rather lonesome. The prince was occupied constantly in hearing complaints and as the conversation was carried on in Georgian, or in Lezgin and Georgian, it was of course entirely unintelligible to me. The weather also was very raw and cold and the wind blew right through our crazy little room so that after the sun began to go down I couldn't be comfortable anywhere.

---

80. Presumably here Kennan means the Ginukhs, of the Ando-Tsez ethnic group, who numbered some 200 individuals in the 1950s. He seems to be correct that they live to the right (i.e., north) of his route, in the Avarskoe Koisu valley. I have not yet been able to identify a specific village of theirs. See *Narody Kavkaza*, 1:463 and map facing page 22. In his "Island in the Sea of History," 1094, Kennan says the aoul of Inookh had 50–60 houses and was located "in the headwaters of the Andiski Koisu."

On the morning of Sept. 30th at half past seven we set out to cross the great range. Vanno, the prince's servant, remained behind with all the heavy baggage. Mahmout the young Lezgin and the other Circassian went to visit their families in another valley so that our party consisted only of the prince, Maxime, 2 men and I. The day was pleasant but rather cool and a few heavy cumulus clouds occasionally hid the sun. The road for a short distance up the valley was good but we soon began to ascend one of the tremendous foothills of the great range in a series of zigzags among birch, beech, maple, oak and elm trees. At a height of a couple thousand feet or so the timber disappeared and we came out on the high bare pasture ground of the Lezgins, which were covered only with grass. Here it suddenly began to snow and I put on my boorka, but it was only a flurry which soon passed over. A little farther on toward the top of the mountain, a couple of Lezgins in ragged shoubas, caps and kinjals came running up to the prince with some sort of a complaint. They were tending a great herd of sheep on the high mountain pastures.

In the course of 2 hours from the time we started we reached the summit of the podnyem[81] and began making our way along the edge of a great ridge[82] leading up to the principal range. The views from this ridge were grand. Its top was not more than 6 feet wide and on each side yawned tremendous valleys 2000 feet in depth, completely shut in by mountains. Occasionally, far below, we could see a patchwork of cultivated fields which marked a Lezgin village looking like half a dozen yellow cotton handkerchiefs spread out to dry or a little collection of saklas looking like small square match boxes. In front the ridge rose still higher and higher, hiding that part of the snowy range, but to the westward it lay in full sight with only its summit hidden in clouds. To the northward lay the first snowy range which we had crossed, rising over a troubled sea of lower hills bare and brown. There was no timber in sight anywhere and the landscape, although grand in its contours, was deficient in coloring and had a gloomy, threatening aspect. Up the narrow crests of two or three winding ridges we rode until at last the ridge rose steeply into a high snowy mountain[83] whose top was hidden

81. *pod"ëm:* ascent.
82. Probably the Bogos Ridge.
83. Probably Nunikas-Tsikhe (3119 m; 10,232 ft).

in clouds and before us across a deep narrow valley was the range of the Caucasus.

Up this snowy mountain I could trace in 8 or 10 sharp zigzags the road or path we were following until it was lost in the clouds but it was so steep that it did not seem possible for anybody to get up it even on foot and the mountain seemed to be a peak detached from the principal range which it would be no object to ascend or cross. On our left was this snowy mountain, at the end of the ridge along which lay our road, on our right was a very deep, narrow gorge between this ridge and the next parallel one and at its end we could see high snowy peaks whose tops were enveloped in clouds. Our road did not as I at first supposed run up this isolated peak. The zigzags were a Lezgin road leading nobody knows where and we turned off to the right and descended by about 20 more zigzags to the bottom of the gorge.

Son of Mollah Nazr Ellin fell from horse and went out of his mind. How could he go out of his mind when he never had any mind.[84]

Vladikavkaz[85]

THE ROAD THROUGH THIS GORGE LAY IN THE BED of the stream over rocks and stones, or on ledges here and there in the faces of the cliffs, first on one side and then on the other. In many places we were obliged to dismount and drag our horses over as best we could. Here and there the brook was bridged by immense masses of solidified glacier-like snow which even the hot summer's sun had not been able to melt away and in one place we rode in the bed of the stream for 5 or

---

84. As the next heading indicates, clearly there is a break in the narrative about the trip, during which he recorded this digression, set off as if he is quoting. This is part of one of the humorous tales about Nasreddin Khoja which are popular in the Middle East. Kennan cites several of the Nasreddin Khoja stories later in his "Unwritten Literature," 444–45.

85. If in fact he wrote this in Vladikavkaz, where he arrived October 13, he was recording the continuation of his story about crossing the Main Caucasus Ridge on September 30 at least two weeks after the event. Judging from his published "letter home," dated October 16 (see below), he was using the time to catch up on his writing.

"Lezgins" on a mountain trail in Dagestan. Painting by Theo. Horscheldt. Markov, Ocherki: *facing 432.*

6 rods[86] under such a snowy bridge which was 3 or 4 feet above our heads. The ceiling of this snowy grotto had melted out into regular architectural figures for which I don't know the name. Thus, side view [*sketch*]; view from below [*sketch*].

Finally at the end of this gorge we came to the glovni krebet[87]— the great dividing ridge and stopped to consult as to the advisability of taking lunch before crossing. In view of the threatening appearance of the weather it was decided to go on at once and take lunch on the other side. Our saddles were adjusted, girths tightened, and we began the ascent. The ridge or spur on our left rose higher and higher as it approached the glovni krebet until its top was sprinkled with snow and swept with grey clouds. Its whole slope—very steep—was glare rock without a vestige of vegetation, and down it in slender white threads rushed hundreds of mountain rills bursting out here and there into filmy cascades, tumbling noisily over jagged ledges of volcanic rock—trickling swiftly in an almost transparent film over a smooth slope and finally uniting into several larger streams and tumbling with a hoarse roar into the bottom of the gorge. In front was the glovni krebet rising in a steep slope strewn with huge jagged boulders and seamed by a deep, irregular gash from top to bottom through which foamed another torrent of rock-tormented water.

At a height of 1000 or 1500 feet could be seen the beginning of snow and above that all was hidden in clouds. Stopping a moment here and there to breath our horses we slowly made our way upward in a series of steep zigzags in the left side of the ravine through which tumbled the torrent from the melting snow. As we went higher and higher, the whole wild desolate panorama of Southern Daghestan opened behind us in a perfect chaos of mountains. Through the gorge up which we had come could be seen the ridge along the crest of which we had approached the glovni krebet—its top now touched by grey storm clouds and its whole slope thrown into black gloomy shadow. As we approached the snow line, we caught occasional glimpses through the clouds over the before-mentioned ridge of the first snowy range. The road was horrible—

86. rod: 5.029 meters.
87. *glavnyi khrebet*, referring to the Main Caucasus Ridge.

blocked up with rocks, wet and slippery with melted snow. Just at the snow line, we crossed the mountain torrent before-mentioned and began ascending in steep zigzags on its left bank, our ears filled with its roaring. In a few moments we entered the clouds, lost sight of everything except the snow on which we stood and to the roaring of the mountain torrents succeeded a deathly stillness.

We had reached the region of frost and perpetual snow. For an hour or more we climbed slowly and laboriously upward in a dense clammy mist through which I could see nothing except the form of Prince Jorjadze riding a few rods in advance and an occasional black rock projecting out of the snow. The snow and sky were so blended together by the mist that the prince now and then seemed to be riding through the air high above my head. The cold was quite severe as we neared the summit and as I had nothing but my blue overcoat I was in a constant shiver. At last a cold piercing wind which began to blow suddenly in our faces announced the summit. We could see nothing, but knew that the wind came from the other side. We stopped a moment to rest our horses and Prince Jorjadze, pointing downward through the fog, said "there lies Kakhetia" and if it was only clear you could see the valley of the Alazan for 100 miles. Mentally anathematizing the clouds, I began to descend. We had not gone down more than 600 feet when the clouds began to break away under us and at the tower of Shamyl which stands on a bluff 10,400 feet above the sea, there suddenly opened beneath us a great rent in the clouds through which appeared the green sunny valley of Kakhetia.[88]

As the gap in the clouds slowly widened, there opened before us the most magnificent picture I have ever seen. Far, far below our feet lay the warm green valley intersected by scores of glittering streams like winding silver threads, dotted with vineyards, and orchards and rising in one long gentle cultivated slope to the heights of Tomburg.[89]

---

88. The tower marks the pass across which Shamil kidnapped the Georgian princesses Chavchavadze and Orbeliana. He later exchanged them for his own son, whom the Russians had captured. Baddeley, *Russian Conquest of the Caucasus*, 449–51. See Introduction above.

89. He writes the last part of this description around the pages (169–70) with his annotation of the musical performance at Dzhengutai earlier in the trip.

[Journal, 191–92, apparently written in Vladikavkaz after October 13][90]

Residence of Prince Jorjadze, Eniseli, Kakhetia, Oct. 3rd, 1870

MY OTHER NOTE BOOK IS ENTIRELY FILLED UP WITH Daghestan and I must begin a new one for Kakhetia. Being very tired from the long days journey of Sept 30th, I did not get up on the morning of the 1st until 9 o'clock. After tea, I proceeded to take a survey of the premises. Prince Jorjadze's house is a large stone and brick building whose front appears something in this style [*sketch*]—In [the lower row] are arches opening upon a high piazza floored with a divan at one end. Above this piazza is a balcony of the same size with wooden arches and curtains which can be drawn in bad weather so as to close it. Opposite the central arch, door opening into large empty hall. Best rooms above. Garden behind the house and vineyard just across the creek. Prince's wife middle-aged lady of middle height with tolerably regular features, fair complexion, grey eyes whose lids have a way of half closing as if she were near-sighted. Losing[?] hair [. . .] too.[91]

[Journal, 203–5, written in Vedeno, October 23]

The Prince's household consisted of himself and wife, one daughter aged about 8 and one son of 4 or 5. Besides these there were two other men— I should think chief steward and superintendent of wine department[92] and the other a sort of a poor relation—also a prince. The latter was a tall, thin man of 60 with scanty white hair who made me a present of a Lezgin pipe. My life during the 5 days I lived there was monotonous but pleasant. Rose in the morning about 8:30 or 9, drank tea or coffee, and then lay around on long divan and smoked one of the prince's big Georgian pipes till one o'clock, when we had dinner. Dinner was served sometimes on the long wide balcony in front, which was hung with about

---

90. This is the first entry from the second of the two journal notebooks. I have supplied the page numbers from this point, since Kennan numbered pages only in book one. The second notebook begins with page 189.

91. One line is illegible; then he records Jorjadze's address (see Appendix).

92. Prince Jorjadze and his family were vintners.

50 highly-colored views of Vesuvius and the bay of Naples, sometimes in the room in which I slept. Began generally with soup—excellent soup too by the way—and ended with peaches and grapes. Sometimes we had very curious dishes—for instance boiled chicken with some sour herb like rhubarb, covered and hidden with sour cream. Again, ox's stomach entrails, brains, and feet, boiled and eaten with the soup and garlic. Wine flowed like water. After dinner I sometimes took a nap, sometimes sat on the lower balcony and watched and listened to the Georgians who came to the prince with complaints. They were a ragged, unkempt, wild-looking set generally and reminded me of Italians. All had the same black hair, eyes, eyebrows, and lashes and dark olive complexion and gesticulated a great deal when they talked. Late one evening four or five came in covered with blood and bruises, each one complaining

Ruins of the Jorjadze family church. Photo © Chris Allingham.

The fortress of Ananuri, which Kennan would pass on his way north from Tbilisi. Photo © Daniel C. Waugh.

that he had been the victim of a murderous assault at the hands of the others.

Sometimes their complaints were of the most trifling character— For instance a Georgian sold a sheep to a Dedoiskoi Lezgin[93] for 4 RS and he appealed to the prince for redress. Over such a case as this they would talk for 2 or 3 hours. I wondered that the prince didn't lose his temper. About half past five we drank tea on the lower balcony, the prince generally sitting with his wife on the divan at the end and listening to

---

93. The Dido peoples live in the highest, most isolated region near the Georgian border. The Dido language belongs to the Avaro-Andi-Dido division of the Northeast Caucasian language family. See Wixman, *Peoples of the USSR*, 57.

three or four ragged, barefooted Georgians who had some complaint to make. At 9:30 or 10 we had supper of soup, zharkoi,[94] fruit and wine served on the long divan in my room, all sitting around the cloth cross-legged in Asiatic style.

[Kennan MSS, LC, Box 64, envelope "Miscellaneous Scraps," 108–9]

On the estate of Prince Jorjadze, a tract of land half as large as an American county, I counted 14 churches and cathedrals, all empty and deserted and at the present time there are not people enough left on that area to fill a single chapel. Every church was fortified like a medieval castle with moats and draw bridges and its high stone walls and flanking towers were loop-holed for musketry and cannon. In these churches the unhappy Georgians took refuge from their Mohammedan enemies and fought to the last. So terribly destructive were the raids of the Caucasian mountaineers down into these beautiful valleys that the last Georgian king despairing and hopeless abdicated his throne in favor of Russia. [. . .]

94. *zharkoe:* roast meat, usually game.

THROUGH THE LANDS OF CHECHNYA TO THE DAGESTAN HIGHLANDS

[Kennan seems to have written nothing in his journal between October 3 when in Eniseli and some time after October 13 in Vladikavkaz. He was still catching up then on his description of the final part of the trek over the mountains and in fact recorded his last observations on Eniseli only on October 23. We know from his expense list (see Appendix) that he spent a night in Telavi on his way to Tbilisi. The silence in his narrative about events after leaving Eniseli probably is explained by his having written the details in letters home. One or more of these letters, dated Sunday, October 16, when he was in Vladikavkaz, apparently served as the basis for a lengthy published description of much of his trip to that date, published in the Norwalk, Ohio, newspaper, *Reflector*. A battered copy, without date or page numbers, is in Kennan MSS, LC, Box 64. Excerpts here, somewhat rearranged, fill in some of the gaps in the travel narrative. Clearly he invents some details and dialogues.]

Tiflis

[. . .] TRAVELING BY POST OCCASIONALLY IS THE greatest nuisance in the world. For instance, I come to Tiflis, live for four days,[1] see everything I care to see, and want to leave for Vladi Kavkaz; I go to the post station to enquire about the diligence which is advertised to leave every day at 4 PM regularly. I learn to my surprise that there is no regularity about it. The diligence leaves when passengers enough appear to fill it, and not before. I enquire of the official at the

1. In developing this yarn, Kennan seems to have inflated (by about a week) the number of days spent fighting the bureaucracy in Tbilisi. Apparently he left Eniseli on October 5 and left Tbilisi for Vladikavkaz on October 10.

View of Tbilisi(?). Photo from Kennan archive.
Courtesy of Library of Congress.

A bazaar in Tbilisi. Painting by Theo. Horscheldt. Markov, Ocherki: *351.*

counter when the next diligence will probably go. He doesn't know; probably in two or three days.

"Can I engage a seat?"

"No. Seats can't be engaged till the diligence is ready to start."

"But how am I to know when the diligence is ready to start?"

"Come in and enquire."

"But when shall I come in?"

"Come in tomorrow morning and then day after tomorrow and the next day and when passengers enough get together we will tell you."

This wasn't very satisfactory, but on the following morning I make my appearance. No passengers. The next day—no passengers. The third day—no passengers.

I enquire of the official at the counter if this is the way the thing usually runs. He replies indifferently that it is.

Street scene in Tbilisi near Botanical Garden. Markov, Ocherki: *336.*

"But when will a diligence probably go, in a week—ten days—two weeks—or when?" [. . .] He doesn't know and evidently doesn't care.

With this I give the diligence up in disgust and conclude that I'll get a traveling pass and go on my own account. I appear at the proper office, exhibit my passport, and ask for a "padarozhna" or traveling pass to Vladi Kavkaz. The official turns the passport upside down, examines it critically in that position until he happens to notice that the American eagle is standing on his head, then turns it sideways and examines it still more minutely. He asks if I have permission from the police office to leave the city. I reply that I didn't know it was necessary. He assures me that it is indispensable and that when the police give me a written permission to leave, then he will give me a padarozhna.

[. . .] I go at once to the police office, produce my worn and tattered passport once more and ask permission to leave the city. The official scrutinizes the curious document, looking at me now and then as if there were a strong probability that I was a criminal trying to escape from justice. Finally he looks at his books [. . .] and asks why I didn't notify the police of my arrival in the city. I become provoked and enquire why the police didn't notify me that there was such a regulation. Nobody asked for my passport when I arrived. [. . .] I enquire again if I can have permission to leave the city. He replies that the police office in its official capacity doesn't recognize the fact of my being in the city, that I have never been "written in" to its books and that, technically, I am not in Tiflis at all (!!), that when the police office has recognized the fact of my arrival, it will proceed to consider the advisability of my departure.

Upon this I beg respectfully to announce my arrival and ask if I cannot be "written in" and "written out" at once.[2] He looks at the clock and says it is after office hours and that it is impossible to write me in today. He says the next day is Sunday—a holiday.

"Well then Monday."

"Monday is also a holiday" and he smiles as if he were announcing some delightful intelligence. [. . .] Tuesday he says I may come in again, and taking my passport I leave in a high state of disgust. Tuesday morning I make my appearance a second time in a little better humor, feeling quite sure that *now* I'll succeed in getting out of town. The official

---

2. Presumably here Kennan is calquing the Russian *vpisat'* and *vypisat'*.

meets me with an impassive countenance and I explain the whole situation over again and ask to be "written in." He takes my passport, keeps me waiting half an hour and finally returns it to me with the announcement that I am now "written in."

"Well," I reply, "I want to be 'written out' so that I can leave the city."

"We can't 'write you out' today," is the discouraging response.

"Why not?"

"Because two days must elapse between 'writing in' and 'writing out' so that if any person objects to your leaving he can have time to enter his protests and give his reasons."

"Then I can't be 'written out' until Thursday?"

"Not until Friday morning," is the pitiless reply. "You should have sent in your passport as soon as you arrived, then by the time you were ready to leave we could have given you permission."

There is nothing to be done, so I wander around the city two days more in a higher state of disgust than ever. Friday morning I appear for the last time at the police office [and claim my document, then on to get my padarozhna and horses. I'm informed that permission to leave has to be written on stamped paper.] I hand over two roubles, thinking to myself that stamped paper is an expensive luxury, and in course of time I receive the "svedaitelstvo."³ Upon examination I find that the stamped paper costs twenty kopecks—the extra rouble and eighty kopecks probably goes into some official pocket.

Armed with this indispensible document, I go once more to the Government treasury after my padarozhna. The room is full of other applicants and I wait an hour before anybody looks at me. At last I buttonhole another official and present my case. He tells me to sit down a little while and he will see to it. I sit down and the "little while" stretches into another hour. At last I get disgusted and walk outdoors to smoke a cigarette. The official [. . .] hurries after me and says he will see to my case. I tell him that my case is very simple. I want a padarozhna to go to Vladi Kavkaz. He says I must write out an "obyavlenia." I can't write Russian and haven't the slightest idea what an "obyavlenia" is, but tell him if he'll write it out I'll sign it.⁴ [. . .] After another hour he presents me with

3. *svidetel'stvo:* certificate.
4. *ob"iavlenie:* statement.

the document [which, for all I know,] may be a profession of belief in the dogmas of the Greek church, [and] I sign it. Taking my passport, my permission to leave, and my obyavlenia and pinning them all together, he then goes to another official and presents them for his inspection. The latter reads them all over deliberately and says all right.

Official No. 1 then carries the documents to official No. 3, who also reads them over and finally gives official No. 1 a sheet of stamped and signed paper on which the padarozhna is to be written. Official No. 1 brings me a book in which he has written a profession of faith or something of that sort and requests me to sign it. All the preliminaries being thus duly observed, official No. 1 proceeds to write out the padarozhna. In course of time he brings me the [. . .] order for two horses, and my passport, and says he shall have to charge me six roubles and seventy kopecks! [. . .] He then adds that I have not paid for writing out the "obyavlenia." I enquire how much and he leaves it to my generosity. I throw him fifty kopecks, grab my hat and run, mentally resolving that I'll give my head for a foot ball sooner than apply for another padarozhna.

By this time it is late in the afternoon, but, hoping to get away before dark, I hurry to the post station and demand horses. The official looks at me in astonishment as if I had asked him to give me the moon for a soup plate! He finally observes that I'm a poor, ignorant foreigner and tells me coldly that there will be no horses until the next Tuesday—five days! This is a quencher. After having been four days in getting a padarozhna, and paying eight rubles and seventy kopecks, I am informed that I must wait five days for horses. At last the official looks over his books more closely and finds horses unoccupied for 4 o'clock the next day. [. . .] The next day I appear, present my padarozhna, and ask for horses. He says he shall have to charge me twenty-five rubles and eighty kopecks. [. . .] I had expected to pay sixteen and enquire why it is so much. He replies with an offended air that 25.80 is the regular price for three horses.

"But I don't want three horses," I remonstrated, "my traveling pass is for *two* horses not three."

"That don't make any difference, after the 15th of September travelers are not allowed to take less than three horses."

"But I'm traveling alone and I have no baggage whatever; is it possible that two horses can't draw a single man?"

The official insists that I must take three horses or none and I had to submit. [. . . He] told me to send after the horses in an hour [which I did,] but it was not till after 3 hours that the horses finally came and I rode out of the city of Tiflis, with a firm resolve never again to travel post in the Caucasus. The post system as it is managed there is nothing but organized robbery and imposition. [. . .] From [Vladi Kavkaz] to Daghestan and back I'm going to hire private horses, and in Daghestan I have a special order from the Governor. [. . .]

I have been tormented incessantly for three months with fleas and shall continue to be tormented by them probably till I get out of the country. [. . .] I had ten times rather sleep outdoors on the snow in a Siberian storm with the thermometer at 20 below zero than to sleep as I have for the last hundred nights. [. . .] In Timour Khan Shoura [. . .] I slept three nights on a small table [. . .] with my feet on the window sill, without mattress, bedding, blankets or anything over or under me. [. . .] I believe I haven't slept with my clothes off but once since I left St. Petersburg; that was when I lived with Prince Djordjadse. I have also seen just once, in the same place, sheets, pillows with cases on them, and comforters. As a general thing, I have slept as I am sleeping now, on a board, with a piece of felt under me, a blanket over me and my overcoat for a pillow. [I don't mind] sleeping on a board or a stone pavement if it is free from fleas, but [. . .] to lie on a board and be tormented by fleas so that you can't sleep—to get up in the morning with one eye swelled up so that you can't open it, and one lip so that you can't half smoke—that's misery. [. . .] However, taking my whole trip together from America here, I can't complain. I am ready to suffer from fleas another three months for the sake of seeing as much more that is strange, curious and beautiful. Daghestan paid me for all the hardships and inconvenience that I endured in getting there and in traveling through it.

[. . .] The title of my lecture will have to be changed. When I adopted it, I had no idea what the nature of my material would be, and I expected to pay the most attention to the region south of the great range between Tiflis and the Black Sea. This part of the country may properly be called "The Land of the Golden Fleece," for it was here that Jason and his Arganautic Expedition came in search of that precious wool. As it happens however, I haven't been there at all; don't know anything about it, so that I have chosen a new title for my forthcoming lecture—"Mountains and Mountaineers of the Caucasus." My information relates entirely to the great range from the Dariel pass to the Caspian Sea, and the life, manners, and customs of its wild inhabitants [...]

[...] There are many magnificent landscapes in southwestern Daghestan between the two snowy ranges which equal, if they do not surpass, any part of the Georgian military road. The most remarkable part of the latter is the Dariel gorge. That is really wonderful, and in its way it is unsurpassed by anything which I have ever seen. The road from the station of Lars begins to be shut in closer and closer by enormous, precipitous mountains; the descent becomes steeper, the cliffs on both sides approach nearer and nearer to the perpendicular, until at last you enter a dark, tremendous canyon only thirty or forty feet in width, through which boils and roars the river Tersk [=Terek] between perpendicular walls of black rock seven or eight hundred feet in height, in the face of which has been blasted out a narrow road. When you are in the center of this defile you cannot see its entrance or its outlet: you are in a tremendous *well* in the mountains, with walls of rock seven or eight hundred feet in height on every side and only a little patch of blue sky appearing far over your head, as if resting on the edges of the precipice. The most insensible person cannot help being impressed with the grandeur of this pass. It would be a fitting gateway to the infernal regions! When the upper part of it is filled with clouds as is frequently the case, or when a thunder storm sweeps over it, it must be a fearfully gloomy place. [...]

Here I am again on the north side of the mountains, less than 200 miles from the place where I began my Caucasian wanderings. I arrived here on Thursday, after a very pleasant but hot and dusty trip of two days and a half from Tiflis. [...] I made the acquaintance on the Volga steamer of some Russians who were going to Vladi Kavkaz and through their representations I had been induced to stop in Daghestan. One of them was named Stryker and Friday morning after my arrival here I started out to hunt him up and report progress. When I parted with him in Petrovskoe he was very much concerned about my safety and success, and expressed a great many fears that I would not be able alone to make my way along the north slope of the mountains to this place, as I *then* intended, on account of the wildness of the country and its inhabitants. I assured him that I would get through somehow, and we

The Darial George. Painting by R.G. Sudkovskii. Markov, Ocherki: *facing 80.*

parted with the understanding that in ten days or so I would call upon him in Vladi Kavkaz.

Instead of going along the north slope of the mountains to Vladi Kavkaz, [I] crossed them by a bridle path directly into Kakhetia. Ten days passed, fifteen, twenty, and still there were no tidings of the American "pootashestvenik"—American traveler—and at last when nearly a month had elapsed, Stryker gave me up for lost. When I made my appearance Thursday morning he looked at me as if I had risen from the dead. "Where have you come from!" he exclaimed in astonishment. [. . .] "I expected to see you three weeks ago!"

"I came from Petrovskoe," I replied.

"But where have you been so long? It doesn't take a month to come from Petrovskoe to Vladi Kavkaz."

"No, but I came via Tiflis, and that's a circuitous route." [. . .]

"How did you ever get from Petrovskoe to Tiflis without passing here?"

I explained that I had been over the whole of Daghestan, crossed the snowy mountains into Kakhetia, crossed Kakhetia into Georgia and finally had come from Tiflis to Vladi Kavkaz by the Georgian military road. All he could do was to look at me in astonishment and shake his head. [. . .] "Vot shto znacket americanski pootashestvenik."[5] [. . .] he exclaimed at last. "I thought you wouldn't be able to get to Vladi Kavkaz and here you come from Tiflis by way of Timour Khan Shoura, Goonib and the snowy mountains!" [. . .] He looked at me [. . .] as if I had come from the North pole by way of the moon.

[. . .] I have been here three days now and shall remain until Wednesday[6] when I start for a *second* trip through Daghestan! I shall quite likely go directly back to that flea-infested settlement of Timour Khan Shoura from which I started more than a month ago. I shall follow, however, an entirely new route by way of Groznoi, Weden, Botlekh, and Khoonzakh, crossing the region inhabited by the Checkenses and returning through the settlements of the Terskoi Cossacks to Vladi Kavkaz. This will be my last trip. As soon as I return I shall start at once for home by way of Tiflis, Kutais, Poti and the Black Sea.

5. "There's an American traveler for you!"
6. October 19.

THROUGH CHECHNYA TO DAGESTAN

[Journal, 193–99]

Samashkinski Station, 33 versts west of Groznoi, Thursday, Oct. 20th, 1870

WE GOT A PADAROZHNA YESTERDAY MORNING AND wanted to start at once for Groznoi and Veden, but as usual there were no horses and we couldn't get away until after dark. It was a cold and foggy night and as we rode out through one of the arched gates of the wall which surrounds Vladi Kavkaz, we lost sight of everything except a few scattered campfires here and there, surrounded by faint halos of mist. Our equipage was a regular butcher's cart without springs, drawn by four horses, and we all piled in on the bottom and made ourselves as comfortable as we could. The first station we passed pretty well, stopped at the second where three Russians, one of them an officer, were discussing the Russian educational system in a room about ten feet square, filled with clouds of blue smoke. There was evidently no room for us to sleep here so we went out. From here we had a stupid yemschick[7] and three still more stupid horses.

The fog settled down denser and denser and it finally began to rain. Before we had gone 10 versts, we lost the road and from that time till 2 o'clock we knocked around over a miserable steppe beside the Soonzha River, capsized once more into a ravine, Zamber was pitched out 4 times and I once, got all mud, wandered around through high, wet grass and weeds on foot in search of the road, tumbled into mud holes, got all burrs, and had a hard time generally. Zamber cursed the driver and the driver cursed his horses and then, leaving us beside the pavoska,[8] he would wander away in search of the road and be gone so long that we would give him up for lost until somewhere or other we would hear a faint halloo— At last, about 2 o'clock we reached some station or other, and tired, wet and covered from head to foot with mud and burrs, we stretched ourselves out on the floor and slept about 4 hours. From that station to this one we had good horses and made good time. Road runs along a level steppe with low distant mountains on each side. Station master here a

---

7. *iamshchik:* coachman.
8. *povozka:* carriage.

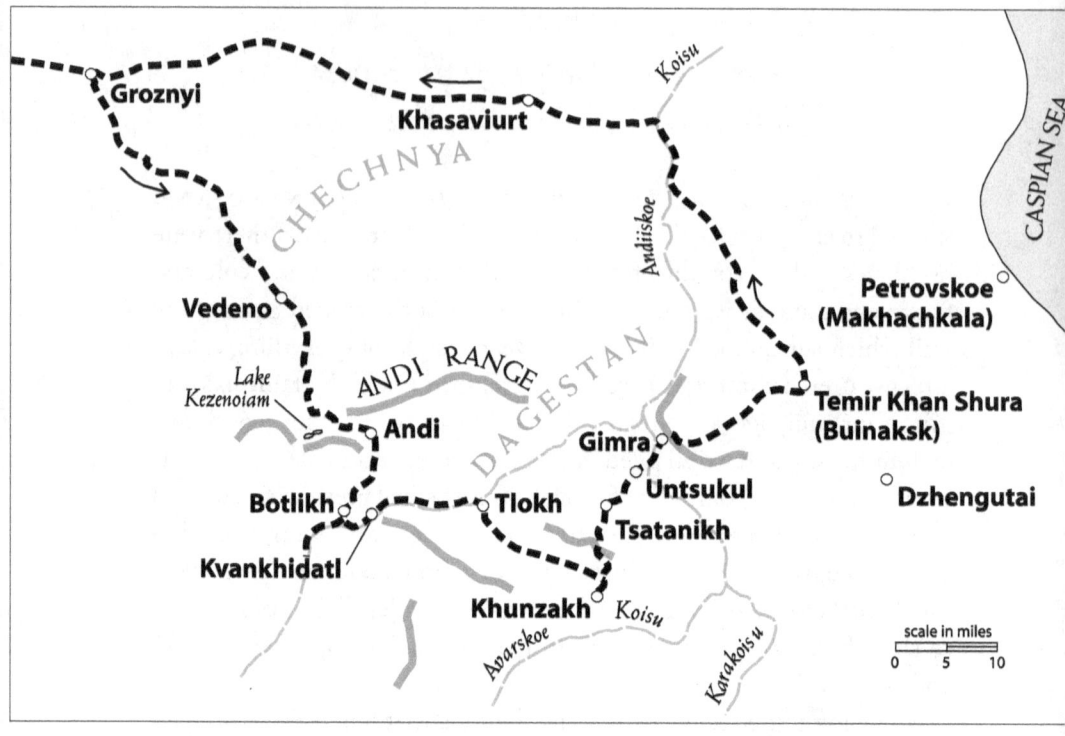

Map 4. Kennan's route from Groznyi to Temir Khan Shura.

Pole—great admirer of America—tall, slender, smooth-faced man, Nachalnik[9] of station and an old man who was in Moscow when Napoleon captured it. Said with pride that he had travelled everywhere and seen everything.

Dookhan or Tavern on the Steppe, 14 versts from Groznoi, Oct. 10th—O.S. [=Oct. 22, N.S.][10]

GROZNOI SCATTERED IRREGULAR TOWN ON STEPPE, but I don't know much about it because it rained all the time I was there and I didn't go out of the house till today. Stopped at a very decent hotel, read Russian for occupation and played billiards for amusement. Made acquaintance of young Jew named Gleinber—most intelligent man I've seen in 2 months. Owns and reads Buckle, Darwin, Huxley, Lyell, Maury, Shakespeare, Byron and all most noted English French and German authors—to say nothing of the classics. Takes Russian magazines and papers and is well-posted with regard to America and American institutions of which he too is a great admirer—reads also Spencer and Draper and Mill.

Left Groznoi at 2:30. Muddy road, one horse cart with roof over it, lazy horse and incompetent driver. Horse stops to think about once every 2 mins. At last I get out my whip and driver and I play a duet on his back until we get him into a run. At dark we reached this tavern, a wattled house that wind blows right through, fire on ground in corner, smoky as a Korak yourt, big, square lantern. Proprietor, a Chechenets, sells mushrooms and watermelons. Finally, make raise of bread and samovar and stop for night. Have just drunk tea and am going to sleep in pavoska. Weather cloudy and cold, a little snow. Smoke in my eyes. Must stop.

9. *nachal'nik:* manager.
10. O.S.: Old Style. Until 1918, Russia used the Old Style Julian calendar, which Kennan begins to follow here. In the nineteenth century, O.S. dates were twelve days *earlier* than the New Style (N.S.) Gregorian calendar.

Veden [=Vedeno], Oct. 11ᵗʰ [=Oct. 23]

I'M AS TIRED TONIGHT AS A DOG BUT I MUST TRY and write up my journal. We slept horribly last night in our miserable cart called by a complimentary figure of speech "pavoska." The wind blew so that I became chilled through in less than two hours, the straw on which we lay was uneven so that our heads were on two mountain ranges and our hips in a valley, the pavoska was so short that I couldn't lie at full length, and my knees ached from being doubled up, and finally our miserable horse kept pulling the covering off me all night in order to get at the hay underneath, so that I only slept a few hours and shivered away the rest of the 11 hours of the night. The dookhan, open at both ends and roofed with bushes, was so cold and smoky that we could not sit up there so we turned in at 7 o'clock. At half past 5, our yemschick harnessed up and drove off. From that time till half past ten we tried to travel and by kind of hammering our horse with a big stick and 2 knouts simultaneously, succeeded in keeping him in motion nearly half the time. The driver, however, had to walk. As soon as he would get on the pavoska the horse would stop. Mud everywhere very deep.

At 1/2 past ten we reached a government station with a stone fort 75 or 80 feet square, round towers at 2 opposite corners, slits for musketry. Opposite was a dookhan where we stopped to drink tea. Here we got with great difficulty half a pound of bread, which was all we had to eat till we reached here. Started from there at 1 PM. Went 25 rods and horse began stopping again.

["A Tenth-Century Barbarian," 201]

The horse that fell to my lot on that particular morning was so weak from sickness or starvation that he could hardly be forced to move at all, and after riding behind him at a slow, plodding walk for three or four hours, I abandoned the whole outfit and started ahead on foot for the fortified post of Veden, leaving the driver to follow with the blanket and saddle-bags which made up my scanty equipment.

[Journal, 199–201]

Zamber proposed walking and I agreed, so we walked 22 versts to Veden in 4 and 1/2 hours. Road up ravine rising gradually, steep, timbered sides, leaves orange, yellow and brown. Cossack pickets, 3 or 4 little tents trimmed with green, and a wicker cage on top of a pole in which sits the caraoul.[11] No one allowed to pass after dark unless he is armed. Am too tired to write any more tonight.

Veden—Oct. 12th, morning O.S. [=Oct. 24]

THE ROAD FROM THE LAST STATION TO VEDEN RUNS along the river or stream called Khoikhoolaoo [=Khulkhulau], following the right bank and rising gradually on the hill sides. In front appeared a range of mountains not very high, covered with recent snow. Behind at the mouth of the ravine lay a Chechense aoul and the fortress of Ersenoi. The weather cleared away about 11 o'clock and the sun came out very hot so that walking was very hard work, especially as we had nothing to eat since the day before except a quarter of a pound of bread each. As the sun sank, however, the long shadows of the hills on the right covered us so that it was even too cool. At the head of the ravine we turned away a little to the right round the end of bluff and then to the left and began the ascent of the long hill leading up to the plateau on which Veden is situated. This hill was just a verst in length but it seemed to be at least 3. At last, however, we came out on the summit. In front on the south was the range of mountains which we had seen from the ravine and which rose directly from the plateau. On the west and north were high, wooded hills and on the east the great snowy range of Ande. In the foreground were the white walls of round towers of Veden, and a little cluster of houses from which rose columns of smoke. The sun was just setting behind the western hills, tingeing the Ande range with red but leaving the level plateau in darkness. A short distance from the top of the hill, we begged some sour black rye bread from a couple of soldiers whom we met and went limping on our way rejoicing.

["A Tenth-Century Barbarian," 201]

I had eaten my last pound of black rye bread and was becoming weak from hunger and fatigue. Two or three miles from Veden I came to a

---

11. *karaul:* guard.

Cossack picket's shelter—a high mast with ladder-like crossbars, on the top of which there was a small platform inclosed in wattled bushes. In this crow's-nest, watching the road, sat an armed sentinel in Cossack uniform, who hailed me in Russian and ordered me to stop.

"Who are you?" he demanded.

"A traveler," I replied.

"What kind of a traveler?"

"Amerikanets."

"Where are you going?"

"Into Daghestan."

"Are you armed?"

"No."

"What are you doing on these roads alone at nightfall, and without a weapon?"

"My pistol was stolen from me," I explained, "and since then I've had only a pocket-knife. Why weapons? Is the road dangerous?"

"At night, yes," he said. "My orders are to stop every man after sunset unless he is armed and can take care of himself. But it isn't quite dark yet, and if you walk fast you can reach the post in an hour. You may go."

Reflecting upon the possibilities suggested by this encounter, I quickened my steps. An hour and a half later, towards the end of which I was again halted by an armed sentry, I entered the fortified post of Veden, where I found a place to sleep and a rather scanty supper of black bread, goat's-milk cheese, and tea.

[Journal, 202–3, 206–11]

It was already quite dark when we entered the gates and made our way through the muddy streets to Zamber's house, where I stopped for the night. Tea and afterward lunch of bread, eggs, and cheese. Jews will not eat meat killed or cut up by a Christian or Mohammedan so that they don't have any very often. Had to go without meat yesterday and shall probably have to go without today. Called upon the Nachalnik of the Okroog (or rather his assistant) this A.M. and got promise of assistance. Weather foggy last night but clear again today. I'm awful hungry.

Veden, Oct. 12th, 9:30 AM O.S. [=Oct. 24]

WALKED AROUND A LITTLE YESTERDAY BUT DIDN'T see anything particularly remarkable. Weather still clear and warm. Had a dinner of unclean meat alone yesterday as it was impossible to buy any Jewish meat so my host couldn't eat with me. Spent the evening with a good looking young Jew whose name I don't know. Leave today at 11 am for Ande, Botlikh, Khoonzakh, Gimre, and Shoura. Nachalnik of the Okroog gives me an otkrytyi list.[12]

[. . .] Chechense Aoul—Khorochoi, October 12th, O.S. [=Oct. 24]

LEFT VEDEN AT NOON TODAY UNDER GUARD OF AN ill-looking millitaioner[13] armed with rifle, postol, sabre and kinjal. Rode away to the eastward across the plain on which Veden is situated and entered a ravine where a company or more of soldiers was at work on the new road to Daghestan. Here at the mouth of the ravine were also several camps not far one from another. Tents square pitched with 5 poles. In front was a mountain up which ran a road in seventeen zigzags. Ravine bare and treeless on both sides and very steep. Small stream at bottom. Just above the mouth of the ravine we entered upon the new road and followed it to this aoul. Stopped at sakla of the Starshena. Small square house of clay with hard clay floor fireplace to left of door—beds, comforters, etc. piled up opposite door and immense copper and metallic platters 3 or 4 feet in diameter hung up all around. Little girl about 7 years old was left to do the hospitable as the Starshena and his wife were absent. She spread down a mat on the floor, put a pillow on it, and then retired.

It was dark and dismal in there, so I finally came out to stroll around a little and see the place. Heard there was a Russian officer here and concluded to introduce myself. He was just at dinner. Met[?] me very

---

12. *otkrytyi list*: permit to procure horses, here written by Kennan in Cyrillic. At this point in the journal, 203–5, he flashes back to Eniseli. I have placed that passage earlier

13. *militsioner*: policeman.

kindly, insisted upon my taking dinner with him, and I have been ever since. He is living in a low, clay whitewashed sakla with no furniture but a couple of rude wooden bedsteads, a couple of iron camp chairs and a wooden table. Two saddles were placed on saddle blocks opposite the door, 2 plaited whips and a kinjal were hung over the fire place, bridles were suspended here and there from wooden pegs, bottles, tea canisters, etc., stood round on ledges in the walls, and on a shelf opposite the door were a few books, maps, etc. [. . .]

Oct. 13th, Rus. Style [i.e., O.S.; =Oct. 25]

WE WERE FAVORED WITH A REMARKABLE DISPLAY of the Aurora Borealis at 10 o'clock last night. This ravine opens upon the plain of Veden exactly north of here and the whole triangle between the black mountains was filled with a red mist cut by long slender lances of white light which shot nearly up to the zenith. Taking the whole scene together the dark bare mountains, the blue starry skies overhead and a glittering planet just resting on the edge of the eastern range, the scattered flat-roofed saklas in the bottom of the valley and the Aurora playing away in the north and shooting up from behind the mountains—it was a beautiful sight.

The Capt. has been here since March superintending the construction of this road. The height of this aoul above the sea is 3326 ft. according to his measurements; of Veden 2460 ft., of Lake Ilezan 6130 feet, of the pass over the Ande range 7377 feet. [. . .][14]

Aoul of Ande—Oct. 13th, Evening [=Oct. 25]

I LEFT CAPTAIN CHERKASSOF'S SAKLA THIS MORNing about 9 o'clock under guard of his interpreter Achmet and a milliaioner. The Captain gave Achmet a brimming tumbler of vodka before we started. He stuffed a chunk of bread into the breast of his beshmet, put boiled eggs all around his head in the turned up part of his papakha, and announced himself ready to start. I shall remember Capt. Cherkassof

---

14. I have transposed a few lines on the lake ("Achmet says . . . Trout lake") to another section below.

at least until I get out of the Caucasus. I haven't been so well fed since I left Tiflis as I was in his little sakla. We spent the whole evening yesterday in smoking, eating supper, and discussing America, the French war, telegraphs, Auroras Borealis, and I don't know how many more subjects.

[A key source for this part of Kennan's journey is the two-part article he later published which features his guide Akhmet and describes rather dramatically Akhmet's understanding of customary law. The selection here reproduces much of the previous section from the journal, but with the addition of a certain amount of judgmental verbiage and the literary embellishment of dialogues. Comparison of the journal and article tells us a lot about Kennan's literary technique. He may have even made of the one encounter with the little girl two such encounters, although the incidents could in fact have been separate ones. "A Tenth-Century Barbarian," 201–4]

Monday morning, equipped with an open order for horses and an escort from the commandant of the post, and attended by a semi-civilized mountaineer in the Russian service who carried a small arsenal of antique silver-mounted weapons, including dagger, saber, rifle, and two pistols, I started on horseback for the Andiski Khrebet.[15] Early in the afternoon, after a ride of three or four hours across a high plateau and through a narrow, rocky, and very wild gorge, we came squarely up against the mighty and almost precipitous mountain wall which separates Chechnia from Daghestan. The steep western slope of the titanic ridge was treeless, and up it, like a whitish snake, ran a tortuous bridle-path, which climbed in seventeen zigzags to the snow-powdered summit, eight thousand feet above the level of the Caspian Sea. At the base of this great range stood a small collection of flat-roofed, clay-colored adobe houses known to the Chechenses as the aoul of Khorochoi, where my escort had instructions to turn me over to the *starshina*[16] of the settlement, and then return himself with the two horses to Veden.

The head man and his wife both happened to be away from home; and in a low, dark room hung around with ancient weapons and huge circular trays of copper or bronze I was turned over to the starshina's daughter, a timid little girl about seven years of age. As she could not speak

---

15. The Andi Ridge.
16. *starshina*: elder or village head.

Russian, she was unable to talk with me, and, frightened by the strange dress and appearance of the first foreigner perhaps that she had ever seen, she extended to me a sort of symbolical hospitality by laying down a cushion for a seat on the bare clay floor, and then fled. Tiring of solitude in the gloomy room, and longing for something to eat, I went out of doors, wondering what I should do next. In that wild and unfrequented part of the Caucasus, without horse, guide, interpreter, or food, I had, naturally enough perhaps, a feeling of helplessness and perplexity; but there is always a way out of the most discouraging situation, and when, in an exploration of my environment, I found between the village and the mountain a little encampment of Cossack tents, I felt almost at home again.

"What are you doing here, boys?" I inquired of two sunburned Cossacks in white tunics and high-top boots who were washing dishes beside a low-spirited fire.

"Building a road, your High Nobility," they replied, with a friendly grin.

"Up the Andiski?"

"Just that."

"Where is your commanding officer?"

"Captain Cherkassof? He's over there in the whitewashed sakla by the big rock." Five minutes later I was introducing myself to Captain Cherkassof and explaining to him my difficulties and needs.

"Of course you'll stay with me to-night," he said, with cordial Russian hospitality. "You're simply a godsend! I haven't seen an educated man in three months. I can't offer you much," indicating with a sweeping gesture two camp beds, two high-pommeled saddles on blocks, three homemade chairs and a bare pine table, "but you're more than welcome to what there is. I've got plenty to eat, and something to drink."

"Meat, drink, and a bed are what I want most," I said, laughingly. "I haven't had a square meal in a week, and I'm tired enough to sleep on a mattress of barbed wire."

In the course of half an hour my blanket and saddle-bags were brought from the house of the starshina, and I sat down at the bare pine table to the most satisfying meal I had had in a week—cold boiled mutton, eggs, bread and butter, honey, delicious purple grapes, and red Caucasian wine. My host, Captain Cherkassof, who had been isolated for six months, was even more hungry for news and companionship than I was for food; so we talked science, literature, art, Russian affairs, world politics, and the state of the eastern Caucasus all the rest of that day and far into the night.

I was glad to find that a trip through western and central Daghestan was regarded by Captain Cherkassof as perfectly practicable and reasonably safe. The Russians had pacified the country only in part after their long war with the mountaineers, and I had been told by almost everybody whom I had consulted that if I ventured far back into the interior, away from the Russian posts, I should take my life in my hands.

"Daghestan," Captain Cherkassof told me, "is a wild country [. . .], the state of society that of the tenth century—or possibly I might say the first. We haven't been in control long enough to change things much, and in many of the mountain aouls you might easily imagine yourself in ancient Gaul in the time of Caesar."

At breakfast the following morning I brought up the important question of ways and means, and I asked Captain Cherkassof what chance there was of getting horses, an escort, and an interpreter for my proposed trip.

"There will be no trouble about horses and escort," he replied. "The starshina will have to give you those on your 'open order' from the commandant in Veden. The question of an interpreter is more difficult. The mountaineers in Daghestan speak fifteen or twenty different languages, and you ought to have a man who knows at least five or six of them. How long a trip do you expect to make?"

"I though I would go to Timour Khan Shoura," I replied, "by way of Andi, Botlekh, and Khunzakh. It may take a couple of weeks. I can't stay in the mountains much longer than that, anyway, because winter is coming on and the passes will be blocked with snow."

Captain Cherkassof thought for a moment, and then said: "Suppose I give you my interpreter. I can spare him for two or three weeks. He speaks Russian fairly well, and knows seven of the mountain languages besides. He is an Avar by birth, and is better acquainted with the people of Daghestan than any other man I know. He's a barbarian, of course; but you won't mind that. Grip him firmly and hold him with sea-urchin mittens, and you won't have any trouble with him."

"I'll take him," I said, "if you can spare him and he'll go."

"Oh, he'll go fast enough," replied the captain. "He's a born adventurer and such a trip will just suit him."

"Mahmoud," he said to his young assistant, "go and find Akhmet and bring him here."

Ten minutes later the interpreter silently entered the room, greeted Captain Cherkassof with a formal military salute, took off his high, muff-shaped sheepskin hat, and stood at attention. He was a tall, athletic man, perhaps fifty years of age, with a rugged, deeply lined face and the fierce blue eyes that one sees now and then among the Highlanders of Scotland. His closely clipped and bristly hair was sprinkled with gray, but his beard and mustache had been dyed a bright, peculiar red with henna. The broad white seam of a scar crossed his forehead above and between the eyes, and seemed to give an added fierceness to the naturally stern expression of his face. He was dressed in the long-skirted black coat of the Daghestan mountaineers, with a row of ivory ammunition tubes across his breast, and the silver galloon of a red silken under-tunic showing as his throat. From a silver-studded leather belt hung diagonally across his body in front the long, straight dagger known in the Caucasus as kinjal; and thrust through the belt, in the small of his back, was a heavy single-barreled pistol with a globular butt. Both weapons were richly mounted and the sheath of the kinjal was ornamented with arabesques of silver niello work. As he stood there, with impassive face, paying no attention to me, but gazing fixedly at Captain Cherkassof, he was a striking and impressive figure.

"Akhmet," said the captain, "this is a foreign traveler from the other side of the great ocean, who is about to make a trip into Daghestan. He wants an interpreter. Will you go?"

"Why not go, if it is ordered?" replied Akhmet, briefly.

"Well, I order it; how soon can you be ready?"

"As soon as I can get on my horse. How far am I to go with him?"

"To Timour-khan-Shura. From there you will come back to me."

"Slooshiyoo's'.[17] Does he speak Russian?" pointing rather contemptuously at me with his thumb.

"He does, and he will tell you where he wants to go. Take good care of him—you'll answer for him with your head."

"Slooshiyoo's'."

"Be off, then, and get your horse. Take food to Andi."—the first

---

17. *Slushaius'*: Yes, sir! (literally: I am listening, sir.)

large aul in Daghestan. "The starshina will furnish a mounted guard and another horse."

Half an hour later Akhmet and I, with a heavily-armed Chechense horseman as escort, were climbing the zigzag road that led to the summit of the Andiski Khrebet. Just before we started, Captain Cherkassof had given the red-bearded interpreter, as a farewell stirrup-cup, a brimming tumbler of colorless Russian vodka, but I could not see that it had the slightest effect upon him. His scarred, saturnine countenance showed no change of expression, and he did not speak either to me or to the Chechense escort until we reached the crest of the titanic divide and looked out from a height of eight thousand feet over the wild, rugged landscape of western Daghestan. Then, at sight of his native Avaria, his face seemed to brighten a little, and, turning to me, he pointed out the approximate location of his birthplace; the five-thousand-foot precipice of Gimry; the deep, gloomy gorge of the Andiski Koisu; the cliff-girdled mountain of Gunib, where the great Caucasian leader Shamyl made his last stand against the Russians; and above and beyond them all the white, snowy peaks of the main range stretching away in a long, serrated line toward the coast of the Caspian Sea.

On the snow-powdered summit, we stopped a few moments for lunch. Akhmet doffed his muff-shaped wool hat and took out of the space between the crown and the facing a thin pancake of unleavened bread, a piece of dried meat, and a couple of hard-boiled eggs. Meanwhile I produced from my saddle bags some cheese and white bread, half a cold fowl, and a bottle of red native wine, which Captain Cherkassof's boy had put up for me before we started. My experience not only with tenth-century barbarians, but with savages of the stone age, had taught me that it is always good policy to share food and drink; so I gave Akhmet part of my lunch, including the wine, and took in return a part of his. This immediately improved our social relations.

Two or three days passed before the subject of homicide came up again, and by that time Akhmet and I had made some progress toward intimacy. He had discovered that, although I was a foreigner, from a country of which he had never heard, I was nevertheless a human being with some sympathetic intelligence; and I had found that although he was a tenth-century barbarian, his social behavior in certain situations showed as much tact, consideration, and delicacy of feeling as mine.

One day, for example, about noon, after climbing three thousand feet or more up an almost precipitous mountain slope, we rode into a high mesa village where the only inhabitants seemed to be boys and girls from four to ten years of age. These children, of course, did not live there alone all the time. The adult members of their families had gone down into a neighboring valley to harvest Indian corn, and they had left the younger boys and girls at home to tend the babies and keep house.

Without knocking for admittance, Akhmet threw open the door of the best-looking dwelling in the settlement and walked in. The only occupants of the house were two little girls, apparently about six and nine years of age. At sight of two strange men, one heavily armed and the other dressed in a terrifying foreign costume, the children seemed to be half paralyzed with the shock of surprise and fear; but they soon rallied, and the elder, remembering that in the absence of her parents she was invested with the duties and responsibilities of the family, beckoned us to follow, and, conducting us to the guest chamber, invited us to take seats on a broad, rug-covered divan. Then, bowing to us with a courtesy that was half womanly and half childish, she retired. Five minutes later her little six-year-old sister came in, trembling with fear, and offered to us on a huge circular bronze tray two bunches of grapes—the only refreshments they had been able to find in the house that seemed to them worthy of our acceptance. The poor little tot was so frightened as she approached me that her trembling shook the tray; but she knew her duty, and, rallying all her spiritual forces, she performed it with a courage that was as admirable as it was touching. It may well be doubted whether two New England children left alone in the house and surprised by the sudden incoming of a cowboy and a bashi-bazouk would have given such an exhibition of the two noble virtues—hospitality and courage.

But the behavior of Akhmet, the mediaeval barbarian, was equally surprising. Not only did he strive in every way to encourage and reassure the children, but he treated the elder girl especially with as much respect and deference as if she were de jure, as well as de facto, the "lady of the house." When we took our leave, he bowed low to her, with bared head, and thanked her with what might fairly be described as "ornamental earnestness" for the shelter and hospitality that we had enjoyed.

Journal, 211–16, 209–10, 216–24]

Our road today from Capt. C.'s dwelling ran in a series of long zigzags up to the mountain lying east of the aoul. When we had gone 7 miles we could still talk with an inhabitant of the village by raising our voices and at a distance of 10 miles by the road it was still possible to shoot a rifle bullet directly into the aoul. It lay directly under our feet for 2 or 3 hours. The road wound round and round following all the salient and neutering[?] angles of the mountain and was frequently so crooked that we could see it on four sides at the same time—that is, it appeared in front, behind, and on both sides. It is a good specimen of Russian engineering in the Caucasus.

From Veden to Lake Ilazam there is not a place where a span of horses cannot be driven at a trot up or down with any kind of a wagon or carriage although the road crosses the Ande Krebet at a height of 7377 feet. Everywhere it is cut or blasted in the steep slopes of the mountains, sometimes supported by a stone wall from beneath, sometimes guarded from water from above by two deep trenches cut at such an angle as to catch all the water from above and carry it one way or the other to regular sluices across the road. In many places, the road is blasted out of solid rock for 2 or 3 miles. Everywhere it is about 14 feet in width level and safe and with very moderate grades. After ascending to a height of about 5000 feet above the sea without making more than three miles in horizontal distance, the road runs in one long gradual slope along the side of the ravine following all the sinuosities of its bluffs and lateral gullies—now coming out on a tremendous buttress at a height of 1000 feet or more above the bottom of the ravine, then running back a mile or more into a side gorge—turn out again upon another bluff. The ascent here is very gradual. At last about 1 o'clock PM we came out on the pereval[18] 7377 feet above the sea and there opened before us on the other side a scene of remarkable grandeur. Away on the right 75 miles or more distant, appeared the white, sharp, ragged peaks of the glovni krebet, covered everywhere with snow, glittering in long smooth slopes in the

---

18. *pereval:* mountain pass. Here, Kennan is crossing the ridge of mountains marking the border between Chechnya and Dagestan, the pass in question probably being the Kharami (in fact 2177 m; 7142 ft).

sunshine, and deepening to a pearly blueness in the shadows of its ravines, and rising here and there to a height of 12,000 feet in apparently inaccessible peaks. In the foreground was a perfect chaos of huge irregular mound shaped mountains, breaking off here and there in great precipices, cut by deep narrow ravines, and covered everywhere on their northern slopes with snow. Directly south of the pereval there seemed to be a river and on its eastern side ran a long row of high bluffs separated from another by deep gullies and rising gradually to a high bare ridge which hid the base of the glovni krebet. I could not tell certainly whether a river ran under these bluffs or not as I could not see the bottom of the ravine but there appeared to be one. Directly under our feet to the eastward in a deep chasm among enormous mountains lay Lake Izalam, its waters so darkly blue that they appeared almost black.[19] Achmet says the large lake is called Isalam—it is about a verst and a half in length and very deep. In some places the Russian soundings found no bottom. Near Isalam there is another smaller lake called Farelnia or Trout lake.[20] Along the right side of the lake rose steep, almost perpendicular precipices and in their faces was blasted out the government road to Botlekh. The road and lake, however, wound around the end of a mountain and were lost to sight. Turning away to the left from the government road, we ascended gradually 200 or 300 ft higher and rode along the crest of a ridge in an E.S.E. direction toward Ande. From two or 3 points on this mountain road the views to the S.W. and E.S.E. were magnificent. In the latter direction lay the glovni krebet, rising in white majestic cliffs and peaks above a chaos of nearer mountains and seeming to be only 10 or 12 miles distant, while in the former appeared a deep gap between two enormous snowy ridges, through which we could see a deep, bare valley and a long vista of new mountains 50 miles beyond. The outlines of Daghestan scenery are grand, but they lack coloring and filling up. The mountains everywhere were perfectly bare and brown where there

---

19. This lake, which Kennan spells first "Ilezan," and then "Izalam," appears to be the lake now called "Kezenoiam," which the modern map glosses as "Goluboe" (sky blue). On the top of page 206, Kennan had jotted notes: "Farelnian Ozera, Ilzelan— so called by Tartars; Farelnian Ozera— Ilzelan is the large lake. Farelnan is the small one—Go first to Ilzelan." The small lake does not appear on the 1:200000 scale map.

20. *forel'*: trout (Russ.).

was no snow and there was not a tree to be seen within 50 miles in any direction. On some of the less precipitous slopes were scattered here and there 100 or more huge[?] rocks but nothing more. The pictures which presented themselves to the eye were wild, grand, but desolate.

I have tried to write down here a mountain song which Achmet sang today on the road but I have had poor success. Achmet forgets it and loses himself if he tries to sing it slowly and there are so many accidentals in it that I can't catch it.

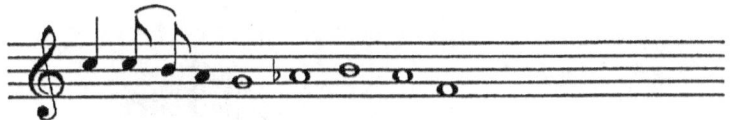

At the top of the ridge over the village of Ande we stopped for a few moments to rest and eat. Achmet's eggs—the few which were not broken—2 I believe, and a piece of bread. From there we descended the mountain on foot leading our horses. On the right was a very high precipitous ridge sprinkled with snow and on the left a slope growing steeper and steeper and terminating in what appeared to be limestone cliffs. The formation of this whole valley is limestone and it crops out everywhere white as milk. Passed two or three men drawing hay down the mountain side on a sled with a team of oxen and about 1/2 past 2 saw Ande. The aoul is situated on the left bank of a small stream which runs along the foot of the steep ridge before mentioned and when we saw it nearly all the village was shadowed by the ridge. It lies partly on a high slope 60 or 70 feet above the bed of the stream and partly under the cliffs and is a large aoul. The houses are of stone like all the Daghestan aouls I have seen and are scattered around in such a helter skelter style that you can't tell whether you are walking in a street or on the roof of somebody's house. There are no streets at all—nothing but narrow winding passages between the irregularly-built saklas. On every roof almost are one or two haystacks and against every wall are plastered 15 or 20 round plates of cow dung drying for fuel—on the roofs are also stacks of this material. The most noticeable building in the aoul is the mosque which is a large but low square edifice of stone with a flat roof and a round stone minaret about 40 or 50 feet in height, loopholed for musketry with a sort of gallery and narrow windows round the top. The chimneys of the saklas here are more ornamental than any I have seen, being more or less regular pyramids of clay with holes in them—thus for the escape of the smoke [*sketch*]. The Chechense chimneys, on the contrary, are of this shape [*sketch*].

The dress of the women here is noticeable for the huge pillows or cushions which they wear on their heads. These cushions are 3 or 4 inches thick, project an inch or so over the forehead and come down to the ears on each side. They are covered generally with striped or figured calico in gay colors. Over these cushions are fastened veils of white cotton cloth

*Daghestani women. Photo from Kennan archive.
Courtesy of Library of Congress.*

which hides the neck and ears and hang down behind almost to the feet. They wear blue cotton trousers and dresses ornamented about the breast with silver just as did the women of Bezhuta. The dress of the men is the huge shuba of black sheepskin and long wooled black caps of southern Daghestan. We stopped at house of Starshine. Room without windows, low, fireplace with 2 or 3 white cheeses over it on a shelf, a Persian mat half covering the clay floor, a long shelf opposite door on which are huge earthen and metallic pitchers of antique shapes, two or three big metallic tasses and a couple of Russian trunks. On the right side of door is a peg on which hang sabres, pistols, kinjals etc. Big bag of wool in one corner. Hurry[?] upon my arrival, a samovar was hunted up, stuffed with cow dung, lighted, water boiled and tea made. After tea I strolled out on roof of 1st story and watched women coming to spring below house for water, group with glittering copper and metal pitchers on their backs, gossiping. Curious arrangement of stables—one in 1st story under room in which I am writing and one a little farther uphill on roof of first story. Achmet says that the head cushions of the women originated in an attempt to keep their heads from being broken by their husbands. Supper tonight consisted of plates made of bread: round, thin, 12 or 14 inches in diameter, a wooden bowl of boiled mutton and another of mutton broth thickened with rice and eaten with huge wooden spoons, 1/2 doz. hard boiled eggs, shelled, and a plate of grapes. All very good. I'm tired and am going to bed.

Ande—Oct. 14, morning [=Oct. 26]

HAVEN'T FELT VERY WELL YESTERDAY AND TODAY. Something which I have eaten has disagreed with me. Saw a woman this A.M. dressed in . . . [21]

["A Tenth-Century Barbarian," 205–7]

As we rode together day after day through the wild gorges of western Daghestan and sat together night after night in the guestrooms of mountain houses, I encouraged Akhmet to talk frankly about his early life. At first he seemed reticent and reserved, but, finding that I was making an honest effort to understand his environment and look at things

---

21. He never completed the sentence.

from his point of view, he gradually gained confidence; and finally related to me without any attempt at justification or self-defense, the most extraordinary stories of adventure, lawlessness, and crime that I had ever heard. It did not seem to occur to him that I might be shocked by the purposes he avowed and the actions he described, and he told me the story of his life just as he would have told it to a brother-barbarian of whose perfect comprehension and sympathy he felt sure.

One day, for example, he gave me in a matter-of-fact but graphic way an account of an attempt that he made in early manhood to kill an aged Kumik and carry off the latter's young wife. It happened, he said, when he was a young and unmarried man about twenty-five years of age. He had started one summer day with a raiding party of twenty-five or thirty Avars on a cattle-lifting expedition in the territory of a hostile clan. In riding through a Kumik village, on the way to the scene of action, Akhmet happened to see in the street a very beautiful young Kumik girl. With the impetuosity of his age and temperament, he fell in love with her at sight, and, halting his party, he proceeded to make inquiries about her. To his great disgust, he found that, although she was only sixteen or seventeen years of age, she was already married to an old Kumik. That such a pearl of young womanhood should be married at all was bad; that she should be married to a despised Kumik was worse; and that she should be the property of an old man—a man three or four times her age— was simply intolerable. It was a violation of the laws of nature which ought not to be permitted. In less than half an hour Akhmet made up his mind to kill the old husband and carry off the young wife. Making known his intentions to his companions, he let them go on the raid without him. He then called together the head man and three or four leading Kumiks of the settlement and explained to them that he was a sword-maker, and that he had come to the village for the purpose of taking a house and beginning there the manufacture of kinjals.

No question seems to have been raised as to the sincerity of Akhmet's professions, and he was able in a few days to rent a house and settle down. His first move was to give one evening a sort of house-warming, to which he invited all the villagers, including the old Kumik and his young wife. Then, with his horse in readiness, he went out and lay in wait for the old Kumik, intending to ambush him, kill him, and carry off the girl. The old Kumik, however, seems to have become suspicious of Akhmet at an early stage in the proceedings, and instead of coming to the entertainment, he and his wife remained quietly at home.

Having proceeded thus far in his narrative, Akhmet stopped and seemed to be lost in gloomy reflections.

"Well," I said, "what did you do then?"

"Do then? One night, after dark, I tried to bring him out as a peacemaker. I got up a sham quarrel with one of my neighbors and sent for him to act as arbitrator."

"Did he come?" I inquired, as Akhmet again paused.

"No; the cowardly old pig. And it was so dark where I watched that I came near killing another man in his place."

"Wouldn't it have been simpler," I asked, "to climb into one of his windows some night and kill him at home?"

"Kill him in a house!" exclaimed Akhmet, apparently shocked. "In our Daghestan you can't kill a man in a house."

"You can't? Why not?"

"There is no adat for it. It would be dishonorable. You mustn't kill even your blood enemy in a house."

This exposition of tenth-century ethics left me dumb with amazement. According to Akhmet, you might honorably invite a man to an evening party and kill him while he was coming as your guest to your entertainment, or you might properly ambush and murder him when he was coming at your request to act as arbitrator in your quarrel; but it would be disgraceful to kill him in a house. He must be assassinated in the open. [. . .] I cannot now remember all the stratagems to which Akhmet resorted in his effort to get the old Kumik out of doors, where he might be killed with perfect propriety and in strict accordance with the customary law, but they all failed. The suspicious husband and his young wife never left their house at night, and never in the daytime unless they were accompanied by friends enough to protect them.

["Murder by Adat," 479–80]

In the eastern Caucasus at that time murder for the sake of robbery was not common, and was little to be feared; but in the wilder parts of the country the danger of provoking assault by giving offense inadvertently was one to which the inexperienced traveler was always more or less exposed. Individual conduct and social intercourse were regulated only by adat; and the mountaineers, who all carried deadly weapons, had not only a keen sense of personal dignity, but a sort of fierce, sensitive pride, which impelled them to resent instantly anything that had even the appearance of an insult. Careful as I was to avoid words or behavior that might be misconstrued or taken amiss, I got into difficulty with a mountaineer in whose house we spent a night soon after we entered Daghestan. The misunderstanding was the result of my offering him money.

He had given Akhmet and me shelter overnight and had taken care of our three horses, and it seemed rather shabby to go on our way without paying for our food and lodging. Just before we started, therefore, in the morning, I offered him two rubles. He barely glanced at the money, and then, putting his hand quickly to the hilt of his long, double-edged *kinjal*, he gave me the most searching, penetrating, and at the same time menacing look that I had ever encountered. I saw instantly that I had blundered, and I have no doubt that my face looked like that of a reprimanded school-boy as I hastily put the two-ruble note in my pocket. Just at that moment, to my great relief, Akhmet came up, and the mountaineer, turning to him, said with stern dignity, in which there was still an undertone of menace: "Tell your foreign traveler that we mountaineers don't sell our hospitality." Akhmet, with quick wit, explained that I had no thought of offering money to him—still less of insulting him. My intention was to have the two rubles given to the servant who had cooked the food. The mountaineer was appeased, but there was still a flush of anger in his face as he withdrew his hand from his kinjal.

"It isn't safe to do that," said Akhmet to me as we rode away from the village. "In our Daghestan you can't offer money to a man in whose house you have been a guest. It is a deadly insult."

[Journal 224–42]

Botlekh [=Botlikh], Oct. 15th, 10:30 AM [=Oct. 27]

WE LEFT ANDE YESTERDAY MORNING ABOUT 10 o'clock. The scenery in the vicinity of that aoul is remarkable for its wild, savage barrenness and the grandeur of its outlines. The aoul lies as nearly as I can estimate at a height of about 4000 feet above the sea. It is situated on the edge of a deep stony ravine between a high snow-covered ridge on the south and a long gradual barren slope on the north. Leaving the aoul we crossed the stream by a stone bridge skillfully thrown across it in a single arch and began a gradual ascent on its right bank, going around the edge of the before-mentioned high ridge. The following is a rough sketch of the country [*map sketch*]. The country on the left bank of the stream below Ande is a perfect chaos of high bare whitish limestone hills cut by deep gorges, separated by small plains more or less level, and cut out here and there by the action of water into a thousand fantastic shapes. As we ascended on the end of the ridge the whole region opened before us like a map.[22] On the left were huge barren hills cliffs and gorges with a large aoul built on the brink of a precipice 200 feet in height. Lower down and farther to the eastward on a gentle slope lay another aoul and through the gorge S.E. of us appeared the valley of the Andeski Koisu blue and hazy with distance and beyond it a triangular view of a great snowy range. More to the eastward lay the huge blue and white mountains of Koonsakh [=Khunzakh] and N.E. appeared over a nearer ridge the distant range of Ande. As we turned away to the right, we lost sight of this picture but when we reached the crest of the second range there opened before us to the west and south the most magnificent view I have yet seen in the Caucasus. We stood on the western end of the second ridge, on the brink of a precipice nearly 2000 feet in depth. Looking to the westward, there appeared the Andeski-Krebet with the government road running in long sharp zigzags down its barren sides and N.W. another huge ridge more than 7000 feet in height, covered on top with snow and breaking off about half way down in precipices 200 or 300 feet high. This ridge was cut with deep narrow gorges out of which ran little mountain streams in white limy[?] channels and along its side ran a couple of white thread-like roads or bridle paths. Directly under our feet 2000 feet down lay an aoul on the top of a high mound shaped hill cut out into little terraces for cultivation which looked like irregular flights of steps leading up to the aoul. The hill on which the aoul stood broke off on the S.W., W. and N.W. in precipices 200 or 300 feet in height and the summit was accessible only by paths leading up at the foot of the cliffs on which we stood. The aoul was so

---

22. Here he is probably ascending to the Rushukha Pass (1715 m; 5626 ft).

far below us that it looked more like a nest than a village and the herds of sheep and cattle browsing around it were nothing but crawling ants. On the other side of the stream on another precipitous hill lay a second aoul. Directly in the south appeared the Andeski Koisu issuing from a tremendous gorge in the first snowy range, turning to the eastward and lying stretched in silver threads through the valley of Botlekh. From this stream rolled up the gigantic foot hills of the glovni krebet, becoming gradually covered with snow, interacted by deep, gloomy gorges, and rising at last to the sharp jagged peaks of the great range glittering in the sunlight a snowy white and deepening in shadow to a pearly blue. North of the Andeski Koisu lay the tree-embowered aoul of Botlekh like an oasis in this desert of barren mountains and rocky gorges. The scene was perfectly indescribable. In the distance lay the white peaks of the great range, visible for 100 miles to the westward, and in the foreground a chaos of mountains, precipices, deep gorges, cliffs, terraced hills, aouls, glittering thread-like rivers, herds of cattle, sheep and goats, vineyards, walnut trees turned canary color by frost, and here and there the white zigzag lines of mountain roads lying like wounded serpents among the barren mountains. In all Daghestan I have seen only a few views which can be compared with this one and only one which surpasses it—viz the view of the Kakhetinski valley from the summit of the glovni krebet. The Georgian military road can show nothing equal to this or to the latter. We stopped a few moments on the brink of the precipices at the end of the ridge and sitting down on the very edge of an overhanging mass of rock 2000 feet above the aoul and nearly 7000 feet above the sea I tried to fix the wonderful picture in my memory.

Then, remounting, we rode down the zigzag descent on the south into the aoul of Botlekh. Botlekh is situated on the left bank of the Andeski Koisu and on the right bank of a small stream which falls into it. It is surrounded on all sides by barren mountains and itself lies on bluffs over the stream so that its saklas are very irregularly disposed. The bluffs and hill sides have been cut away into successive walled terraces which are planted with vineyards and walnut trees and a part of the stream has been carried in a long canal into the aoul so that it runs through every street between the houses and can be turned over every terrace. It is this system of irrigation which has made Botlekh an oasis in a desert. The aoul itself is not remarkable for anything except the foliage, gardens, vineyards, etc., which surround it and the irregularity of its construction. Riding into the aoul we stopped at the house of an Armenian merchant and I sat down on a bag of grain in his lafka[23] while Achmet hunted up a place for me to stop. In a few moments a mountaineer with silver cartridge tubes on his breast and a henna-dyed beard came to me with an invitation from Prince Chefchavadze's adjutant to make his quarters my residence during my stay. Of course I gladly accepted. The Adjutant was a handsome young man of about 24 or 5, with light brown hair and a long brown moustache, no beard, regular handsome features and a very pleasant expression of countenance. He received me with the greatest cordiality and at once offered me tea. Noticing that he spoke the Avarski language I asked with some surprise how he had learned it. He replied that it was his native tongue, that he was an Avaretz by birth, and spoke Avarski better than Russian. I should never have supposed that he was a mountaineer. After tea about 6 o'clock we called upon Prince Chefchavadze spent the evening there and took supper. He lives in a large, handsome stone house elegantly furnished in eastern style with luxurious divans, cushions, pillows, etc., lace curtains, easy chairs, and Persian carpets. Walls ornamented with costly Asiatic weapons richly ornamented with gold and silver chasing, disposed in fanciful figures. In the centre, a huge silver-mounted Georgian drinking horn. Walls neatly papered with blue. Spent the evening in talking and playing chess. Had an excellent supper with sherry claret and champagne.

Botlekh, October 16th, 8:30 AM [=Oct. 28]

TOOK A WALK YESTERDAY MORNING AROUND THE aoul and the adjutant related to me some interesting facts with regard to life and customs of mountaineers which I will note down here. First mountain etiquette. He said that very frequently when travelling he met a dozen or more mountaineers with whom he was not acquainted. One of them would come up to him with outstretched hand and begin, "Salaam aleikoum"—"Salam Aleikoum"—"How is your health, Are you well?"—"How is your father's health? Is he well?" "Thank you my father is very well!"—"And your mother, does she enjoy good health?" "My

23. *lavka:* shop.

mother, thank God, is also well"—"And how are all your relatives?"—"All perfectly well."—"And what is the condition of your house?"—"My house is in good condition."—"And how do your sheep flourish?"—"My sheep, thank you, are all doing finely."—and so on with a dozen more questions relative to the health and prosperity of the questioned and all his relatives and belongings. At last the man finishes when the second one approaches and goes through the same routine. After the 2nd or 3rd and so on, every one of them heard the answers which were made to the questions of the first man but nevertheless they must all go over the same ground again. The Adjutant met some mountaineers yesterday as we rode to the half tunnel, but he cut them short in very summary style by exclaiming impatiently "I am well, my father is well, my mother is well, all my relatives are well, my house is in good condition and my father's sheep are flourishing. If you and your relatives are all well, thank God I am very glad."

The mountaineers notwithstanding their generous hospitality are very close with regard to money and frequently bury it like misers. Such a case happened a few days ago at Khoonzakh. A man had 400 silver and gold roubles. He buried them secretly no one knew where and shortly afterward was accidentally killed by falling down a precipice. The money now is irretrievably lost as no one knows where it is hidden.

The mountaineers of Daghestan were known to the Georgians under the general name of Lyegae or Lesge—probably a corruption of Lyake the name of a tribe S. of Goonib who have always enjoyed a certain prominence in pride of power and influence. Strabo and Plutarch undoubtedly took this name from the Georgians as they were at that time in communication with Rome, and from them also the Russians have adopted the title of Lezgins which they apply to the mountaineers of Southern Daghestan generally. Relics which have descended from the Crusaders are still to be found in the Caucasus. Among the Toochets[24] especially there are still in existence great numbers of straight broad cross-

---

24. The Tushetians are an Eastern Orthodox people who live in the north of Kakhetia, across the Main Caucasus Ridge from the Dido peoples. In the next entry, Kennan calls them "Toovchinni," which sounds like their name for themselves: "Tushuri." Wixman, *Peoples of the USSR*, 200. Baddeley refers to them as "Tousheens."

handled swords, suits of armor with white crosses on them, steel helmets with veils of chain mail and the weapons of the middle ages generally. Knaz Chefchavadze saw a Crusader's sword for which he offered 500 roubles. Previous to the invention of gun powder they were worn in southern Daghestan and various parts of the Caucasus but since then they have been simply handed down from father to son as relics. Traces of Huns in Daghestan.[25] Goonib in the native language is Goonee or Hoonee—place of the Hoons. Khoonzakh may also be connected with them.[26]

Aoul Khlokh [=Tlokh]—Oct. 16, 7:30 PM [=Oct. 28]

TO CONTINUE WITH THE FACTS LEARNED FROM Adjutant. The Toovchinni are Christians, but whether they have always been so or not the Adjutant did not know. They were long accustomed to make raids into the territory of the Dedoitse, kill as many as possible and, cutting off one hand from every dead man, carry it home and nail it on the wall of their house. 3 or 4 years ago almost every sakla in Toovchima was ornamented in this way with the black fleshless hands of murdered men. During the reign of Shamyl there were 7000 executions directly or indirectly through his orders in Daghestan.

On the afternoon of the day following my arrival, we made a trip up the Andieski Koisu to what the Russians call the "half tunnel"—a very wild deep precipitous gorge in the mountains about 12 miles from Botlekh. The road through this gorge is certainly a very remarkable one, being a mere footpath hewn out in the face of the precipice on the left side in this style [*sketch, section of cliff face with protruding ledge*]. It rises in some places to a perpendicular height of 100 feet or more above the stream. In places this path has caved away entirely for a few feet and across these gaps have been thrown flying bridges of two stringers, half a dozen cross pieces, and a few bushes. It's enough to make a man's hair stand on end to cross them on foot—to say nothing of riding over them.

---

25. This comment may reflect Kennan's having in hand a published pamphlet on the Huns in Dagestan. See Appendix.

26. Baddeley mentions this theory that the name "Khunzakh" can be traced to the Huns, but does not find the evidence conclusive (*Russian Conquest of the Caucasus*, xxxi).

In places, the stone roof over the path is only about 5 feet from the path itself, so that riding is utterly impossible. From tall horses they are even obliged to take off the saddles.

The scenery throughout this gorge is extremely wild and as we returned by moonlight it looked still wilder. We reached the village about 7:15, drank tea and went over to the prince's. Played 2 more games of checkers: won one and drew one. Went to bed at 12:30. Adjutant tells gortze that I am man from another world. They enquire "Where did he light?" Near town we met girls singing. When they saw us they stopped. Adjutant asked them why and they said because they were girls! Instance of musical pokhabnosti[27] related by Adjutant.

[Journal, 257–59]

During the walk of the Adjutant and I in Botlekh we visited the mosque. It was a large, square flat-roofed stone building, with very small windows and an earthen floor covered with Persian mats and carpets. One ceiling was upheld by long rows of pillars. On one side was a flight of stairs leading down into the bath room and on the other a flight leading up to the roof. Facing Mecca was a large sort of [28] wooden pulpit, elaborately carved, in which the moolah read the Koran and prayed. On the pillars which supported the ceiling, here and there were pasted elaborately illuminated certificates from Mecca. It is customary when a man intends to make a pilgrimage to Mecca to give notice to that effect (especially if the would-be pilgrim is a poor man) and take up a collection for his benefit. Every inhabitant of the aoul gives as much as he can: 10, 20, 50 roubles, with the condition that the pilgrim shall pray for him in Mecca. The pilgrim when he arrives prays for every man who has contributed to defray his expenses, and brings back to each one a certificate to prove that he has really prayed for him.

27. *pokhabnost'*: obscenity.

28. The narrative here is written around notes that apparently had been jotted on the page at an earlier point: "Aoul Antzookhoul—Oct. 21[=Nov. 2]. Left Botlekh yest. AM. Passed aoul of Tsatunikh. Sea of Fog. Poti, Nov. 14 [=Nov. 26]." This is an important clue to the fact that much of Kennan's narrative of his return journey through Dagestan was not composed until he was on the boat on the Black Sea, heading for Istanbul weeks later.

[Journal, 242–57]

Koonzakh—Oct. 18th [=Oct. 30]

LEFT BOTLEKH DAY BEFORE YESTERDAY ABOUT noon. The road from the village ran down one of the many water-worn gullies which intersect the barren hills in that vicinity to the fortress of Preobrazhenski. This is an open stone fort with crenellated walls, barracks, round corner towers pierced for cannon and musketry. It has been entirely abandoned as a post on account of the deadly fevers which prevail in that vicinity during the summer months. The Andeski Koisu overflows the lowland along its banks in the spring and leaves a deposit of black earth which under the influence of an almost tropical sun breeds malignant fevers. Even Botlekh itself although it lies at a height of 2000 feet or so above the sea is not entirely exempt. The climate of Botlekh is a remarkable one. Lying in the midst of mountains 2000 feet above the sea, not far from the snowy range, it has an almost tropical climate and the weather throughout the winter is almost always warm and pleasant. Snow occasionally falls to a depth of a few inches but rarely lies longer than one day. Even now, as late as Nov. 1st, the weather there is as warm as June so that it is uncomfortable to ride horseback in the sunshine. Grasshoppers are as thick as in midsummer and the foliage of the fruit and nut trees has only just begun to turn yellow. Passing Preobrazhenski fort, we rode along the left bank of the Koisu to Preobrazhenski Bridge. Of this I have a photograph so that a description is unnecessary.[29] All along the right band of the Koisu from the polu-toonell[30] ravine nearly to Klokh, there are the ruins of a stone wall built during the time of Shamyl, probably to defend the approaches to Avaria. It runs up over

---

29. Kennan purchased some photographs of Dagestan while he was there and provides at least a partial list on page 176 of the journals (see Appendix). The National Geographic Society has some of his Caucasus photographs and the rest are in the Library of Congress Photograph Collection. Many of the photos were used to illustrate his *National Geographic* article, "An Island in the Sea of History," supplemented by some of the elegant views of the Caucasus mountains taken by the noted photographer Vittorio Sella.

30. *polu-tunnel'*: half-tunnel.

bluffs in places to a height of 200 or 300 feet and its construction must have cost a good deal of labor.

Crossing Preobrazhenski Most,[31] we entered a deep, wild ravine between indescribably bare, desolate mountains, climbed to a height of 150 feet and entered the aoul of Inkhelee [=Inkhelo]. This aoul, like all Daghestan aouls almost, is built on the slope of a precipitous mountain over the Koisu, its saklas rising one above another like seats in a theatre. Owing to limited space between the mountain and the stream, its houses have all been built together in one solid mass, with no openings whatever between them, and the streets run underneath like dark narrow tunnels. From these underground streets flights of stairs or rude ladders lead up into the houses. The first story opening upon the streets is always occupied as a stable for cattle, the second and third stories are occupied by the family. The second story is generally dark and has no opening to the air whatever but the third story of every house, owing to the steepness of the slope, rises above the lower ones and has generally an open balcony.

From the time we entered the aoul, we rode constantly through dark, narrow, subterranean passages which reminded me of the catacombs: dirty, filled with manure and offal of every description, ill-smelling and filthy to the last degree. We rode, I should think, at least a quarter of a mile in this way, underground in almost total darkness through a passage not more than 4 feet wide, bending our heads low over our saddle bows to avoid striking them against the beams of the houses overhead. On each side were stone walls cut here and there with doors opening into foul black dungeons called stables and at intervals appeared cross streets running vertically up and down the mountain at an angle of 45 degrees. Occasionally we met women with copper water pitchers on their backs and little donkeys half hidden by loads of hay, straw, wood, and the passage was so narrow that they had to take refuge either in a stable or a cross street to allow us to pass. Taking it altogether, Inkhelee was one of the most curious aouls I have ever seen.

Emerging once more into daylight which fairly dazzled our eyes after the darkness of the underground streets, we descended again to the bank of the Koisu and rode along it through a very deep ravine to the bridge of Khonkhodatel [=Kvankhidatl]. Although it was only a little after noon,

31. *most*: bridge.

the sunlight did not begin to reach the bottom of this ravine and evidently would not reach it again before February. Of Khonkhodatel bridge I have a photograph. Akhmet—although he was "Akhmet Avarski"—did not venture to ride over this frail swinging bridge but dismounted and led his horse to the other side. The bridge sways up and down to the footsteps of a horse in a decidedly alarming style but it seemed to be strong enough and safe enough. The inhabitants of Khonkhodatel gain a scanty livelihood by making salt. 2 versts or more beyond the aoul there are four or five salt springs and by these the Khonkhodatelski are supported.

The method of extracting salt from the water is original. In the first place they level off a flat of ground 15 or 20 ft square on the bank of the stream, beat it down hard like a floor and cover it with fine black sand which is found in the bed of the creek near by. Over this sand they then sprinkle the salt water from the springs and allow it to evaporate. This sprinkling and evaporation go on for several days until the sand becomes impregnated with salt. It is then shovelled up by the women into baskets which they carry and fill on their backs and empty into wooden boxes about 4 ft long and 2 wide which stand near by. When these boxes are filled with the salted sand, water is gradually poured into them and after dissolving and taking up the salt the water trickles through openings in the bottom and falls into troughs which are prepared for its reception. From these troughs it is bailed out with wooden bowls and emptied into skins, which are strung across the backs of mules or donkeys and carried to the aoul. Here the water is emptied into large kettles and boiled down. The whole process is managed exclusively by women. I did not see a single man at work anywhere. It is attended throughout with great difficulty. There is no wood anywhere near the aoul and it is brought half a dozen sticks at a time on donkeys from a distance of 10 or 15 miles. The sale of this salt, however, is the only source of revenue which the inhabitants have.

Riding on beyond the Khonkhodatelski salt works between terribly steep and desolate mountains, we entered a little more fertile region. The valley of the Koisu widened out a little and gave room here and there for oases of nut trees, fruit trees, and vineyards whose green and canary-colored foliage seemed strangely out of place among the barren, treeless, vegetationless mountains. A little farther on, the ravine widened still more and we entered what I called "Earthquake Valley." The formation of this valley struck me as being very peculiar. On both sides there were the most wonderful upheavals of sandstone strata which I have seen in Daghestan. The valley looked as if it had originally been a high plateau covered with horizontal strata of grey sandstone rock in this way [*sketch of strata*]. I could imagine that during an earthquake or internal convulsion of some kind, the bottom of this plateau (so to speak) fell out and sandstone strata unsupported from beneath broke in the middle and fell in this way [*sketch*]— It is very evident from the appearance of the sides of the ravine that the valley was made by a subsidence of the centre and not an upheaval of the sides and this is also shown by the opposite slopes of the strata themselves.

On the Southern side of the ravine these strata rose almost perpendicularly to a height of 1200 feet and were covered on top with snow and the slope was so steep that nothing could grow on it except moss and here and there tufts of grass. From top to bottom it was simply bare rock. The scenery from the centre of this valley looking to the westward was very wild, owing to the immense broken slabs of sandstone rock which lay on both sides just as they fell, and rose to sharp broken edges 300 or 400 ft high. Riding along the left bank of the Koisu between vineyards hanging full of yet ungathered grapes, past 3 or 4 common aouls posted on the heights of the left shore, we reached just before dark the American bridge of Klokh. This is simply a square open box [*sketch showing girder framework*] strengthened by an arch which has been recently added. Crossing the bridge, we entered a narrow street leading to the aoul of Klokh and made our way up the hill with difficulty between scores of little donkeys loaded with wood baskets of grapes, enormous bundles of hay and straw, women with metallic pitchers of water on their backs or bundles of cornstalks, men and boys.

We stopped with the Starsheena and were made tolerably comfortable. Drank tea and in course of time had supper of boiled mutton and broth with vinegar, coarse dark wheat bread, strong, sweet native wine, white grapes and walnuts. The Starosta's house, unlike most Daghestan aouls, was built around an open court on the floor of which lay great heaps of yellow corn. On the following morning we had breakfast of mutton fried in grease with vinegar and small round flat cakes of boiled corn bread. Also a new thing which Achmet declared was a triumph of Daghestan gastronomical science. We drank about 2 bottles of our host's wine—that is, Achmet drank a bottle and a half and I half a bottle, ate a few more grapes which were very sweet and nice and about 1/2 past 10 am we finally got started. I was very tired when we reached Klokh on account of a hard-trotting horse but I changed him there and hired another for a rouble and a half. Saddles of mules and donkeys in western Daghestan this shape [*sketch*]—mere frames of sticks.

Knaz Chefchavadze told me that in the Darinski or Darginski Okroog there existed at the time of the Russian conquest a perfect republican form of government. The obshestvo was divided into 7 cantons, each of which elected one representative or more to a general assembly by which all general questions were decided. They had also a president, but he could do nothing without the sanction of the Assembly over which he presided.

["Murder by Adat," 480–82]

In a high, lonely aoul where we happened one day to be storm-bound, [Akhmet asked . . .] whether, in my country, a man who had killed another could make peace with his blood-seekers. I replied that in most cases a man who killed another in my country was hanged or imprisoned for life by order of society; but that in some of our mountains where blood feuds were carried on I thought they were fought out to a finish.

"In our Daghestan," he said, "you can almost always make peace after a while by paying an indemnity. But sometimes you can't. Once, in an *aoul* south of Gunib, where I was hard pressed by my blood enemies, I had to take refuge in the house of a man whom I hardly knew, and I lived there night and day for three months."

"Do you mean without going out?"

"Yes. Four men with rifles watched that house constantly. How could I go out? I tried to make peace with them, and even offered them four horses, a dozen sheep, and six rolls of woolen cloth; but they wouldn't listen."

"Was the owner of the house willing to keep you all that time?"

"He had to—that's the adat. In our Daghestan you can't turn a man out of a house when his blood-seekers are there watching for him. But when winter came on they went back to their homes. They lived more than sixty miles away, and they couldn't lie in wait for me forever.

"It was there that I got married," continued Akhmet, after a moment's reflection. "Living in the house night and day, I fell in love with a daughter of the man who gave me refuge."

"Then it wasn't such a bad thing for you after all," I suggested.

"In one way, no," he replied. "But in another way it was. There was another man who wanted the girl, and the night that I was married he tried to spoil me."

"How spoil you?"

"He hid under one of the windows of the mosque, and during the ceremony he tied knots in a cord and tried to work evil magic on me. I heard of it, and the next time I saw him we fought. That's where I got this scar," pointing to his forehead. "He nearly split my head open with his kinjal, but I had a pistol in my left hand, and I shot him and stabbed him before he could strike again. Then I had to go into kanle, and it was a bad business. He belonged to a strong family, and his brothers hunted me like a wolf. I didn't see my wife again for nearly a year, and it was two years before I could make peace."

"What do you do when you want to make peace?" I asked. "Is there an adat for that?"

"Yes; but the adat is not the same in all parts of the country. There are different adats."

"Tell me, then, just what you did when you made peace with the men who hunted you like a wolf."

"Well, first I let my hair grow. That was a year and a half after I killed the man who tried to spoil me, or perhaps more. Then some of my friends went to my blood-seekers and said: 'Akhmet is letting his hair grow—it is more than two inches long already.'"

"But what had your hair got to do with it?" I asked in amazement.

"When you let your hair grow long," he replied, "it means that you are sorry and want to end the feud. According to the adat, you must do that first. Then your relatives or friends open negotiations. Well, my friends talked and argued and bargained for a long time—two or three weeks. My enemies were willing to make peace, but the terms were too hard. There were four of them, and the father and eldest brother of the man I killed would not forgive me unless I would agree to pay a large indemnity and to join their family."

"But I don't understand," I interrupted. "How could the father whose son you had killed want you to join his family?"

"I don't mean that they wanted me to live with them," explained Akhmet. "They only wanted me to take on my shoulders their blood feuds. I was known to be a good fighter, and they wanted me to help them kill off their enemies. But I didn't like to do that because their enemies were not mine, and they had a lot of them."

"Tell me one thing more," I interrupted again. "Are your blood feuds between whole families or between individuals? If a member of your family were killed, who would take up the feud? And would the avenger have a right to kill any member of the other family?"

"According to our Avar adat," said Akhmet, "the oldest brother is the first avenger; but there may be more than one. In my case there were four, because in the fight that started it I began the attack. But my four bloodseekers wouldn't have had a right to kill any one but me. In some of the clans families fight families, but our adat doesn't allow the killing of a blood enemy's relatives. That would be as bad as killing a man in a house."

"All right," I said. "Now I understand. Go ahead."

" . . . I was willing to pay an indemnity, but not to join the other family and take up its feuds. My friends did all they could for me, but my bloodseekers—may eagles drink their eyes!—gave me no peace; and after I had been shot at two or three times from ambush my wife persuaded me to yield." Again a gloomy and savage expression darkened Akhmet's face as he recalled his humiliation, and for two or three minutes he stared silently into the embers of the cowdung fire.

"Well," I finally said, "what then? Did you make peace?"

"Yes," he said, with bitterness; "after an accursed ceremony of blood adoption, I made peace." Again he relapsed into silence. He seemed disinclined to tell me any more, but by means of cautious and sympathetic questions I finally drew from him the following story:

After the arbitrators had settled the terms of peace, Akhmet had to return to the Lezgin village of Mukar, where his blood enemies as well as his wife's family lived, and there go through the ceremony of blood adoption. He was taken first to the house of the father whose son he had killed, and was there called upon to press his lips to the bared breast of his victim's old mother. This, apparently, was intended to be in part fictitious acquirement of kinship, and in part a sacred and solemn undertaking to assume the dead son's liabilities in the matter of offensive and defensive feuds. Akhmet had killed the son—he must therefore take the son's place. When, however, he was brought into the presence of the bereaved mother, she cursed him vindictively, and struggled so violently when compulsion was attempted that this part of the ceremony had to be abandoned.[32]

"She fought like a she-wolf," said Akhmet, "and I was so shamed and humiliated that I was ready to cut my own throat."

On the following day the ceremony of making peace took place in front of the village mosque. At the appointed hour Akhmet removed his outer clothing, wrapped himself in a burial shroud, belted about his waist the long, double-edged *kinjal*, which was the only weapon he was allowed to carry, and went alone to the open space in front of the village mosque, where, assembled in a semicircle, were all the male members of the hostile family. Taking off his sheepskin hat, so as to show the long hair that signified repentance, he drew his kinjal from its sheath, took it by the point, and presented the hilt to the oldest brother of the man whom he had killed. Then, standing before them unarmed, bareheaded, and in a burial shroud, he bowed low, as an intimation that he gave himself up to the men whom he had injured and was ready to be killed and buried if such should be their will. For a fateful moment the killer and the relatives of the killed gazed at each other in silence. Then the oldest brother of the murdered man returned the kinjal holding it in turn by the point, and with his other hand stroked gently Akhmet's long hair. From that moment the homicide was safe; but he had become an adopted member of another family and without forming any new ties of family affection he had acquired a new set of family feuds.

[Journal, 259, 261–64]

Khoonzakh—High plateau west of aoul 5000 ft above sea. Aoul and fortress stand on brink of a tremendous crack in the earth 200 ft wide and 500 or 600 deep, both sides precipitous. Into this canyon fall two or three streams in beautiful cascades 150 ft or more high and run down it in rapids to the Avarski Koisu, which lies in a deep blue ravine to the

---

32. Chenciner writes that when a son was born to the ruler of the Karakaitags, people who have now assimilated with the Dargins, "he was sent from village to village to be suckled by all the women who could, in order to make him foster-brother of his entire generation" (*Daghestan*, 81).

southward out of which rises Chemodan Gora[33] like a huge trunk [sketch]. The water of the falls near the fortress is frequently taken up by wind and sifted in rain all over the fort, not a drop reaching the bottom. From the edge of the precipices on the eastern side of the principal gorge criminals were thrown by order of the Khans. The plateau of which I have spoken lies between two low mountain ranges running nearly

33. *Chemodan Gora:* suitcase mountain. His sketch shows something like a steamer trunk or large suitcase with a handle projecting from the top, which would explain the Russian nickname for the peak. This probably refers to a peak marked at 1382 meters (4534 ft) located just south of the bend where the Avarskoe Koisu turns

Khunzakh. Markov, Ocherki: 505

E. and W. and opening on the western side into the valley of the Andeski Koisu. It is the largest plateau in Daghestan and is thoroughly cultivated, there being aouls all over it in every direction. No trees to be seen from Khoonzakh, wood being brought, I believe, from the Avarski Koisu.

Found Longfellow's *Evangeline* here in Khoonzakh, as well as Thiers' *Consulate and Empire* and Buckle's *History of Civilization in England.*[34]

Steamer Vesta, Turkish port of Ordu, Nov. 17 R.S. [=Nov. 29]

I LEFT KHOONZAKH OCTOBER 20TH [=NOV. 1] UNDER guard of Achmet and two good-looking mountain Cossacks who had been detailed by Major Teekheenof as my convoy. Achmet had acquired in Khoonzakh a new horse and a new pistol, the former borrowed and the latter bought (as he claimed for half price). It was a hard-looking weapon (at least it seemed so to me) but Achmet declared that it was very valuable and that if its owner had been at home when he bought it, he wouldn't have got it for double what he paid! Riding away in a northerly direction from the aoul of Khoonzakh, we began the ascent of the mountain range to the north up which a government road had been cut in two or three long zigzags. At first we did not follow the road but took a short cut up a steep precipitous bluff by a foot path. As we ascended a little we caught sight of a sea of fog which filled the valley of the Andeski Koisu and all the region around Antsakhoul, Botlekh and Ande, but which did not reach at all the elevated plateau of Khoonzakh. On the summit of the 1st mountain range, somebody had erected a pole and leaving my horse with the convoy I made my way up to it on foot to see the surrounding country. The view in all directions was very fine but particularly so to the S. and E. where lay the deep blue valley of the Andeski, Avarski Koisu and on the other side Chemodan Gora, Goonib and the snowy mountains. To the westward I could see the moun-

---

from E. to N.E. between Khunzakh and Gunib (the road to Gunib leaves the river at this point). Just below this peak is the village of Karadakh (presumably "Kara dag," or Black Mountain). The peak apparently rises abruptly out of the river plain, and would be prominently visible from the Khunzakh plateau.

34. Inserted from page 257.

tain ridge of Ande with the government road running in a sloping white line down its bare, precipitous side, the ridge between Ande and Botlekh, and the ridge from which we had descended into Ande. To the north the view was cut off by the 2nd mountain range. The intervening valley and the north slope of the first range were covered with snow. After admiring the scenery for a few moments I remounted my horse and we rode down into the valley and up on the 2nd ridge from which we caught sight of the precipice of Gimry. Descending from the 2nd ridge, we left the government road entirely (which turned away to the right toward Shoura) and, following a gorski footpath, rode up a gentle slope to a high bluff and descended on foot through a wild, stony, rugged ravine to the aoul of Tsatanikh. Here Achmet met many acquaintances as usual. Riding through the aoul we came out at a distance of 2 or 3 versts upon another high grassy bluff overlooking the whole country to the Gimrinski spooska, a perfect chaos of mountains lying in the greatest confusion far down under our feet. Beyond them all rose the precipice of Gimry. On the summit of this bluff we stopped to lunch and unpacked the saddle bags which Major Teekhenof had so bountifully provided. I found there vodka, a bottle of wine, bread, excellent meat pies, cold roast beef, a couple of cold boiled chickens, etc.

[Journal, 264–71]

Samsoun—18th [=30th] 1870

AFTER LUNCH WE DESCENDED ON FOOT THROUGH another long, precipitous, rocky ravine which ended in the splendid pass or gateway of Antzakhoul. This was a pass about 75 feet wide between two walls of volcanic rock at least 600 feet in height. Through the pass ran a small stream which occupied nearly all the bottom of the ravine. From the walls of rock on the right and left burst unexpectedly as we entered two beautiful cascades 125 or 150 feet in height, the spray from which wet us as we rode past. High up on the cliffs could be seen other smaller cascades tumbling 12 or 15 feet and then gliding in a smooth film of water over a steep slope, then bursting out again into a cascade. High over our heads hung 2 or 3 small stunted storm-beaten pines, the only vegetation to be seen in the pass. Behind us was the mountain from which we had descended. On either side, rugged walls of rock between which appeared only a narrow strip of blue sky and in front, through the pass between immense masses of rock which had caved away from the summit, appeared the aouls of Gimry and Antzakhoul and the towering Gimrinski Spooska with a path like a grey thread running up it in zigzags and disappearing in the clouds.

The scene was indescribably wild and grand. The pass that is the narrowest part of it was only about 150 feet in length and it gradually widened out into a wild gloomy ravine with bare, almost precipitous mountains on each side which supported a roof of clouds. High up on the left side was the aoul of Antzakhoul embowered in canary-colored trees and vineyards which presented a strange contrast to the bareness of the surrounding scenery. A little farther on the valley widened still more and on each side of the stream was a narrow strip of fertile soil which was planted with vines and purple with grapes. Soil here was evidently precious, for in one place I saw an immense boulder whose top had been industriously covered with earth and planted with vines. Just before dark we began to ascend the left side to Antzakhoul. The aoul was situated very unevenly on a sort of shelf which broke in one place the slope of the mountain and through it ran several deep ravines which were crossed by high narrow wooden bridges. The road ran up in zigzags cut out of the mountain side and over it hung trees smothered with grape vines from which hung huge clusters of white and purple grapes which were within reach of our hands as we rode underneath.

Halfway between Ineboli and Stamboul—Nov. 20th [=Dec. 2], 1870

CROSSING THREE OR FOUR HIGH NARROW WOODEN bridges under one of which was a spring where 5 or 6 women were getting water in big metallic pitchers we entered Antzakhoul. The aoul filled with trees and grape vines where foliage was just turning canary-colored, presented a very pleasant contrast to the bare mountains around. Achmet seemed to know everybody as usual. The whole population almost flocked to shake hands with him. We stopped at the sakla of the Starsheena, which was a well-built stone house with a flat roof, a piazza and a courtyard. His youngest wife, a very fine-looking girl of 18 or 20, was unloading wood from a couple of diminutive mules as we entered and Achmet with gallantry quite unusual in a mountaineer set about helping her. The guest room of the Starsheena's house was very clean and neat—on the rafters and ceiling were written in a large, clear Arabic hand verses from the Koran. The whole side opposite the door was occupied by silken and cotton velvet pillows and cushions the dowry of the Starsheena's last wife. On the left hand side hung tassels, etc. There was only one window and a low square door, but between them was a well-constructed clay fireplace. The Starsheena presently made his appearance and fixed me a bed under the window. Laid down and caught cold, in 5 minutes could hardly speak loud. Wrapped myself up in my Ande Shouba and took a sweat while supper was being prepared. Round flat pancakes of bread, very good mutton broth and magnificent grapes for which Gimry and Antzakhoul are famous.[35] Achmet shows me grave yard where his father was buried. Says Antzakhoul is bravest aoul in Daghestan. I ask how he comes to know everybody everywhere. He says that several years since he killed a man and had to flee from blood revenge and take refuge in Antzakhoul. I ask why he killed him. Achmet explains, "He said a bad word to me. I drew my kinjal. Batz! and it was done." How many men have you killed in your life time—sixteen. Nasha Dagesta: vsorovno oobeet chelovek oobeet Kooreetaw.[36] Says he was well received by the inhabitants and lived there a year and that was how he happen to be acquainted so well in that aoul.

[*The previous exchange served as the basis for an expanded dialogue in Kennan's later article, "A Tenth-Century Barbarian," 204–5.*]

About half-way down the eastern slope of the range, we passed through a village of closely packed, flat-roofed houses, which suggested in general appearance a pueblo of the Arizona Indians. As we rode through the narrow, hall-like streets, all of the old and middle-aged men who were

---

35. Since the notes of pages 270–72 are increasingly cryptic and disorganized, I have rearranged them into the actual sequence of the journey without special comment for each fragment.

36. *Nashim Dagestantsam, vse ravno ubit' cheloveka, ubit' kuritu:* For us Dagestanis, it's all the same whether you kill a man or kill a chicken!" I have reconstructed the somewhat ungrammatical Russian here. The word *kurita* (Kennan's kooreetaw) is dialect for chicken.

Street scene in a Dagestani aul. Photo © Chris Allingham.

sunning themselves and gossiping in front of their houses rushed forward to clasp hands and press thumbs with Akhmet, who seemed to know them all and to speak with fluency their guttural, clickful tongue. As we rode out of the village I remarked casually to the interpreter:

"That sounds to me like a very difficult language; how did you ever learn it?"

"Oh," he replied, nonchalantly, "many years ago, when I was young, I killed a man and had to flee to this village to escape his blood avengers. While I was living here I learned the language."

This explanation Akhmet made in a perfectly matter-of-fact way; as if killing a man were a natural episode in normal human experience. I was a little startled to find myself associated in that wild and lawless region with a homicide; but I did not think it prudent to ask for details. "Very likely," I reflected, "he killed the man in self defense, so that he isn't really a murderer." But I soon discovered that I had not yet got back, mentally, into the tenth-century atmosphere.

We slept that night in another village, ten or fifteen miles farther along, where the people spoke another language, but where Akhmet seemed to be as much at home socially and linguistically as he had been in the first one.

"How did you happen to get acquainted with these people and learn this language?" I asked, as we were smoking and drinking tea together early in the evening.

"Many years ago," he replied, "when I was young, I killed a man, and I went into *kanle* here."

"What do you mean by going into *kanle*?" I ventured to inquire.

He looked at me in apparent surprise, as if I had asked what he meant by saying that he "went into the house when it rained." Then, as the thought occurred to him that customs might be different in another coun-

Street scene in a Dagestani aul. Photo © Chris Allingham.

try, he patiently explained: "When you kill a man" (as if I were likely ever to kill a man!), "the *adat* says that you must take refuge in some distant village, where his blood avengers are not likely to follow you. I took refuge here, and it was two years before I could make peace with my blood-seekers. May they stand before God with blackened faces!" he added, fiercely. "They were stiff-necked, and I had to pay them five horses."

Slowly I began to get the tenth-century point of view. Killing men and "going into kanle" were not extraordinary occurrences, and the state of society in which such things happened was perfectly normal.

"How many men have you happened to kill, Akhmet?" I inquired.

He laid down his pipe and began to count them up on his fingers—hesitating reflectively now and then, as if in doubt. Finally he said, decisively: "Fourteen; besides some Russians that I killed in battle; I don't know how many of them there were."

"How did you come to kill the first man? Was it in a fight?"

"Not exactly a fight. We had a dispute, and he said a bad word to me. I drew my *kinjal* and—*bats*! It was done."

I made no comment, and Akhmet, taking my silence as a possible indication of disapproval, inquired in turn:

"What do you do in your country when a man says a bad word to you?"

"Knock him down," I replied, "or perhaps call the police; it depends on circumstances." Akhmet snorted contemptuously. "In our Daghestan," he said, "it's only a step from the bad word to the kinjal" (a Caucasian proverb). "What do you carry weapons for?"

"We don't carry weapons."

"Then don't you ever kill anybody; or go on raids, or protect your cattle, or avenge blood?"

"Never; we don't have to; we are protected by the law."

"Humph! Yours must be a sheep's life."

I ought, perhaps, to have made my statements with some reservations and exceptions; but I did not see how I could do this or furnish the necessary explanations without finally casting reflections upon the character of Akhmet himself, and at that stage of our acquaintance it did not seem wise to say anything that might be construed as a "bad word." I had already heard, moreover, the significant and oft-repeated Daghestan proverb, "Hold your tongue and you'll save your head." I therefore contented myself with saying that different peoples had different customs—a trite but reasonably safe remark.

[Journal, 270, 272]

Went to sleep early. Following morning started for Shoura—dense fog [at] Asiatic suspension bridge, ride over it on horseback. Achmet dismounts and walks. Gimri. Tremendous cliff disappearing above in fog at height of 300 or 400 feet. Begin ascent of first long zigzag. Gloomy defile. Place where Kazi moolah[37] was killed and where stood a fort in time of Shamyl. Echo. The ascent of the first zigzag through a long dark wild gloomy defile occupied three quarters of an hour or more during which we ascended into the fog and lost sight of everything.

Constantinople—Nov. 23rd [Dec. 5], 1870

RUINS OF FORT WHERE ACHMENT SAID KAZE MOOLAH was killed. Bed of ravine. Ascent of zigzag 2nd. Enter fog—at height of 2000 feet get above fog. Misty Niagara. Sea of clouds. Islands of mountain peaks. Grand view. Lunch. Ride down other side. Enter clouds again. Come out near an aoul. Send escort for vodka. Koomik aoul clay saklas—quite neat. Achmet relates his exploits in driving off cattle in this vicinity during the war.

Timour Khan Shoura, Oct. 22nd [=Nov. 3]

["Vagabond Life" lecture, Kennan MSS, LC, Box 73]

By caravan to the Black Sea[38]

FASCINATED BY THE MAGNIFICENT SCENERY OF THE wild adventurous life of the mountains, I could not make up my mind

---

37. Kazi Mullah (Ghazi Muhammad ibn Isma'il al-Gimrawi al-Daghistani) was the first Naqshbandi imam to lead resistance to the Russians (1830). He was succeeded in 1832 by Gamzat Bek (Hamza Bek ibn 'Ali Iskandar Bek al-Hutsali) and in 1834 by the third imam, Shamil. See Gammer, *Muslim Resistance*, chapters 6–8.

38. Kennan's journal contains only a few clues as to the rest of his travels after he parted company with Akhmet (presumably in Temir Khan Shura). Most likely

to start for home until the fast-lessening store of Russian rubles in my money belt warned me that I must. I had barely enough money left to take me even with the most rigid economy to London. When I finally decided to go I was at a little Russian post on the north side of the mountains known as Vladi Kavkaz and the coast of the Black Sea where I expected to take steamer for Constantinople was more than 150 miles distant. I could not afford to hire a carriage to take me there and was just revolving in my mind the possibility of walking when there passed through the town one day bound for my destination a long caravan of loaded four-horse wagons from European Russia. I succeeded in making arrangements with one of the drivers to carry me through for four dollars, I to find my own provisions and ride on a bag of flour. There were several other vagabonds in reduced circumstances accompanying the caravan.

Our caravan was more than a week in reaching its destination, during which time we lived chiefly on black bread and turnips and either slept in gloomy Oriental caravanserais or lay down on the ground under the soft, clear Caucasian sky. On the 26th of November [N.S.] tired, hungry and whitened from head to foot with flour I arrived at the port of Poti and presented myself at the police headquarters.

The official in charge glanced at my well-worn passport, discovered that I was an American and then, dropping it, stared at me with open-mouthed astonishment. He might well be surprised. The closest observer never would have recognized in the deplorable object before him the well-dressed, prosperous looking tourist who had landed at St. Petersburg five months before. I came into the Russian Empire on the first of July with a trunk and two large valises. I went out of it on the 28th of November with the clothes in which I stood and an old pair of carpet saddlebags. I sailed for Constantinople in a steamer of the Black Sea Navigating

---

he went from there via the route north of the mountains, passing through the Chechen lowlands to reach Vladikavkaz. To reach the Black Sea port of Poti he retraced his steps through the Darial Pass on the military highway and after Tbilisi passed through Kutais. See his comment at the end of the first selection in Part 3 above.

Company, taking a second class passage between decks with 300 Mecca pilgrims.

I thought I had seen vagabonds before but those pilgrims, many of whom had come from the northern slopes of the Himalayan Mountains across half Asia were the hardest looking specimens of humanity I had ever encountered. Persians, Khivans, Tartars, Caucasian mountaineers and dervishes with single dirty blankets wrapped around their gaunt naked bodies. As we approached Trebizond the Sea grew rough—the steamer began to pitch about in an uncomfortable way and one of the pilgrims became sick. The poor fellow had never been on the water before in his life; did not know sea sickness even by name and supposed of course that he was about to die.

The moolah was called to prescribe for him and after reading a chapter of the Koran over his body without producing any perceptive effect, he called for a pen and ink and a saucer, wrote a verse from the first chapter of the Koran on the inside of the saucer, poured in a little water, rubbed off the writing and mixed it in the water with his finger, and gave this infusion of the holy volume to the sufferer to drink. Something had the desired effect. The poor wretch stopped vomiting, the priest went away to mix up a text for another victim and the skeptical American stood by lost in admiration. My only regret as I watched this performance was that the Mohammedan method of administering sacred literature in solution was not in vogue in America during my youthful days. If I could only have had the proverbs of Solomon, hymns and the Westminster catechism written on a big platter and washed off with a tumbler of water so that I could have swallowed them at a draught—how many tearful hours I should have been spared.

Arrived at Constantinople on the 3rd of December [N.S.] and, finding that there would be no steamer up the Danube in five or six days and that my means would not admit of my living at a European hotel, I was compelled to take refuge with the Mecca pilgrims in a Turkish caravanserai on the Stambul side of the Golden Horne. Here I lived for a week in a state of semi-starvation which was partly the result of poverty and partly of my ignorance of the Turkish language. This delay still further reduced my pecuniary resources.

[Journal, 273–89]

Constantinople, 23rd [=Dec. 5]

ENTERED BOSPHORUS 20TH ABOUT 6 PM. COULDN'T get practika because it was too late. Fired shells at us 3 times from port on left to signify that we must anchor. Came to anchor opposite quarantine below 2 red lights. Old ruined castle on summit of eastern hills, small village on either side. Morning of 21st, sent 3rd officer for practika. Steamers darting here and there; we whistle impatiently for return of officer. Comes at last, we get our anchor and start. Beautiful scenery up the strait. Dependent, however, for its beauty largely upon architecture. On both sides high rolling hills crowned with villages, castles, and mosques. Very fine view where two immense stone castles command the harbor. Long boats rowed by 8 or 10 men in Miaragiaran [?] style carrying passengers like omnibuses—little caiaques. Palace of English ambassador. Palace belonging to Sultan on the left. Constantinople—Golden Horn on left covered with mosques and tall dark cedars.[39] High hill on right thick with houses. Anchor just below bridge. Tremendous confusion as usual. Fight our way into a boat at peril of our lives among motley crowd. Land at customs bourse. Baggage examined on gangway; examination trifling. Grand dispute with boatmen and hire porters. Start for Hotel de Paris. Narrow muddy streets. Turkish cities white sepulchres. Comfortable quarters but dear. Send to Legation and get letters. Walk once up and down the principal street, get run over, buy an English paper and return to hotel where spend balance of day. Yesterday morning started out in search of cheaper quarters.

Crossed bridge to Stamboul. Ragged, dirty Spaniard in dirty fez without a tassel tied round with a dirty handkerchief, long, dirty European coat, over coat, Turkish short trousers, bare legs below knee and patent leather slippers accosts us and offers his services, "You know Moses?" Certainly. "Well me Moses." Told him that I had read discred-

---

39. Kennan landed in the Galata (Pera) section of the city, across the natural harbor of the Golden Horn from Istanbul proper. To reach the Topkapi palace, the nearby Cathedral of Sancta Sophia, and the other major monuments of the city, he crossed the Galata Bridge.

itable accounts of a certain Moses. He claimed that he was not that Moses but another one called Moses Guiseffi. We went with his assistance to hire rooms. Visited about a dozen caravansarais and at last found a bare room for 15 francs and 5 francs for key. Door iron with tremendous bolts and key weighing about a pound, windows grated. Went to hotel, breakfasted and brought my things here, after which went to mosque of St. Sophia. Asked a dollar to go in. Traded with him and got in for 15 francs instead.

Magnificent building. After this went to see Turkish museum where Moses said were "all the dead mens in silver etc." Plaster figures dressed to represent various types of Turkish Empire. Ancient arms, armor, etc. From here went through bazaar and bought fez. Also looked at lots of other Turkish merchandise. Returned to room and Moses left me. Man came in to ask if I wanted dinner. Couldn't make him understand Eng. or Russian.[40] He goes off and brings another Turk in dressing gown. Pantomime for 15 minutes, which ends with the supposition on the part of the Turks that I want water to drink. Turk No 2 goes off after Turk No 3. Pantomime again. 3rd Turk concludes that I want brandy. Parle vous francais. Turk No 2 rushes off and brings Turk No 4, who speaks French. Situation still as bad as ever. Make Turk No 4 understand at last that I want dinner. Soup, beefsteak and whatever else they've got. In course of time it comes. Soup, stew of mutton and greens, fried beef and potatoes and raw dough sweetened and powdered with cinnamon. Ate dinner and went to bed. This morning heard somebody yelling out what sounded like "coffee" in the court. Called him and ordered a cup and a bread ring about a foot in diameter. Coffee proved to be diluted sweetened glue powdered with cinnamon—utterly undrinkable. Ate the bread ring covered with seeds, pitched the glue out of the window and am now awaiting the arrival of Moses and further developments.

40. Interesting that Kennan had gotten so used to communicating only in Russian, his one foreign language, he was still trying to use it and was continuing to record some Russian words in his journal. In Istanbul at the time, if there were any Russians, they probably would have spoken French; it was only with the collapse of the Soviet Union and the influx of suitcase traders that Russian would become common on the streets of this cosmopolitan city.

Rooschuk, a Turkish town on the Danube, Dec. 8, N.S.[41]

MOSES ARRIVED IN COURSE OF TIME AND WE WENT to a cafe near my lodgings and had coffee. After coffee went over to Pera in search of my tavarish[42] in the Hotel de Paris. Didn't find him at home. Bought a guide to Constantinople and returned. Sent Moses off after a nargileh and bought one of the two which he brought for my inspection. Took a smoke to try it—tasted like an old burnt boot. At 5 o'clock I ordered dinner: beef and potatoes a la turque, macaroni and eggs with butter in Asiatic style, and glue pancakes with butter, cream, and honey. Latter tolerably good, only very sweet. Went to bed at 7 o'clock to escape skooka.[43] Fleas bit me all night and I woke in the morning with both eyes bunged up as if I had a fight. [. . .]

> [The Journal continues for another five pages, 279–85, which have been omitted here. Instead, here is the summary of the end of his trip, from the "Vagabond Life" lecture, Kennan MSS, LC, Box 73.]

When I finally sailed I had to take a deck passage across the Black Sea to the mouth of the Danube. The month was December, the weather cold, and at night I could only keep warm by wrapping my heavy Caucasian wool cloak around me and lying down beside the smokepipe. I knew there would be money waiting for me in London. The question which I anxiously debated with myself every night was "Can I possibly reach London before my money entirely fails?" I economized in every imaginable way. I went up the Danube in the hold of an Austrian steamer with the offscourings of the Turkish Empire and three principalities. I lived for a week almost wholly on bread and water, took a third class passage through Hungary, Austria, & down the Rhine, &, on Christmas

---

41. Rusçuk (now Ruse) is in Bulgaria, which in 1870 was still part of the Ottoman Empire. The narrative here is still about Istanbul.

42. *tovarishch*: comrade.

43. *skuka:* boredom (Russian). Curious word choice here, perhaps reflecting long hours of listening to bored Russian officers assigned to the North Caucasus, or, who knows, possibly an indication Kennan had started *Eugene Onegin* in the volume of Pushkin he had picked up in St. Petersburg (" . . . No, Bozhe moi, kakaia skuka . . . ": Onegin lamenting in the first stanza the boredom of sitting with his sick uncle).

Eve rolled into the railway station of Charing Cross in London with triumph in my heart and two shillings & sixpence in my pocket. I paid two shillings for a cab, drove to the Euston Hotel, invested my last sixpence in a cigar—a luxury that I had not been able to afford for weeks—& sat down, penniless but happy to smoke & meditate upon the vicissitudes of vagabond life.

APPENDIX

[The following reproduces sometimes difficult to decipher pages of Kennan's notes largely bound at the back of the two journal books. As many travelers do, Kennan used those pages to jot down expenses, addresses, and other odds and ends. Reproduced here are only those items that seem particularly relevant to the Russian and Caucasian part of his trip. I have provided in brackets and footnotes suggestions for deciphering abbreviations and partly legible words.]

[Page 172: a brief German-English traveler's phrase book. Page 173 is blank.]

Die Grentza [Grenze]—Boundary
Dos Tsolhaus [Zollhaus]—Custom house
Die Effectin[1]—Baggage
Vo heen moos Ich gain-mid diesen billet[2]—Where must I go with this t[ic]k[e]t
Statzion—Station
Dae tzveite platz [Der zweite Platz]—The second floor

1. Effekten: effects, but most likely referring to financial instruments.
2. Wohin muss ich gehen mit diesen Billet?

APPENDIX

On fardt[? fährte/fährt]³—Train tsoog [Zug]
Vee feel browkht [?] man tsa allen [?]⁴
Gast house [Gasthaus]—Hotel

[Page 174]

Fleas at Shoura. Etiquette of meeting friends. Lincoln G. E. and S. twins. Wild men in mts. Lang. specimens—no active verbs. Fear of mtn foods. Smoking cigarettes to [. . .]. Prince. Henna dyed beards and nails. Accusing man by suspicion. Oath by marriage. Time of Shariat. Woman marrying man who had murdered her sister's[?] husband. Prayers. Prayer certificates. Call to prayers. Leaving child's face dirty. Man from another world.

[Page 175]⁵

Aug. 27th—On hand—			RS 837.
27	—Grostchick [gruzchik: porter] to Bellevue		.40
"	"	" Depot	.80
"	Fare to Moscow		13.
"	Dinner and cigarettes		.75
"	Tea		.20
"	"		.20
"	Fruit		.50
			15.65
28	Tea		.10
"	Grostchick Moscow		1.
"	Dinner		1.
"	Tea		.65
"	Money bag		4.
"	Grostchick		.15
			6.90

    3. Perhaps Kennan has mixed Russian and German here: on (=it, Russ.), fährt (=is going, Ger.)

    4. Wiefiel braucht man zu allen? = How much for everything?

    5. Kennan's own pagination ceases with page 174; I have assigned the remaining numbers only to pages with text on them.

APPENDIX

29	Grostchick	.75
"	Pistol Holster	2.50
"	Tower of Ivan Veleekee[6]	.75
"	Dinner	1.

[Pages 176–177: presumably a list of purchased photographs]

1) View of Goonib from Keherski Heights
2) House of Shamyl at Goonib
3) Ruined aoul Goonnie
4) View of Sattinefski Most (Bridge)
5) Timour Khan Shoura
   View Western Daghestan
6) Aoul Moinnee[?=Muni] on road to Botleh[=Botlikh]
7) Preobrazhenski Bridge and tower
8) Salinova Aoul Konkedatel[?][7]
9) Asiatski Bridge at "
10) Aoul Ande
11) Andeski Ravine
12) Aouls Goonka and Gogutt[?][8]

Types

1) Girl Adzhee, daughter of an inhabitant of Booglerick, Tim[our] Khan Sh[oura], Dist Tavlor
2) inhabitant of Kazaneeshe[?] Sooleman Aitek Oglee
3) Cadi. Dag. narodno sooda[9]
   Mahomet Tyeer [?]-born in Karag.T[imour] K[han] Sh[oura] U[ezd]
4) Deputy from village of Jenguti—Aki Bey Mooza Oglee
5) Shoormaki Militia horseman Goro-Omar
6) Arakanski woman Pateena—wife of Ali
7) Doctor Goonip Obdoo Vagap Mustafa Oglee

6. The bell tower of Ivan the Great (=Velikii) (completed in fact in the time of Tsar Boris Godunov, ca. 1600) in the Moscow Kremlin. Presumably there was an admission fee to climb to the best view over Moscow from the top.

7. Presumably the salt-producing ("salinova") aul.

8. Gunkha and Gagatli, just N.E. of Andi.

9. Kadi. *Dag[estanskii] narodn[yi] sud['ia]:* A *kadi.* Dagestani folk (i.e., traditional Muslim) judge.

APPENDIX

Groups
  1) Members of Andeski Doovana
  2) Militia of Knaz Chefshoodza aoul Karatee
  3) Same from aoul West Dag.
  4) Doovana members Botleh
  5) Suite of Shamhul Tarkofskoi
  6) Shamhul Tarkofskoi and son
  7) Group of Kirghis

[Page 178]

Tartar words
Yok—No
Yakshie—Good
Adam—Man
Sa oo—Thank you

[Page 180]

Expenses	RS
Aug. 21—Fare to Vwiberg	2.40
Tea at station	.10
Change 1 RS	1.
Petrovskoe to Shoura (pavoska) [povozka: carriage]	2.50
Shoura to Joongootai 2 horses	1.
Joongatai to Goonib "	6.
Goonib to Kakhetia	15.
Maxime for services	1.

[Page 181]

Mem—Book in Georgian lang. called Slovar [*slovar'*: dictionary (Russ.)] and raiche [?*rech'*: speech, language (Russ.)][10] Gaverilla—by Typographia[?] Loris Melikova[11]—Teflis.

  10. Perhaps here something like *rechegovorilo*, which we might understand to be the equivalent of a *rechnik* or phrasebook.
  11. *Tipografiia Loris-Melikova*, presumably the Tiflis publisher of the book.

APPENDIX

Predvornoi Photograph—na maista Kavkazki[12] Edward Vesley—Tiflis.
Fsevalot[=Vsevolod] Alexandrovich Seeshep[?=Sychev] Peotr Petrovich
Koobleetski
Sotninkee[13]
Essentookhe
Kontsilaria 1st Terski Battery[?]

Bechterof and Shubert at Shoura
Lev. Gregovitch Shtryker
Na Alexandrofskom Perspective [?][14]
Chefchowdsa [=Chevchavadze]

[Page 182]

Curiosities

Photographs—Circassian kinjal. Cross and Elijah from Smolensk Graveyard. Finnish money. 2 curious stones from Imatra. Little kinjal. 3 cigar holders. 1 smoky topaz bottle seal and one small weight seal from Nizhni; Tartar pipe from Timour Khan Shoura. 3 photographs from Nizhni. 27 photographs from Shoura. Purple and white grape seeds from Shoura.
Doctor Kostemerefski—Timour Khan Shoura
Red cheeks—miershaum pipes and red mustache in car window

[Page 184]

When child is very handsome his face is not washed because they say that if any one glances at child they will become sick.
When man drives wife away cannot marry another till after 3 months.
In 1865 in district of prince, child was found. All women—that is unmarried in settlement were examined that is breasts examined for milk. The one who was in fault was buried to hips in earth and stoned to death—every man and every woman could throw 1 stone.
If a Christian kills or cuts up an animal Lesghians will not eat it.

---

12. *Pridvornyi fotograf—na mesta kavkazskie:* Court-appointed photographer for the Caucasus.

13. Probably *sotniki*, indicating both named held that officer rank in Cossack regiments.

14. *Na Aleksandrovskom prospekte:* on Aleksandrov prospect (a street address).

APPENDIX

[Page 185]

20 kopecks, piece of calico and paper for stolen horse.
Man under suspicion must justify himself by witnesses.
Graves of warriors at Gotschob.
Naibs authority 1500 smokes—assembly of village deputies.
Shaking hands.
Punishment for smoking.
Touching hats after dancing.
[. . .] to leave things as they were [. . .] Shamyl.
[. . .] dancing prohibited under
[. . .]ing [. . .] away from settlement
Skid with stones in for thrashing.
Shaking hands—Lezgins do not shake but simply hold and press.
[*illegible—4 lines*]

[Page 186]

Asses

Innook 28 [. . .] and peculiar language not found in any other part of Caucasus.
If man shoots deer and deer dies from bullet before he can cut his throat he wont eat him, believes it to be sinful.
bread etc. was divided among poor. When drouth women get together and march in a[. . .] round hills singing Allah il Allah [. . . . . .] one hill, on another and another. Men get together with moolah and collect all stones they can find, moolah says prayer over every [. . .] stones then put in basket and put in creek.
In case of pestilence they dig arch in ground[?] moolah stands on top and sprinkles with water people and cattle as they pass through. Diseases they say can't pass through.

[Page 190][15]

Bot of S. Watkins and Co St. Petersburg
Sagvolat[?] 9 Francs
[sketch]
O Goonakh Daghestana Sazerefa[?]

    15. Beginning of second notebook. Page 189 is cover inscription: "Caucasus No. 2. Prince Djordzadsi's House to Vienna."

230

APPENDIX

Small brochure published in Tiflis.
Vsemirnoi puteshestvennik [world traveller (written here in Cyrillic)].
Article with regard to Shaksee Vaksee.

Inkhelee	8.	meals	5
Khonkhadatel	25.		9 Francs
Khlokh	20.		

[Page 192]

Tifliski Goobernia[16]
Telavski Ooyezda
Selenia Ennesille
knaz Georgi Davidovich Djordjadzi
Akime[?] Feedootoofa Groonboora[?]
Left Vladi Kavkaz for Groznoi Wednesday.

[Page 290]

Maksoot Ali Khanof
Shtats Rot. Meister
Timour Khan Shoura
Mansut Ali Khanov [*in Cyrillic*]

[Page 294]

Ovakim Keghamian
Tiflis Caucase
Chez Moatafoff[?]
Ovakim Keghamian
Vienne Leopol.
Schtoss
Chez Gregor
Abouloff

[Page 295]

Petrovskoe to Shoura	2.50
Shoura to Joongatai	1.—

16. Here he records Prince Jorjadze's address: Tifliiskaia guberniia, Teliavskii uezd, Selenie Eniseli(?), Kniaz' Georgii Davidovich Djordjadze.

APPENDIX

Joongatai to Goonib	6.—
Goonib to Telaw [=Telavi]	15.50
Vanno for Services	2.—
Maxime	2.50
Hotel bill Telaw	2.80
Telaw to Tiflis	10.—
	42.80

[Page 296]

Na Kavkaz
G. Tiflis
B. B. Afanasiofa
Chinovnik Tif. Skladochni
Tamozhni[17]
Mahometa Ansookski

[Page 297]

Maksut Ali Khanov
Kavkaz s. Khunzakh [in Cyrillic]

17. *Chinovnik Tiflisskoi skladochnoi tamozhni:* official of the Tiflis customs warehouse.

AFTERWORD

Autumn 1996

FILMMAKER CHRIS ALLINGHAM AND I WENT TO THE Caucasus to follow Kennan's route from Dagestan to Georgia. We wanted to recapture what it must have been like for this intrepid American as he explored highland Dagestan, and find out how much has changed over the last century—and how little. Our goal was to cross from Dagestan to Georgia over the Main Caucasus Ridge, the journey that Kennan made in the company of Prince Jorjadze. We also visited a few towns and villages farther south than Kennan was able to go. It was not possible to repeat the second half of Kennan's journey, in which he entered Chechnya from Georgia via the Georgian Military Highway and from there dropped into Dagestan again. Russian troops were being withdrawn from Chechnya while we were in the Caucasus from September to November 1996, but it was still a war zone and travel there was out of the question.

The bombed-out rubble of Groznyi, Chechnya's capital, just to the north of our route testified to the scorched-earth tactics used by the Russian Army in its two-year campaign to subdue the tiny republic, a flash point of ethnic nationalism. Forty thousand Russian troops invaded

AFTERWORD

Groznyi in December 1994, two years after the pugnacious leader of the republic, Dzhokhar Dudayev, declared its independence from Russia. Sixty thousand died in the ensuing war, most of them civilians.[1] The August 1996 accord that ended the war deferred any decision on the future status of Chechnya until the year 2001.[2]

Events since Kennan crossed the Caucasus in 1870 shed light on the most recent debacle in the region. Modern boundaries in the Caucasus are largely an artificial construct. When Shamil and his Murids were fighting the Russians, there were no national entities of Dagestan or Chechnya. Peoples of the region traditionally identified themselves by their clans and villages rather than as members of a nation. (The terms "Chechen" and "Chechnya" are labels adopted by the Russians, taken from a lowlands Chechen village.) The Soviets carved the North Caucasus up into nearly a dozen pieces, lumping together unrelated peoples and fracturing natural alliances in an attempt to suppress opposition to rule from Moscow. In other words, the Russians created an enemy by waging war against this ethnic group for decades, but then resettled Russians, Ukrainians, and other colonizers on their traditional lands, thus leaving the Chechens with a national identity and a reason to hate Russia.

Actually, they had plenty of reasons to hate Russia. Although the Caucasian Wars came to an end not long after Shamil's capture, rebellions continued well into the twentieth century, with Chechens taking an active role in the uprisings. In 1944, accusing them of collaborating with the Germans, Stalin deported the entire Chechen nation (along with several other North Causasian Muslim peoples) to Central Asia. When they were finally allowed to return in the 1950s, their homes had been expropriated and their historical bitterness had hardened.

---

1. That is, 50,000 civilians, at least 6,000 Russian soldiers, and 2,000 to 3,000 Chechen fighters. See Carlotta Gall and Thomas de Waal, *Chechnya: Calamity in the Caucasus* (New York: New York University Press, 1998), 360. These figures are only for the period to the 1996 "peace."

2. How quickly our reportage becomes dated! As this book is being edited in 2002, a second war has been fought and peace is not in sight, even though the Chechens now can manage only small guerrilla attacks in the face of the same kind of brutal Russian tactics that General Ermolov had advocated in the early nineteenth century.

AFTERWORD

Although the peoples of Dagestan and Chechnya were allies in their resistance to the Russians in the nineteenth century, Dagestan did not get drawn into the recent war on its borders and we found that most people did not sympathize with the Chechens in their standoff against Russia. In fact, they resented the hardships that war had forced on Dagestan, including economic disruption caused by the severance of rail service from Makhachkala to Russia, and the blow to Dagestan's flourishing post-Soviet tourism industry.

In Kennan's day, Petrovskoe was a sleepy Russian outpost. Today, renamed Makhachkala, it is the capital and hub of Dagestan, a republic that is now Russia's southern border in the Caucasus. Dagestan enjoys some political autonomy, but is heavily dependent on Moscow. Federal subsidies prop up the economy of the region, which lacks the Caspian oil reserves that promise to transform its southern neighbor, Azerbaijan, into the next Saudi Arabia. Dagestan has a population of just over two million. About 350,000 people live in Makhachkala, a dusty industrial city bearing the indelibly dreary imprint of Soviet architecture; a couple hundred thousand more live in several other cities. But two-thirds of Dagestan's population lives in villages and hamlets scattered through the highlands.

The logistics of our journey were simpler than Kennan's—we traveled in a donated four-wheel drive Chevy Blazer. If I had to ride a horse, I doubt I could stomach some of the trails Kennan covered. We made our way inland from the Caspian coast, up the hogbacks of the eastern Caucasus where they begin the climb toward the crest along the border with Georgia. The roads are mostly unpaved, heavily potholed hairpin serpentines up and down steep mountainsides that made us grateful for our Blazer's good brakes. With tunnels now connecting some of the mountain valleys by road, it's easy to become disoriented in the labyrinth. But these tunnels have taken some of the terror out of travel in Dagestan. We reached Gimra via a tunnel bisecting the mountain instead of down the treacherous slope that was Kennan's route. In other aspects, the scenes presenting themselves to the traveler haven't changed much in a century. We passed giant bundles of straw that looked as though they were walking on their own legs, hiding the women doubled over beneath them. The villages still balance at the tops of the ridges, sometimes more than a thousand feet above the river valleys.

AFTERWORD

The usual pattern in societies that do a lot of sheep herding is for people to live in the lowlands and move to the mountains during the summer months for their animals to graze. In Dagestan, people live year-round in the highlands, but each community has wintering lands for the sheep in the flat northern part of the republic where it abuts Chechnya. As we drove higher into the mountains with winter fast approaching, our progress was frequently halted by woolly roadblocks, herds tumbling across in great rivers of white and brown.

There are virtually no hotels outside of Makhachkala, nor anything resembling a restaurant. Produce and a few other foodstuffs can be bought in the farmers' markets held in the larger towns. Like Kennan, we stayed in local homes all across the highlands. Dagestanis are passionate about their hospitality. Kennan noted, "If a stranger arrives in a village, the elder cries out in the streets 'who will entertain the stranger?' and somebody takes him in." We found the Caucasus tradition of treating any traveler as an honored guest remains alive and well. Our support crew included Ziavdin, our driver who also managed our homestay arrangements, and Habibula, who translated for Chris and assisted him as soundman. Ziavdin has been crisscrossing Dagestan for years as an outdoor education program leader; everywhere we went he had a *kunak*. A kunak is a friend who puts one up in another village, an important relationship in the social structure of the Caucasus.

Our hosts invariably put out the best for visitors—the best food, the best beds. At each stop, alcohol in prodigious quantities was pressed upon us despite protests. "This treatment is not reserved for foreigners," explained Ziavdin. "Even if my enemy comes to my door, I will make him welcome. I will feed him and care for his horse and ask no questions. But if I meet that same enemy on the road . . . " He drew a line across his throat.

Tradition holds strong in the highlands despite political change and economic dislocation. We found many of the same rituals that Kennan observed, some of them customs traceable to pagan beliefs predating Dagestan's conversion to Islam. Kennan wrote about *adat*, the customary law of the Caucasus, which dictated the stoning of unchaste women. At one of our homestays, I asked two teenage girls about attitudes toward morality. "Father never lets us get together with boys outside of school," they explained. They confided that in a neighboring village, a girl alleged

AFTERWORD

to be loose was murdered by her brother for bringing shame on the family. We saw ample evidence of the persistence of superstitious practices remarked on by Kennan, who noted that a child's face would be left dirty out of fear of illness. We saw a child whose face had been smeared with ash "to keep him from getting sick." Kennan described the blood feuds carried on in Dagestan in the name of honor. Blood revenge (*kanle*) continues to this day in parts of the highlands. In Kharachi, an aul of 500 or 600 people, there were three murders in the space of a few months.

Kennan's journal notes provided interesting conversation starters. People we met along the way knew the tradition Kennan described of furnishing a guest with a virgin ("with her he can spend the night, but no serious connection is permitted"). They had heard of the ritual of nailing slain enemies' hands to the wall of one's house to shrivel and dry, although these practices have disappeared from present-day Dagestan.

Daily life in the highlands changed surprisingly little during the Soviet era. Russian culture never infiltrated the highlands because Russians never lived in the highlands, and where its influence is apparent, in many cases, it is only skin deep. Kennan noted [Journal, 153], that women did virtually all the work—and they still do. Men spend most of their time gathered in the central square (*gudekan*) smoking and socializing. The *cherkeskas* with bullet-holders stitched into the breast worn by the men who charged Kennan and the Prince in the salute he thought was going to be his final hour, the elaborate sabers in jeweled sheaths—all those trappings survived into the first half of the twentieth century, but the battle pomp is gone now. The warrior tradition in Dagestan has crumbled into legend, a convenient excuse for why men share little of the daily grind. "We must be prepared at any moment to take up our weapons and defend our town and our families," more than one man explained to me.

The society of men and women is strictly divided. Women cover their heads with scarves, but the veil that curtains off their realm is an intangible one maintained by centuries of tradition. They don't mingle with men outside their families, and they don't venture out except on the daily business of hauling water from the spring and working the fields; they keep to their own houses and yards, stacking the cow pie (*kiziak*) walls ever higher. Men didn't know quite what to make of me. I'm female, so by all rights I belonged with the women in the kitchen and the courtyard. But at the same time, I was an American guest. I enjoyed the gender limbo, which allowed me to slip between the male and female spheres.

At the homes of our hosts, we were invariably given the best rooms and served our meals there. We were not invited into the communal room where most of the family sleeps and the women all pitch in with the cooking. But the women were my best source of information, and since I had my own knife, I used helping to peel potatoes as my entry into the concealed women's world. Once they were convinced I sincerely wanted to talk with them, they were very open. They have all studied Russian and use it as their second language, as I do. "Go out in the street without a scarf on?" they laughed at my questions. "People would think we'd lost our mind!"

The ideological pendulum yo-yoed drastically in the 126 years since Kennan's travels across Dagestan. When he was exploring the highlands, Russian influence had yet to seep into the social fabric. In 1996, we witnessed a Dagestan rebounding from debunked Soviet rule. That tragic legacy was brought home to us when we visited the cemetery in the village of Tsovkra with our host, school principal Bakri Bakriev. The pre-Communist graves were in the old Muslim cemetery—the believers on one side of the ravine, the nonbelievers on the other. The field, densely planted with tall, tilting grave markers, testified to the antiquity of this rugged mountain's habitation by humans.

In the early 1920s, Communist zealots ransacked the old cemetery, desecrating graves and toppling headstones. Tending one's ancestral burial plot became tantamount to an anti-Soviet act. Bakri showed me the gravestones of his grandparents, overgrown and in shambles, the Arabic inscriptions obliterated by moss. The stones of his parents were in Russian and much better kept. His father, Magomed, was born in 1880, in time to witness the Russian Empire replace Islamic culture in Dagestan. Bakri's father began his education in the Tsovkra *madrasa* but he finished it in the new Russian school in the valley.

As we walked back through the cobblestone passageways between the houses, Bakri recited the names of his paternal male forebears: Bakri, Dali, Bakri, Bitu, Ramazan, Bakri, Magomed. They were all born and died in Tsovkra, seven generations of Lak patriarchs. (The Laks are one of the approximately forty ethnic groups that make up Dagestan's population of just under two million.) Bakri's grandson, the latest Bakri in the Bakriev line, was the first to be born outside the village.

Economic exodus to the cities is the most significant result of the Soviet system's splintering. Pick one of Dagestan's auls at random and chances are that more than half the village lives in Makhachkala, Kaspiisk, Buinaksk, or Derbent. The Soviet command economy kept collective farms operating and salaries paid even when they weren't profitable. The shift to *market* economic principles left whole swaths of village populations without work.

The village of Khuchni, one of Dagestan's ancient weaving communities, provides an illustration. Until recently, all the women of Khuchni wove for the carpet market. It takes four to five months to finish each rug. They used to sell their carpets for $100 apiece but now, even at that price, there are no buyers. While these exquisite pile rugs and kilims command ten to twenty times that amount abroad, the distribution system in Dagestan has broken down. Khuchni seems a community caught in time, the way of life people knew for centuries suspended and nothing to take its place. The elder generation looks back with nostalgia to Communist days when they received stable salaries and could supplement them by selling their fruit, grain, and carpets at market. Now there is no market, and meager salaries go unpaid for months at a time. To the people of Khuchni and other traditional villages, capitalism means economic collapse, not opportunity. They wait for things to get worse. Women who used to teach their daughters the weaver's skills from a very young age are themselves leaving the looms and taking whatever work they can find. But jobs are scarce, the school and the clinic the only employers in hundreds of communities. The paucity of opportunities in the towns draws most young people to the republic's major cities. These émigrés remain bonded to their ancestral auls, often forging in the city a social circle made up of their relatives and fellow exiles from the same hamlet. This urban village émigré unit is the modern equivalent of the ancient *tukhum*, the clan—so preeminent in Dagestan's social hierarchy.

Dagestan overwhelmed me. I was grateful that filming takes time and we spent a few days in each village where we stopped. Despite a more leisurely pace, I still had trouble keeping as careful a journal as Kennan did. Even though he fell behind when traveling hard on horseback, he worked diligently to fill in the record for much of the most venturesome part of his journey. "I'm tired tonight as a dog but I must try and write up my journal," he wrote at one point.

I had studied some Avar, the language spoken by the largest ethnic group in Dagestan, but I found myself falling back on Russian amid the wild profusion of languages that shift from one village to the next. In Khuchni people speak Azeri (a Turkic language), while Tsovkra is a Lak village (like Avar, a North Caucasian language). Today, Russian is the lingual intersection for Dagestan's population, but people sustain their native languages at home. We stopped in Kakhib, high on a ridge above the Avarskoe Koisu, one of three major Caucasus rivers that water Dagestan, and the route that Kennan and Prince Jorjadze followed up to the crest of the Caucasus. I visited with women at a wedding. Patimat, a thirty-five-year-old woman who left the village when she was in seventh grade, explained to me the importance of language in preserving the tukhum. "My children were born in Kaspiisk on the Caspian, where everyone speaks Russian, but I use Avar with them at home. I even brought them back to Kakhib for a year to make sure they don't forget that they belong to this village." Patimat squatted with the other women relatives in the kitchen readying the food, while her twelve-year-old daughter Abidat prepared to lead the procession of the bride's female relatives carrying the dowry through the street to the home of the groom. The bride, Mariam, had sat next to her match-made fiancé at several weddings earlier that summer, but she had never had a conversation with him. "Aren't you nervous about marrying a complete stranger and moving in with his family?" I asked. She shook her head. An entire room of Mariam's maternal home spilled over with blankets, mattresses, clothing, pots, pans, china, carpets, a garlic press. Mariam, blinded by her opaque veil, clung to her assistants' elbows. Aunts, sisters, nieces, and girl cousins took up armloads of the dowry items. They pressed a plump pillow and an iron into my arms and I marched along with them.

When the mullah began the call to prayer, the procession stopped in its tracks. In 1920, Dagestan's mosques numbered more than two thousand. By Lenin's order, the clerics were eradicated and the mosques systematically destroyed or converted to movie theatres, Communist Party clubhouses, or warehouses. Only twenty-seven mosques survived the onslaught, one of them in Kakhib, where the muezzin has leaned from the minaret five times a day for as long as anyone can remember, his supplication echoing off the steep valley wall. When his voice faded, the wedding procession continued, released from its momentary quick-freeze.

Across Dagestan, mosques are being rebuilt, classes in Arabic reintroduced, Islamic schools opened. Shamil has been resurrected as a post-Soviet hero. Does this denote secessionist sentiment? Bulach Gadjiev, a historian who lives in Buinaksk (Temir Khan Shura in Kennan's day), insists that Shamil's popularity today is as a symbol of Dagestan's historical glories, not a protest. He dismisses the likelihood of Dagestan rebelling against its position as a republic in the Russian Federation. "I'm convinced that Dagestan will never support a fundamentalist government," Gadjiev tells me over lunch prepared by his wife Alla. "Here in Dagestan, we can't imagine the present, or the future, without Russia."

In Bezhta, the last village on the Dagestan side of the Caucasus, we stopped for the night at the home of Sultan Abdulmedzhidov. He was the head of the Bezhta government under the Soviet system. In the out-with-the-old, in-with-the-old politics of perestroika, he's now the democratically elected mayor. Encroaching winter had put a chill in the air and we huddled around the wood stove where Sultan's wife cooked *chudu* in a pan on the stovetop. For a month we'd been eating this staple dish, a wheel of dough stuffed with mutton, potatoes, or *brinza*, a salty cheese that keeps for years in brine—the same fare that Kennan survived on. Our hostess stacked the chudu one atop the other, spreading butter in between the layers until they made a great heap. "How long has your family been in Bezhta?" I asked. "Do you know what they were doing in 1870?"

"My great-great-grandfather was the *naib* then," said Sultan.

Chris and I exchanged grins. Kennan had arrived at the home of the Bezhta naib, or headman, on September 28th, 1870!

Sultan had never heard of Kennan, but he assured us that we were the first Americans he'd ever heard of crossing the Caucasus from Dagestan to Georgia. While our journey involved fewer risks than Kennan's, it was not without uncertainty. We'd skirted the southern border of Chechnya and managed to avoid crossing the path of armed bandits, a spillover from the Chechen conflict. Chechen fighters have sometimes operated out of Dagestan—in the most notorious case, kidnapping dozens of Russian hostages and taking them over the border into Dagestan.

AFTERWORD

In Bezhta, bureaucratic roadblocks threatened to abort our plan to trail Kennan across the Main Caucasus Ridge into Georgia. Because of the war in Chechnya, the border between Dagestan and Georgia was sealed. Permission for our crossing had been denied by the highest levels of the Russian border patrol earlier in the summer, and lobbying on our behalf by the Ministry of Tourism and Dagestan's official representative in Moscow had failed to reverse the decision. The border patrol garrisoned at Bezhta—a gaggle of underfed and underpaid Russian soldiers—had no intention of allowing us to leave Dagestan across the mountains. But then, in a sudden burst of travel serendipity, the commanding officer received a telegram informing him that our itinerary had been approved—by no less than Russian Prime Minister Viktor Chernomyrdin himself.

The reprieve came not a moment too soon. In late fall, the colors were turning fast on the flanks of the Caucasus and we were worried that, like Kennan, we'd end up crossing the high backbone of the Caucasus through fresh snow. We sent our Blazer around over the only track between Georgia and Dagestan passable by vehicles, while we took to foot travel, hiking across steep ridges dotted with patches of a plant resembling labrador tea. Our guide was a local Bezhta hunter who refused all urging to sleep in the tent, insisting that his *burka* (sheepskin cape) would ward off the frost. Ali, a thin man who looked sixty but was only forty-five, also turned down the offer of soup brewed from packages. "This is how I stay healthy," he explained, breaking off several bulbs (not cloves!) of garlic and munching them with bread.

The spine of the Caucasus barely dips below 11,000 feet and only in one place does it ease up enough for a highway to pass through it—the Georgian Military Highway between Tbilisi and Vladikavkaz. Our trail climbed steadily up the bare, windswept hillside. Even though this crossing to Georgia was closed, it obviously had once been heavily used. Historically, this was an important pathway for trade between Bezhta on the Dagestan side and Kakhetia on the Georgian side. The Bezhtans, by their own account, would trade meat and dairy products for fresh fruits and vegetables. According to the Georgians, the Bezhtans would raid their farms and steal them blind. When Georgia was another Soviet republic, there were no restrictions on travel back and forth. In fact, there are still 6,000 Avar families, relatives of Bezhta people, who live in Kakhetia, Georgia's eastern province.

AFTERWORD

Thankfully, the snows waited, and the crest of the Caucasus was still hummocked with brown grass when we reached the top the first week of October as Kennan did 126 years before. We looked down on the Alazan Valley he described as "the most magnificent picture I have ever seen" with "scores of glittering streams like winding silver threads, dotted with vineyards, and orchards and rising in one long gentle cultivated slope."

In those days, the Alazan River flowed down from nearby Mount Borbalo (10,804 feet) through the Pakasi Gorge into Azerbaijan and eventually the Caspian Sea. Now the Mingechaur Reservoir is the end of its line, but the lands of the Alazan are as productive as they were in the nineteenth century, when the Jorjadzes helped to develop vineyards in these fertile valleys that produce every kind of nontropical fruit imaginable.

We had our doubts about finding any trace of Kennan's royal sidekick, Prince Jorjadze. We had nothing to go on but a description of his house and a single reference buried deep in Kennan's journal, which mentions the prince's first name and patronymic: Giorgi Davidovich. But for that detail, there was no way of knowing which of the numerous Prince Jorjadzes was Kennan's escort.

Stalin, himself a Georgian, oversaw the eradication of Georgia's aristocracy. Most of the nobles who did not flee to Europe were executed. During the purges, Stalin is said to have asked Beria, chief of his secret police, what percentage of Georgia's noble class remained. "About 3 percent," Beria replied. "Make that number be 0 percent," Stalin reportedly ordered. Those members of aristocratic families who survived did so by hiding their pasts and assimilating into *homo soveticus*, that exemplary modern creature who renounced his history. Only in the past few years have people dared to take pride in their roots.

Chris and I wandered around cemeteries in the villages that were traditionally Jorjadze lands: Eniseli, Gremi, and Sabue. We stopped people in the streets to explain our mission, but no one could tell us anything. Too many generations had come and gone since our man rode those hills. But sometimes even unproductive searches can be interesting. Locals eager to help took us to meet "The Englishman," an innocent-looking white-haired man whose grandmother Gertrude Cook (a cousin of Captain Cook) had come to Gremi late in the nineteenth century as a governess, married a Jorjadze, and lived there until her death in the 1950s. True to Kakhetia's reputation, our research turned into a progressive wine-tasting party.

The three-hour drive from Kakhetia took us through country as lush as Napa, but the denuded roadside hinted at the price Georgia paid for its independence—a desperate energy crisis that leaves the towns without power most hours of the day, and houses without heat. Almost all of the venerable shade trees that used to line the roadway have been chopped for fuel. We found Tbilisi a much more welcoming place than Kennan described. Since Georgia threw off the Soviet yoke, the capital has grown into an overtly Euro city that seems to flaunt its new freedom. Flush with art shows and cultural events, chic shops selling Italian shoes, and even an authentic British pub, the city stays up late and dresses better than seems possible given the country's dire economy. We stuffed ourselves with garlicky eggplant garnished with pomegranate seeds, chicken in peanut sauce, and *khachapuri,* Georgia's answer to pizza (a chewy dough stuffed with the ubiquitous salty cheese), and relished the soft life after the weeks of cold travel through the Dagestan highlands.

After meeting several Jorjadzes who turned out not to be descended from the line we were tracing, we were introduced to Nana and her brother Temur Jorjadze. We sat around a table in a bare, windowless room at the Adam & Eve Film Studio, waiting for Nana, who was an hour late. She burst in like a gust of wind and talked breathlessly, interrupting herself as the stories tumbled out.

"In this room," Nana said dramatically, "Beria himself censored films. He sat in that corner there, while the directors and actors waited outside the door, quaking."

Modern Georgia prides itself on two exports: wine and art movies. Nana, the great-great-granddaughter of Prince Jorjadze the vintner, turned out to be one of Georgia's premier film directors, a Cannes grand prize-winner and a partner in the private film studio.[3] She had just finished her latest film, a joint French-Georgian production. (*Chef in*

---

3. Kennan variously spelled the prince's name Djordjadze, Jorjadzi, Jorjadze. A century and a quarter later, the confusion with the transliteration of this name persists: Prince Jorjadze's great-great-granddaughter is listed in her film credits as Nana Djordjadze. Her brother Timur gave me a business card: Timur Jorjadze!

AFTERWORD

Love was later nominated for a 1997 Oscar for Best Foreign Film.) She had never heard the story of a Jorjadze helping the first American cross the Caucasus, but she knew her lineage. We could hardly believe our luck.

A few days later, in Nana's apartment, we shuffled through family photographs from the turn of the century and before. "My father was Givi, my grandfather Giorgi, and his father, Ivan," Nana said. She picked up a very old portrait, unlabeled like most of the other images. "This could be him. My great-great-grandfather was born in 1819, Giorgi, son of David." That would be Kennan's prince, Giorgi Davidovich.

We returned east to Kakhetia, to the one-time Jorjadze lands, together with Temur, Nana's brother. Temur, an architect and professor at the university, also holds the rank of fifth dan in karate—one of few Europeans to achieve this level of mastery. Temur showed us the old estate at Eniseli. It was confiscated by the state many years ago and turned into a school. The paint was peeling from the walls and an addition had

Frith Maier and the great great grandchildren of Prince Jorjadze looking at family photographs. Photo © Chris Allingham.

destroyed the symmetry of the once-fine house, but we could still see the columns of the veranda Kennan sketched into his notebook.

The little church at Gremi stands on a promontory giving it a 360-degree view of the Alazan plain. It is being refurbished for Georgian Orthodox services to be held here again after standing silent for most of a century. In the church's wall, beneath the frescoes in the unlit sanctuary, a single broken headstone remembers Dimitri Davidovich Jorjadze, 1821–1883. The inscription (in Russian) notes that he was a *Tainyi Sovetnik* (privy councillor) to the tsar.

"This must be my great-great-grandfather's brother," Temur surmised. "There used to be more tombstones in this church, but they were desecrated," he added, without a shred of bitterness at his ancestors' fate. Nana and Temur, the descendants of Kennan's traveling companion, represent Georgia itself: unassuming at face value, yet incredibly sophisticated. We parted company with them, and with Kennan, reluctantly. Having crossed the Caucasus with this shadow traveler, I felt like I knew him pretty well. The vividness of Kennan's journals shrunk the century dividing me from him and put Dagestan's past within my reach.

REFERENCES

I. Manuscripts

George Kennan Papers. Library of Congress [abbreviated Kennan MSS, LC].

II. Books and articles by George Kennan

"An Island in the Sea of History: The Highlands of Daghestan." *National Geographic* 24 (October 1913): 1087–1140.
"The Mountains and Mountaineers of the Eastern Caucasus." *Journal of the American Geographical Society of New York* 5 (1874): 169–93.
"Murder by Adat." *The Outlook* 113 (June 28, 1916): 477–82.
Siberia and the Exile System. 2 vols. New York: Century, 1891.
Tent Life in Siberia: Adventures among the Koraks and Other Tribes in Kamchatka and Northern Asia. New York: Putnam's, 1889.
"A Tenth-Century Barbarian." *The Outlook* 113 (May 24, 1916): 201–7.
"Unwritten Literature of the Caucasian Mountaineers." *Lippincott's* 22 (October 1878): 437–46; (November 1878): 571–81.

III. *General bibliography.*

A[bbott], L[awrence] F. "Kennan, George (Feb. 16, 1845–May 10, 1924)." *Dictionary of American Biography,* vol. 10 (New York: Scribner's, 1933), 331–32.

Akademiia nauk SSSR, Dagestanskii filial, Makhachkala. Institut istorii, iazyka i literatury. *Istoriia Dagestana.* 4 vols. Moscow: Nauka, 1967–69.

Akademiia nauk SSSR, Institut etnografii im. N. N. Miklukho-Maklaia. *Narody Dagestana: Sbornik statei.* Moscow: Akademiia Nauk SSSR, 1955.

Akiner, Shirin. *Islamic Peoples of the Soviet Union.* London: Kegan Paul, 1983.

Atkin, Muriel. *Russia and Iran, 1780–1828.* Minneapolis: University of Minnesota Press, 1980.

Baddeley, John F. *The Rugged Flanks of the Caucasus.* London: Oxford University Press, 1940.

———. *The Russian Conquest of the Caucasus.* London: Longmans, Green, 1908.

Barrett, Thomas M. *At the Edge of Empire: The Terek Cossacks and the North Caucasus Frontier, 1700–1860.* Boulder: Westview, 1999.

———. "Lines of Uncertainty: The Frontiers of the North Caucasus." In *Imperial Russia: New Histories for the Empire,* ed. Jane Burbank and David L. Ransel, 148–73. Bloomington: Indiana University Press, 1998 (reprinted from *Slavic Review* 54 [1995]: 578–601).

———. "The Remaking of the Lion of Dagestan: Shamil in Captivity." *Russian Review* 53 (1994): 353–66.

Barthold, W., and A. Bennigsen, "Daghistan." *Encyclopaedia of Islam,* vol. 2 (Leiden: E. J. Brill; London: Luzac, 1965), 85–89.

Bell, James Stanislaus. *Journal of a Residence in Circassia during the years 1837, 1838 and 1839.* 2 vols. London: Edward Moxon, 1840.

Bennigsen Alexandre. "Un mouvement populaire au Caucase à XVIII siècle: Page mal connue et controversée des relations russo-turques." *Cahiers du monde russe et soviétique* 5/2 (1964): 159–205.

Bennigsen, Alexandre, and Chantal Lemercier-Quelquejay. *Islam in the Soviet Union.* New York: Praeger, 1967.

Bennigsen, Alexandre, and S. Enders Wimbush. *Muslims of the Soviet Empire: A Guide.* London: C. Hurst & Co., 1985.

Bennigsen, Alexandre, and S. Enders Wimbush. *Mystics and Commissars: Sufism in the Soviet Union.* London: C. Hurst, 1985.

Brower, Daniel R., and Edward J. Lazzerini, eds. *Russia's Orient: Imperial Borderlands and Peoples, 1700–1917.* Bloomington: Indiana University Press, 1997.

Broxup, Marie Bennigsen, ed. *The North Caucasus Barrier: The Russian Advance towards the Muslim World.* London: Hurst, 1992.

Campbell, Charles. *The Transformation of American Foreign Relations, 1865–1900.* New York: Harper and Row, 1976.

Chelebi, Evliia, *Kniga puteshestviia (Izvlecheniia iz sochineniia turetskogo puteshestvennika XVII veka). Perevod i kommentarii. Part 2: Zemli severnogo Kavkaza, Povolzh'ia i Podon'ia.* Pamiatniki literatury narodov Vostoka, Perevody 6. Moscow: Nauka, 1979.

Chenciner, Robert. *Daghestan: Tradition and Survival.* Richmond, Surry, U.K.: Curzon, 1997.

Comrie, Bernard. *The Languages of the Soviet Union.* Cambridge: Cambridge University Press, 1981.

Cunynghame, Arthur. *Travels in the Eastern Caucasus, in the Caspian and Black Seas, Especially in Daghestan, and on the Frontiers of Persia and Turkey, During the Summer of 1871.* London: J. Murray, 1872.

Ditson, George Leighton. *Circassia, or, A Tour to the Caucasus.* New York: Stringer and Townsend, 1850.

Dowty, Alan. *The Limits of American Isolation: The United States and the Crimean War.* New York: New York University Press, 1971.

Dunlop, John B. *Russia Confronts Chechnya: Roots of a Separatist Conflict.* Cambridge: Cambridge University Press, 1998.

Ellsworth, William Webster. *A Golden Age of Authors: A Publisher's Recollection.* Boston: Houghton Mifflin, 1919.

Esadze, Semen. *Istoricheskaia zapiska ob upravlenii Kavkazom.* 2 vols. Tbilisi, 1907.

Fairchild, David. "George Kennan: The Inborn and Acquired Characteristics Which Made Him a Great Explorer of the Russian People." *Journal of Heredity* 15 (October 1924): 402–6.

"The Fall of Schamyl." *New York Times*, October 6, 1859, 4, col. 3.

Fitzpatrick, Anne Lincoln. *The Great Russian Fair: Nizhnii Novgorod, 1840–90.* New York: St. Martin's Press, 1990.

Gadzhiev, M. G., O. M. Davudov, and A. R. Shikhsaidov. *Istoriia*

Dagestana s drevneishikh vremen do kontsa XV v. Makhachkala, 1996.

Gadzhieva, S. Sh. *Odezhda narodov Dagestana XIX–nachalo XX veka.* Moscow: Nauka, 1981.

Gammer, Moshe. *Muslim Resistance to the Tsar: Shamil and the Conquest of Chechnia and Daghestan.* London: Frank Cass, 1994.

———. "Russian Strategies in the Conquest of Checnia [sic] and Daghestan, 1825–1859." In *The North Caucasus Barrier,* ed. Marie Bennigsen Broxup, 45–61.

———. "The Siege of Akhulgoh: A Reconstruction and Reinterpretation." *Asian and African Studies* 25 (1991): 103–18.

Geograficheskoe obshchestvo Dagestana. *Trudy.* Vol. 23. Makhachkala, 1995.

Glavnoe arkhivnoe upravlenie pri Sovete ministrov SSSR et al. *Lichnye arkhivnye fondy v gosudarstvennykh khranilishchakh SSSR.* 3 vols. Moscow, 1963–80.

Henze, Paul B. "Circassian Resistance to Russia." In *The North Caucasus Barrier,* ed. Marie Bennigsen Broxup, 62–111.

Istoriia narodov Severnogo Kavkaza. Edited by A. L. Narochnitskii. *Istoriia narodov Severnogo Kavkaza s drevneishikh vremen do kontsa XVIII v.,* ed. B. B. Piotrovskii. Moscow: Nauka, 1988. *Istoriia narodov Severnogo Kavkaza (konets XVIII v.- 1917 g.),* ed. A. L. Narochnitskii. Moscow: Nauka, 1988.

Jersild, Austin. "From Savagery to Citizenship: Caucasian Mountaineers and Muslims in the Russian Empire." In *Russia's Orient,* ed. Daniel R. Brower and Edward J. Lazzerini, 101–14.

———. "Who Was Shamil? Russian Colonial Rule and Sufi Islam in the North Caucasus, 1859–1917." *Central Asian Survey* 14/2 (1995): 205–23.

Kavkazskoe gorskoe upravlenie. *Sbornik svedenii o kavkazskikh gortsakh.* Vol. 1. Moscow: ADIR, 1992; reprint of original published in Tbilisi, 1868.

Kennan, George Frost. *At a Century's Ending.* New York: Norton, 1996.

Lang, David Marshall. *The Georgians.* London: Thames and Hudson, 1966.

———. *The Last Years of the Georgian Monarchy, 1658–1832.* New York: Columbia University Press, 1957.

———. *A Modern History of Georgia*. London: Weidenfeld and Nicolson, 1962.

Laserson, Max M. *The American Impact on Russia—Diplomatic and Ideological—1784–1917*. New York: Macmillan, 1950.

Layton, Susan. "Nineteenth-Century Russian Mythologies of Caucasian Savagery." In *Russia's Orient*, ed. Daniel R. Brower and Edward J. Lazzerini, 80–99.

———. *Russian Literature and Empire: Conquest of the Caucasus from Pushkin to Tolstoy*. Cambridge: Cambridge University Press, 1994.

Lemercier-Quelquejay, Chantal. "Cooptation of the Elites of Kabarda and Daghestan in the Sixteenth Century." In *The North Caucasus Barrier*, ed. Marie Bennigsen Broxup, 18–44.

Magomedov, P. M. *Khronologiia istorii Dagestana*. Makhachkala: Dagestanskoe knizhnoe izdatel'stvo, 1959.

Markov, Evgenii. *Ocherki Kavkaza: Kartiny kavkazskoi zhizni, prirody i istorii*. 2d ed. St. Petersburg and Moscow: M. F. Vol'f, 1904.

McReynolds Louise. *The News under Russia's Old Regime: The Development of a Mass-Circulation Press*. Princeton: Princeton University Press, 1991.

Meshchaninov, I. I., and G. P. Serdiuchenko, eds. *Iazyki Severnogo Kavkaza i Dagestana: Sbornik lingvisticheskikh issledovanii*. Moscow: Akademiia nauk SSSR, 1949.

Minorsky, V. *A History of Sharvan and Darband in the 10th–11th Centuries*. Cambridge: W. Heffer & Sons, 1958.

Monastyrskii, S. *Illiustrirovannyi sputnik po Volge v 3-kh chastiakh s kartoi Volgi: Istoriko-statisticheskii ocherk i spravochnyi ukazatel'*. Kazan, 1884.

Mostashari, Firouzeh. "Colonial Dilemmas: Russian Policies in the Muslim Caucasus." In *Of Religion and Empire: Missions, Conversion, and Tolerance in Tsarist Russia*, ed. Robert P. Geraci and Michael Khodarkovsky, 229–49. Ithaca: Cornell University Press, 2001.

Narody Kavkaza. Vol. 1. M. O. Kosven et al., eds. Narody Mira: Etnograficheskie ocherki. S. P. Tolstov ed. Moscow, 1960.

Pipes, Richard. *The Formation of the Soviet Union: Communism and Nationalism, 1917–1923*. Cambridge: Harvard University Press, 1964.

Rhinelander, L. H. "Russia's Imperial Policy: The Administration of the Caucasus in the First Half of the Nineteenth Century." *Canadian Slavonic Papers* 17/2–3 (1975): 218–35.

———. *Viceroy Vorontsov's Administration of the Caucasus.* Occasional Paper 98. Washington: Kennan Institute for Russian Studies, 1980.

Robinson, Francis. *Atlas of the Islamic World since 1500.* New York: Facts on File, 1982.

Roskoschny, Hermann. *Russland: Land und Leute.* 2 vols. Leipzig: Gressner & Schramm, [1882–84].

Rossiiskaia akademiia nauk. Institut etnologii i antropologii im. N. N. Miklukho-Maklaia. *Narody Kavkaza.* Materialy k serii "Narody i kul'tury". Bk. 3: Ia. S. Smirnova and A. E. Ter-Sarkisiants. *Sem'ia i semeinyi byt.* Part 1: *Formirovanie, tip i struktura.* Moscow, 1995; and Bk. 4: S. A. Arutiunov, G. A. Sergeeva, and V. P. Kobychev. *Material'naia kul'tura: Pishcha i zhilishche.* Moscow, 1995.

Said, Edward. *Orientalism.* New York: Vintage, 1979.

Salkeld, Audrey, and José Luis Bermúdez. *On the Edge of Europe: Mountaineering in the Caucasus.* Seattle: The Mountaineers, 1993.

Saul, Norman. *Concord and Conflict: The United States & Russia, 1867–1914.* Lawrence: University Press of Kansas, 1996.

Stults, Taylor. "George Kennan: Russian Specialist of the 1890s." *Russian Review* 29 (1970): 275–85.

Suny, Ronald Grigor. *The Making of the Georgian Nation.* 2d ed. Bloomington: Indiana University Press, 1994.

Tolstoy, Leo. *Hadji Murat: A Tale of the Caucasus.* Translated by W. G. Carey. New York: McGraw-Hill, 1965.

Travis, Frederick F. *George Kennan and the American-Russian Relationship, 1865–1924.* Athens: Ohio University Press, 1990.

Tyler, Patrick E. "Chechen Warlord Fights Rebels for Mother Russia." *New York Times,* National edition, July 18, 2001, A4.

Uslar, P. K. *Etnografiia Kavkaza: Iazykoznanie VII, Tabasaranskii iazyk.* Tbilisi: Metsniereba, 1979.

Wixman, Ronald. *Language Aspects of Ethnic Patterns and Processes in the North Caucasus.* Department of Geography Research Paper 191. Chicago: University of Chicago, 1980.

———. *Peoples of the USSR: An Ethnographic Handbook.* New York: M. E. Sharpe, 1988.

INDEX

Page references to illustrations are printed in italics.

Abdulmedzhidov, Sultan, 241
ablutions, 99, 112, 114, 142–43
Achmet. *See* Akhmet
Adam and Eve Film Studio, 244
adat. *See* law: customary (*adat*)
Addala, Mount, 9n1, 134n57
Adyge, 16–17, 30, 101–3
afterlife, belief in, 119, 137, 146
agricultural produce, 82, 84, 93, 97, 111, 113, 186, 204–5, 242
agriculture, 51, 68, 82, 107, 120, 129–30, 147, 149, 157, 186, 195–97, 201, 203–4, 210. *See also* threshing; viniculture
Akhmet (Kennan's interpreter/guide), 12, 180–81, 183–86, 191–94, 203, 205–8, 210, 212–13
Alazan Valley, 7, 8, 38, 42, 118n35, 157, 243, 246
alcoholic beverages, consumption of, 62, 65, 97, 99, 106, 149, 180, 182, 185, 197, 204–5, 236, 244
Alexander II (emperor of Russia), 40
Alexander II (king of Kakhetia), 35
Ali (Dagestani guide), 242
Ali (son-in-law of Prophet Muhammed), 100
Allingham, Christopher, viii, 233
alphabets. *See* language in Caucasus
American Geographical Society, 9
Ananuri, *160*
Andi (Ande), 30, 179, 183, *184*, 189–90, 194–95, 210–11
Andiiskoe Koysu River, 30, 91, 152n80, 185, 195–96, 199, 201–4, 210
Andi Range, 89, 9 1n1, 180, 181, 185, 187, 195
Ando-Tsez ethnic group, 152n80
Anne (Russian empress Anna Ioannovna), 35

253

INDEX

Antzakhoul. *See* Untsukul
apiculture, 129
Apsheron peninsula, 89
Arabs, 29
Armenia, 8
Armenians, 106, 197
Arran, Isle of, 53
Ashura, Shiite festival of, 100n8, 231
Associated Press, 8, 11
Astrakhan, 35, 72n32, 74n36, 78n40, 82, 84–86, 98
aul (aoul). *See* village, mountain
Aurora Borealis, 180, 181
Austria, 222
authors and books read by those whom Kennan met in Caucasus: Henry Thomas Buckle, 18, 175, 210; Lord Byron, 175; *Consulate and Empire* (*Histoire du Consulat et de l'Empire*), 17–18, 210; Charles Darwin, 175; John Draper, 175; *Evangeline*, 17, 210; *History of Civilization in England*, 18, 210; Thomas Henry Huxley, 175; Henry Wordsworth Longfellow, 17, 210; Charles Lyell, 175; Maury (Alfred? Matthew Fontaine?), 175; John Stuart Mill, 175; William Shakespeare, 175; Herbert Spencer, 175; Adolphe Thiers, 17, 210. *See also* Koran
Avaria, 185, 201
Avar khanate, 30, 36
Avars, 240, 242. *See also* Dagestan: mountain people of; Lezgins
Avarskoe Koysu River, 30, 91, 130n48, 134n57, 135n59, 152n80, 208–10, 240
Azerbaijan, 243

Baedecker guide book, 79n42
Bakriev, Bakri, 238–39
Bakriev, Magomed (father of Bakri), 238

Baku, 35, 101
Balkars, 30
Bariatinskii, Aleksandr Ivanovich, 19n38, 103
Beany (travel acquaintance of Kennan's), 54
beggars, 72
Bell, James Stanislaus, 23, 25
Ben Lomond, 54
Beria, Lavrentii, 243, 244
Bering Strait, 9, 117
Berwick Upon Tweed, 55
Bezhta (Bezhuta), 128, 142, 191; description of, 147–52; family tradition in administrative history of, 241; hospitality in, 149, 151, 241; its relations with Georgia, 18, 33, 242; Russian soldiers in, 151, 242
Bezhuda, 142n64
billiards, 54, 99, 175
Black Sea, 8, 102, 103, 169, 218–19, 222
blood revenge, 117, 119, 205–8, 213–16, 237
Bognadala gorge, 91
Bogos Range, 91n1, 134n57, 153n82
Borbalo (Barbale), Mount, 90, 91n1, 243
Bornholm, Island of, 58
Bosphorus Strait, 220
Botlikh (Botlekh), 117, 172, 179, 183, 196–97, 199–201, 210
Breshkovskaia, Catherine, 10
bride theft, 192–93
bridges, 55, 129, 146, 195, 199, 212, 217; "American" at Tlokh, 146n72, 204; Galata (Istanbul), 220n39; at Kvankhdatl, 146n72, 203; Lieutenant Schmidt (in St. Petersburg), 60n14; *most*, 202; Nicholas (*Nikolaevskii most*) (in St. Petersburg), 60; Palace (in St. Petersburg), 64; Preobrazhenskii (across Andiiskoe Koysu), 201, 202

INDEX

Bronson (English traveler in Caucasus), 117
budun (boodoon), 132
Buinaksk. *See* Temir Khan Shura
bundling, 116, 237
burial customs, 115, 137, 138, 208
burka (boorka). *See* dress, *burka* (boorka)
Burns, Robert, 53
Burton, Richard, 23, 101
burvol(ok), 101, 148
Byzantium, 31

Calendar, Julian, xiv, 175n10; Gregorian, xiv, 175n10
California, 135
Cameron (English consul in Tbilisi), 117
Cannes film festival, 244
carriages, 60–61, 66, 68, 82, 87–88, 99, 106, 111, 173, 176, 218; *drozhki* (droshky), 60n12; *kareta*, 61; *povozka* (pavoska), 173; *tarantas*, 99; *telega*, 66. *See also* postal coach
carts. *See* carriages
Caspian Sea, 28, 32, 35, 89, 91, 92, 99, 107, 243
Catherine II (empress of Russia), 83n49
Catholicism, Roman, 121
Caucasus, xii, 6–9; admiration for America in, 172, 175, 181; American interest in, 17, 24–25; British interest in, 25, 117; cultural change in, 17–19, 113; ethnic diversity of, 28; ethnographic study of, 23–24; geography of, 27–29, 89–93; history of, 27–40; mountaineering in, 25; popular images of, 13–14, 17; resistance to Russian expansion in, 101–3; Russian administration in, 19, 24, 40; Russian expansion in, 16–17, 34–40; in Russian literature, 13–14; Soviet policy in, 234, 237–40, 243; travelers in, 13, 23–25, 29, 94, 117, 241. *See also* Chechnya; Dagestan; Georgia; language in Caucasus
Century, 9
Charing Cross railway station, 223
Chavchavadze (princess), 38, 157n88
Chechens, 15–16, 30, 87, 95, 102, 175; deportation of, by Stalin, 234; national identity of, 234; wars of, against Russia, xii, 16–17, 36–39, 103, 234–35, 241
Chechnya, 102n14, 181, 218n38; Russian military presence in, 173, 177–83, 187; Soviet rule in, 234; war of 1990s in, xii, 233–35, 241–42
Chef in Love, 244–45
Chelebi, Evliia, 29, 30
Chemodan Gora ("Suitcase Mountain"), 209–10
Cherkassof (captain, stationed in Khorochoi), 179–85
cherkeska (cherkaska). *See* dress, *cherkeska* (cherkaska)
Chernomyrdin, Viktor, 242
Chernyi Iar (Chernaya Yar), 84
Chevchavadze (prince), 27, 197, 205; adjutant of, 22, 197, 200
Chevy Blazer, 235, 242
childbirth, 118
children, 66, 101, 117–19, 133, 149–52, 179, 181–82, 186, 236–37, 240
Chinese, 76
cholera, 84, 86
Christianity, 31, 114, 121. *See also* Georgia: Orthodox Christianity in; Orthodox Church, Russian
Chukchis (Choukchis), 144
Chukotka Peninsula, 6
Circassians. *See* Adyge
clans, 20, 29, 192, 206–8, 234, 238–39, 240; *tukhum*, 239

INDEX

Cleveland and Toledo Telegraph Company, 3
clothing. *See* dress
Clyde, River, 53
communal government: *jamaat*, 29; *obshchestvo* (obshestvo), 128. *See also* Dagestan: administration and government in; law: customary (*adat*); law: Islamic (*sharia*)
Constantinople. *See* Istanbul
Cook, Gertrude, 243
Cook, James (captain), 243
Copenhagen, 58
corn, Indian, 186
Cossacks, 63, 97, 103, 114, 121, 172, 177–78, 182, 210
cotton, Central Asiatic, 72, 81–82
crafts, 20, 239
Crimean War, 16, 17
Cronstadt. *See* Kronshtadt
Crusaders, myths about presence of, in Caucasus, 20, 27, 115, 118, 198–99
Cumming (Kennan's host in St. Petersburg), 61–63
Cunynghame, Arthur, 23, 101
cursing, 85, 86, 136–37, 213, 216

Dagestan: administration and government in, 116, 139–40, 145–46, 205, 230, 235, 241; Christianity in, 33; curiosity in regarding America, 107, 120; economic life in, 18–19, 33, 120, 235–36, 239; education in, 33 (*see also* education in Caucasus); English travelers in, 117; ethnic diversity of, 28; geography of, 28–30, 89–90, *90*, 91–93 and passim; geology of, 203–4; history of, 28–31, 36–39; Islam in, 30–31, 36–38, 118–20; languages of, 28, 31, 118, 238, 240 (*see also* language in Caucasus); mountain peoples of, 95, 96, 98–99, 117–20, 183–84, *190*, 192, 197, *214*, *215* (*see also* Lezgins); name of, 28, 90; in popular imagination, 6–7; national identity in, 234; relations with Georgia, 18, 32–34, 116, 120, 242; Russian culture in, 237–38; Russian rule in, 7, 114, 120–21, 145, 149, 183, 238, 242; lack of separatist sentiment in, 241; social structure of, 29, 116, 237; Soviet economic policy in, 239; tourism in, 235; warrior tradition in, 7, 95, 97–98, 120, 127, 216, 237 (*see also* weapons); in wars against Russia, 36–39, 235. *See also* dress, Dagestani; dwellings, Dagestani; food, in Dagestan; hospitality: in Dagestan; Islam; law; music, in Dagestani villages; rituals, Dagestani; village, mountain
dance, 123, 141, 144–45, 230
Danube River, 219, 222
Dargins, 208n32
Darginski Okroog, 139, 205
Darial Pass/Gorge, 94, 170, *171*, 218n38
David the Builder (king of Georgia), 33–34
Denmark, 58
Derbent (Derbend), 20, 32, 33, 35, 94, 101, 239
dervishes, 119, 219
Deshlagar, 120
Didos (Dedoitse), 160n93, 198n24, 199
Dikosmta, Mount, 91n1
diligence. *See* postal coach
Ditson, George Leighton, 24
divorce, 107, 117–18, 152
Djordjadze. *See* Jorjadze
Dolper (travel companion of Kennan's), 144
Dolph, J. H., 52, 54
dowry, 213, 240

dress, 58, 62, 72, 93, 121–22; *bashlik*, 114; *beshmet*, 87; *burka* (boorka), 121, *122*, 242; *chariki*, 148n77; Chechen, 87, 94; *cherkeska* (cherkaska), 113, 237; Dagestani, 94, *95*, 114, 129–30, 143, 148–50, 153, 184, 189–90, *190*, 237–38; Kalmyk, 86; *khalat*, 72, 74; *papakha*, 127; Persian, 74, 97–99, 113–14; *portianka*, 74n37; Russian, 60, 75–76, 79, 99; Tatar, 72–74, *75*, 87, 99

Dudayev, Dzhokhar, 234

dukhan (dookhan), 175, 176

Dumas, Alexandre, 25

dwellings, 197; in Chechnya, 179–80, 182; Dagestani, *102*, *104*, 104–6, *128*, 131–32, *141*, 141–43, 147–48, 189–91, 202, 212–13; Georgian, 158–59, *163*, *165*; Kalmyk, *85*, 85–86

Dzhengutai, 116n32, 157n89; musical performance in, 119, 123–26, 148

Dzhurmut River, 135n59

Edinburgh, 50n3, 55

education in Caucasus: Georgian, 33; Muslim, 19, 132–33, 151, 238, 241; Russian, 15, 19, 24, 238

Elbrus (Elbrooz), Mount, 92–93

Elsinore, 58

England, 95

Eniseli, 42, 118n35, 158–63, 243, 245

entertainment. *See* dance; music

Ermolov, Aleksei Petrovich, 37, 234n2

Ersenoi, 177

ethnicity, 20, 28, 234

exile system, Siberian. *See* Kennan, George: *Siberia and the Exile System*

Fairs. *See* markets

family relations, 117–19, 139–40, 146, 149, 152, 186, 191–93, 206–8, 237

Farelnia Lake (Farelnian Ozera; Trout Lake), 188

Fedor Ivanovich (tsar), 35

Finland, 64–70; Gulf of, 58; languages in, 65, 70

fleas, 65, 69, 72, 99, 123, 169, 222, 226

food, 52, 55, 57, 72, 79, 221–22, 242; *brinza*, 149n78, 241; in Dagestan, 93, 97, 99, 105–6, 113, 132, 149, 151, 191, 204, 211, 213, 241; in Georgia, 158–61, 244; *iukola*, 151; *khachapuri*, 244; in North Caucasus, 175, 176, 178, 180, 182, 185, 189; rituals regarding preparation of, 152, 178, 229, 230; Russian, 71; *zharkoe*, 161. *See also* grapes; watermelon

France, 16

Franco-Prussian War, xii, 81n46, 181

Freshfield, Douglas, 25

furnishings. *See* dwellings

Gadjiev, Bulach, 241; Alla, wife of, 241

Gamzat Bek (Hamza Bek ibn 'Ali Iskandar Bek al'Hutsali), 217n37

Gasser (Gazr) (acquaintance of Kennan's in Temir Khan Shura), 114, 117, 121, 122

Gaul, Caesar's, 183

Georgia: changes in since 1991, 243–46; film industry in, 244–45; geography of, 31, 243; history of, 31–34, 161; Orthodox Christianity in, 31, 33, *159*, *160*, 161, 198n24, 246; Persian influence in, 32; relations with Dagestan, 18, 32–34, 116, 120, 198–99, 242; relations with Russia, 34–36; Stalin's policies in, 243; trade of, 32–33, 242, 244. *See also* hospitality: in Georgia; Kakhetia

Georgian Military Highway, 93n3, 94n5, 170, 172–73, 196, 242

German colonies in Russia, 83

Germans, 114

Giant's Causeway, 52

INDEX

Gimra (Gimre, Gimri, Gimry), 179, 185, 212, 213; precipice of (Gimrinski spooska), 121, 211–12, 217, 235
Ginukhs, 115, 152, 230
Giorgi XII (king of Kartlo-Kakhetia), 36
Giuseffi, Moses, 220–21
Glasgow, 50, 53–55; its cathedral, 54–55; St. George's Square in, 54
glavnyi khrebet (glovni krebet), 156. See also Main Caucasus Ridge
Gleinber (acquaintance of Kennan's in Groznyi), 175
Glinka, Mikhail, 62n19
Gochob (Gotschob, Ochaw), 128, 132n50, 133, 146; education in, 132–33
Godunov, Boris (tsar), 35
Goethe, 52
Golden Fleece, Land of the, 8, 169
Golden Horde, 29, 72n32
Goldsmith, Oliver, 26
Goncharov (Goncharof), Ivan Aleksandrovich, 70
gortsy (gortse), 114. See also Dagestan: mountain people of
Grabbe, Pavel Khristoforovich, 36
grapes, 93, 97, 99, 106, 186, 191, 204–5, 212–13. See also viniculture
graves, 123, 146, 230, 238, 246
Great Britain, 16
Greenock, 53
greetings and salutations, 127, 136, 146, 197–98, 212, 230
Gremi, 42, 243, 246
Gretingkov (Geetchinkov) (colonel), 103, 114–15, 120, 146
Gromska (travel acquaintance of Kennan's), 71
Groznyi (Grozna, Groznoi), xii, 35, 99, 117, 172, 173, 175, 233–34
Guckin family (travel companions of Kennan's), 51–52

gudekan, 237
Gunib (Goonib), 91, 94, 115, 116, 117, 123, 127–29, 172, 198, 205, 210; as administrative center, 145; etymology of name, 199; Russian storming of, 39, 103, 185; Shamil's house in, 102
Guria, 36

Habibula (Christopher Allingham's translator and soundman), 236
Haji Murat, 38
Hamlet (prince of Denmark), 58
Harriman, E. H., 11
Hay, John, 49n1
Helmsing (Russian consul in Hull), 56
Himalaya, 219
historiography, Soviet Marxist, 28n60, 33
Hogland, Island of, 58
honor, 117–19, 193–94, 205–8, 213–17, 236–37
hospitality: in Chechnya, 179–82; in Dagestan, 41, 97, 105–6, 112, 115–16, 132–33, 136, 186, 191, 194, 204–5, 211–13, 236–37, 241; in Georgia, 158–61, 244–46; *khoziain* (khazine), 134; *kunak* (koonak), 112, 236
hotels, 175; d'Angleterre (Moscow), 59, 70; d'Angleterre (St. Petersburg), 59, 61, 62; Astoria (St. Petersburg), 59n9; Bellevue (St. Petersburg), 70; Daghestan (Petrovskoe), 99; Ehrenberg (Vyborg), 65; Euston (London), 223; de Goonib (Temir Khan Shura), 122–23; Kaiser (St. Petersburg), 64; Paragon (Hull), 55, 56; de Paris (Istanbul), 220, 222. See also *postoialyi dvor*, 112
Hudson River, 53; Palisades of, 52, 83

258

Hull, England, 55, 56
Hungary, 222
Huns, 199; booklet about, 230–31
Husain (grandson of Prophet Muhammed), 100n10

Ichkeria, 102
Imatra, Falls of, 64, 69
Imeretia, 36
Indians: American, 133; Arizona, 213; Sioux, 95
Inebolu (Ineboli), 212
Ingush, 30
Inkhelo (Inkhelee), 202
Innookh. *See* Ginukhs
intellectual horizons, 175, 181–83. *See also* authors and books read by those whom Kennan met in Caucasus; education in Caucasus
Iran, 32. *See also* Persia; Safavid Empire
Ireland, 50–51
irrigation, 196
Islam, 18–19, 30–31, 238, 239–40; alms in, 151, 200, 230; in Georgia, 32; in Nizhnii Novgorod, 72–73; post-Soviet revival of, 133n54, 241; prayer in, 72–73, 83, 118, 142–43, 149–51, 200, 219, 226, 230; Russian propaganda about, 31; its role in resistance to Russia, 36–39, 146; Soviet efforts to suppress, 238, 240; tithe in, 151. *See also* education in Caucasus, Muslim; graves; law: Islamic (*sharia*); mosques; Shiite Muslims; sufism; Sunni Muslims
Istanbul, 200n28, 212, 218–22; Galata, suburb of, 220n39; Golden Horn in, 219–20; Pera, suburb of, 220n39, 222; Topkapi palace in, 220n39; St. Sophia Cathedral in, 220n39, 221
Ivan the Great (Russian grand prince Ivan III Vasil'evich): Bell Tower of, *71*, 227
Izalam (Ilazam, Ilezan, Ilzelan), Lake, 180, 187, 188
izvozchik (isvoscheck), 60n11

Jason and the argonauts, 169
Jews, 97, 99, 100, 101, 106, 144, 175, 178–79. *See also* Tats
Joongootai. *See* Dzhengutai
Jorjadze, Giorgi Davidovich, 7–8, 40–42, 117, 121–26, 132–34, 147, 157, 231, 243; estate of, in Eniseli, 158–61, 169, 243, 245–46; interest in American Indians, 133; lineage of, 245; role of, in adjucating disputes, 41, 137, 146, 149, 151, 159–60; wife of, 158
Jorjadze family, 40–42, 244–46; Dimitri Davidovich (brother of Giorgi Davidovich), 40, 41n95, 246; Dimitri Georgievich (possible son of Giorgi Davidovich), 41n95; Giorgi Ivanovich (grandfather of Nana), 245; Givi (father of Nana), 245; Il'ia Georgievich (possible son of Giorgi Davidovich), 41n95; Ivan Georgievich (son of Giorgi Davidovich; great grandfather of Nana), 245; Nana, 244–46; Timur (brother of Nana), 244–46

Kaitag khanate, 30
Kakhetia, 8, 32–33, 41–42, 117, 157, 172, 196, 198n24, 242, 244, 245
Kakhib, 240
Kalash, 118n37
Kalmyks (Kalmuck Tatars), 85–86, 94, 95, 98
Kamchadals, 63, 144
Kamchatka, 6, 86n56, 95
kanle. *See* blood revenge
Karadakh, 210

INDEX

Karakaitags, 208n32
Karakhaki *ushchele* (Karakhaki Gorge), 128. *See also* Karalazurger
Karakoisu River, 130n48–49
Karalazurger River, 130n49
Karbala, 100n10
Kardib, 135n59
Kaspiisk, 239, 240
Kavkazets (travel companion of Kennan's), 85–87, 106
Kazan, 72n32, 98
Kazbek, Mount, 93
Kazi Mullah (Ghazi Muhammad ibn Isma'il al-Gimrawi al-Daghistani), 217
Kennan, George: archive in Library of Congress, viii, x, 201n29; attitude toward Bolsheviks, 11; attitude toward Russia, 8–12, 15–17, 34; Caucasus journal, composition/accuracy of, viii, x–xi, 12–13, 17–20, 70n27, 102n13, 119n38, 120n39, 123, 127, 129n46, 147n73, 154n85, 157n89, 162, 163n1, 179n12, 181, 200n28, 239–40; cultural bias, 20–21, 150, 175, 185; early life, 3, 6; employment in telegraph industry, 3, 6; expelled from Russia, 10; expertise on Caucasus, xi, 8–9, 12–23; fictionalization in documentary writings, 6–7, 12–13, 20; in Russian Finland, 64–70; influence, 10–12; as journalist, 8–12; knowledge of foreign languages (other than Russian), 65, 83, 94, 149, 152, 219, 221, 225–26, 228; knowledge of Russian, xi, 7, 21–22, 63, 116, 167, 184, 221, 222n43; love of travel, 7, 24–27; meets Prince Jorjadze, 41, 121–22; photographs purchased by, 201, 203, 227–28, 229; as public lecturer, 8–10; in St. Petersburg, 6, 7, 60–64, 70; religious views, 20, 219; Russian literature purchased by, 13–14, 70; sense of humor, x–xi, 219; in Siberia, 6, 9, 86n56, 116–17; *Siberia and the Exile System*, 9–11; *Tent Life in Siberia*, vii, 6–7, 63; as translator, 9, 11, 14n24, 22
Kennan, George Frost (twentieth-century statesman), vii-viii
"Kennanitis," 11n14
Kerzhenets River, 79n41
Kerzhentza, 79
Kezenoiam, Lake. *See* Izalam, Lake
Kharachi, 237
Kharami Pass, 187n18
Khazars, 29
Khivans, 219
Khonkhodatel. *See* Kvankhidatl
Khorochoi, 179, 181
Khuchni, 239–40
Khulkhulau (Khoikhoolaoo) River, 177
Khunzakh (Khoonzakh), 172, 179, 183, 195, 198, 199, 208–9, 209, 210
Khzanor River, 147n75
kibitka. *See* yurt
kinzhal (kinjal), 74. *See also* weapons
Kizylyar, 35
Klokh. *See* Tlokh
Kodor Pass, 33
koisu, 91n2
Koran, 73, 106, 114, 133, 139, 145, 200, 213
Koryaks (Koraks), 6, 86, 144, 175
Kosternerefski (doctor in Temir Khan Shura), 121
Kostomarov, Nikolai Ivanovich, 70
Krasnoiarsk, 9
Kravchinskii (a.k.a. Stepniak), Sergei, 10

INDEX

Kronshtadt, 59
Kropotkin, Peter, 10
Kumyks, 29, 115n28, 192–93, 217
Kutais, 172, 218n38
Kvankhidatl, 146n72, 202–3

Ladoga, Lake, 68
Lady of the Lake, 54
Laks, 238, 240
language in Caucasus, 21, 23–24, 28, 101, 103, 115, 118, 160n93, 183, 240; Arabic, 19, 31, 103, 123, 133, 146, 241; Avar, 21, 23, 103n16, 115, 152, 197, 214, 241; Azeri, 241; Georgian, 18, 21, 23, 31–4, 41n96, 149, 151; Lak, 241; Russian, 7, 17, 21–22, 40, 178, 181–82, 183, 197, 238, 240, 246
Lars, 170
law: American, 107–8, 216; customary (*adat*), 18–19, 101, 117–18, 137–40, 145, 146, 192–94, 205–8, 213–17, 226, 229, 236–37; Islamic (*sharia*), 18–19, 38, 139–40, 145–46, 226, 230; *kadi* (cadi), 132n51, 227; Russian, 19, 40, 145
Layton, Susan, 14
Lenin, Vladimir Il'ich, 240
Lenormant, François, 23
Lermontov, Mikhail Iur'evich, 13–14, 70
Leshef (acquaintance of Kennan's in Petrovskoe), 99
Lezgins (Lesghians), 102, 114–15, 117–20, 132, 141, 144, 151–54, 155, 207; misappelation of name to all Dagestani mountain people, 102n13, 115n29; etymology of name, 198. *See also* Dagestan: mountain peoples of
Lincoln, Abraham, 107, 120, 226
Loch Lomond, 50
London, England, 56, 218, 222–23

Londonderry, 51
Lutherans, 114
Lyskovo (Leeskova), 79

MacMahon, Field Marshal Marie Edmé Patrice Maurice, comte de, 81
Mahmout (member of Prince Jorjadze's party), 153
Main Caucasus Ridge, 8, 31, 89–91, 92, 92–93, 94n5, 196; ascent to, 153–57, 242
Makar'ev, 73n34
Makar'ev (Makarief) Monastery, 74n34, 80
Makhachkala. *See* Petrovskoe
Mansur (sufi sheikh), 37
Mariam (bride at Kakhib), 240
markets, 17–18, 72, 73–74, 76, 77, 80, 82, 84, 93, 97, 98, 111, 113, *164*, 236. *See also* trade
marriage customs: Armenian, 106; Dagestani, 117–19, 240
married life, 107. *See also* family relations
Marshall (English traveler in North Caucasus), 117
Marshall, A. S., 52, 54, 56, 58, 62
Mas'udi (Arab geographer), 28
Maxime (servant hired by Kennan), 153, 228, 232
meals. *See* food
Mecca, 73, 83, 143, 150; pilgrimage to, 39, 200, 219
Medina, 39
migration to cities, 239
Mikhail (Michael) Nikolaevich (Russian grand duke and viceroy of Caucasus), 40, 111, 114, 120
Milford Junction, 55
Mingechaur Reservoir, 243
Mingrelia, 36

261

INDEX

money: Caucasian, 148; Finnish, 65, 67; Georgian, 33; Persian, 148; Russian, 18, 137–39, 194, 198
Mongols, 29, 32, 72n32, 85n54, 115
Montferrand, August, 60n13
Morrill, Ed, 49
Moscow, 70–71, 175; its Kremlin, 71
Moskovskie vedomosti (Moscofski Vaidemost), 117, 120
mosques, 72–73, 100, 133, 139, 150–51, 189, 206, 208, 220, 221
mourning, 151
Mozdok, 35
Mukar, 207
murder, 101, 117–19, 146, 192–93, 205–8, 213–16, 237
Murids, 30–31, 36–39, 145–46; misuse of term, 36n84
music, 61–62, 71, 73, 74, 81, 113, 114; in Dagestani villages, 119, 123–26, 143–45, 189, 200; "Kingdom Coming" (hymn), 99, 144; "Star Spangled Banner," 54, 55; "Yankee Doodle," 144; Zheezn za tsara (*Zhizn' za tsaria*; A Life for the Tsar) (opera by Glinka), 62
musical instruments, 62, 71, 114; in Dagestani villages, 123, 143–45; *zurna*, 144n69
muzhik (moozhik), 60n10. *See also* peasants, Russian

*N*aib. *See* officialdom, *naib*
Naples, Bay of, 159
Napoleon I (emperor of France), 11, 175
Napoleon III (emperor of France), xii, 81
Naqshbandi sufi order, 37, 217n37
nargileh (hookah), 82, 222
Nasreddin Khoja (Mollah Nazr Ellin), 154
National Geographic Society, 201n29

Nelson (correspondent of Kennan's), 70
Neva, River, 60, 62, 64
Newcastle Upon Tyne, 55
New York Herald, 9
New York Times, 17n33
New York Tribune, 15
Niagara Falls, 68, 217
Nicholas I (emperor of Russia), 40
Nizhnii Novgorod, 72–80; its Kremlin, 77
Nogais, 36
Nogai steppe, 89, 92
Norwalk (Ohio), 6; *Reflector*, 162
Nukatl Pass, 134, 135n59
Nukatl Range, 91n1, 130n48, 134n57
Nunikas-Tsikhe, Mount, 153n83

*O*blomov (Oblomof) (novel by I. A. Goncharov), 70
Obyknovennaia istoriia (Obecknovennia Historia) (novel by I. A. Goncharov), 70
officialdom, 9, 54, 56–57, 59–61, 76, 117, 122, 163–64, 166–69, 174–75, 178–79, 220, 231, 232; *ispravnik*, 117; Ministry of Tourism, 242; *militsioner* (millitaioner), 179; *naib*, 136, 142, 144, 145, 146, 241; *starshina* (starshine; starosta), 133, 179, 181, 204, 212–13. *See also* Dagestan: administration and government in
Oka River, 78
Old Believers, 79n41
One Thousand and One Nights, 120
Oosler. *See* Uslar
oral tradition, 119–20, 154n84
Orbeliana (princess), 38, 157n88
Ordu, 210
Orientalism, 12–15, 20–21, 108–9

INDEX

Orthodox Church, Russian, 76–77, 113
Orzhonikidze. *See* Vladikavkaz
Oscar, Best Foreign Film, 245
Ottoman Empire, 15–16, 29, 32, 222

Pakasi Gorge, 243
Palmer (contact of Kennan's in London), 56
Paris, 81n46
pastoralism, 120, 134, 147, 149, 153, 196, 236
Patimat (Avar woman at Kakhib), 240; Abidat, daughter of, 240
peasants, Russian, 60, 72, 76, 78–79, 111
Pentecost, 77n38
pereval, 187
Persia, 32, 34, 36
Persians, 30, 74, 79, 82–83, 86, 95, 97–98, 100–101, 112–14, 116, 118, 136, 219
Peter I (the Great) (Russian emperor), 35; statue of (the "Bronze Horseman"), 67
Petrovskoe, 85, 86, 106, 170, 172, 239; description of, 87, 94–95, 97–100, 235
Pirnie (travel acquaintance of Kennan's), 54
plow, 129
Plutarch, 22, 198
Poles, 121, 175
Pollock, Sean, 35n80
postal coach, 66, 94, 112, 163–64, 165, 168–69, 173, 175–76
postal communication, xn6
postoialyi dvor, 112
Poti, 172, 200n28, 218
Preobrazhenskii fort, 201
Prussia, 81n46
Pushkin, Aleksandr Sergeevich, 13, 70, 222n43; his *Eugene Onegin*, 222n43

Putnam (publishing company), 50
Putnam's, 6

Railroads in Russian Empire, 64, 70
Ranson (Ronson) (English traveler in Caucasus), 117
Rathlin Island, 53
Rawlinson, Henry, 23
Razin (Rasin), Stenka, 79
Reagan, Ronald, 107n20
religious syncretism, 30–31, 237
Reock, 58
revolutionaries, Russian, 10–11
Rhine River, 222
Ritso (contact of Kennan's in London), 56
rituals, 199, 219; Dagestani, 101, 151–52, 206, 226, 229, 230, 236–37. *See also* law: customary (*adat*)
roads and paths, 66, 68, 94, 96–97, 104, 106–7, 113, 121, 123, 129–30, 134–35, 147, 153, 154, 156–57, 172, 177, 179, 180, 181, 187–88, 195, 199–200, 210–12, 217, 235, 242. *See also* Georgian Military Highway
Rome, 198
Roodnyef (Rudnev), brothers, 120–21
Rusçuk (Rooschuk, Ruse), 222
Rush (correspondent of Kennan's), 70
Rushukha Pass, 195n22
Russian American Telegraph Company, 6
Russian Empire, expansion of, 15–16, 34–39; foreign policy of, 15–16. *See also* Caucasus; Dagestan; Finland; Georgia
Russian Geographical Society, Caucasian Section of, 23
Russo-Japanese War, 11

Sabue, 42, 243
Safavid Empire, 29, 34
Said, Edward, 14

Saima, Lake, 68, 69
saklia (sakla). *See* dwellings, Dagestani
salt production, 203
Samara, 81–82
Samashki (Samashinski Station), xii, 173
Samsun (Samsoun), 211
Saratov (Saratoff), 81
Sbornik svedenii o kavkazkikh gortsakh, 23
Schuyler, Eugene, 22n45
Scotland, 50n3, 53–55; Highlanders of, 184
Scott, Walter, 53, 54
Sella, Vittorio, 201n29
Semipalatinsk, 9
Seratchef (official in Temir Khan Shura), 122
sex, illicit, 117, 152, 229, 236–37
Shamil (Shamyl) (imam), 14, 37–39, 94, 103, 157n88, 185, 199, 201, 217, 234; enforcement of Islamic law by, 38, 145–46; house of, *102*; heroic image of, 13n23, 16, 241; mountains of, 107; tower of, 157
shamkhal, 29
shashka, 87. *See also* weapons
Shiite Muslims, 30, 100–101, 118
Sierra Nevada Mountains, 89
Society of American Friends of Russian Freedom, 10
soldiers, Russian, 60, 229, 242. *See also* Cherkassof; Cossacks; Teekheenof
Solomon, proverbs of, 219
Sortia (queen of Persia), 100
Soviet Union: its annexation of Karelian region of Finland, 64n20; anti-religious campaigns of, 238, 240; its attack on Georgian aristocracy, 243; censorship in, 244; command economy of, 239; its deportation of Volga Germans, 83n49; its nationality policy in Caucasus, 234, 237
Spanish-American War, 11
Stalin, Joseph, 83n49, 234; his efforts to eliminate Georgian aristocracy, 243
starshina. *See* officialdom, *starshina* (starshine; starosta)
steamships and steamboats, 56–58, 60, 81–82, 86, 222; A. A. Zeveke Steamship Line, 78n40; Anchor Line, 50, 51; Black Prince, 53; Black Sea Navigating Company, 218–19; Cambria, 50; Caucasus and Mercury Line, 77–78; Colorado, *77*, 78; Great Eastern (G.E.), 107, 226; Thomas Wilson, 55–58; Tsezarovna Maria (Princess Maria), 78, 82; Vesta (Black Sea), 210; Vesta (St. Petersburg), 60; Wilson and Sons, 56; Zaire, 57
St. Petersburg, 6, 7, 13, 59–62, 64, 67, 70, 218; Admiralty Square in, 67; Gorkovaya Street in, 60; Letni Sad (Summer Garden) in, 61; St. Isaac Cathedral in, 59n9, 60, 62; statue of Peter the Great in (the "Bronze Horseman"), *67*; Vassilli Ostroff (*Vasilevskii ostrov*, Vasilii Island) in, 60–61
Strabo, 22, 198
Stryker (Shtryker), Lev Grigor'evich, 99, 170, 172, 229
sufism, 36–38. *See also* Murids
Sulak River, 35
Sunja (Soonzha) River, 35, 173
Sunni Muslims, 30, 100nn 9, 10, 118
superstition. *See* rituals

Tabasaran khanate, 30
taboos, 152, 178, 229, 230. *See also* law: customary (*adat*)
Tarku, 29, 35

INDEX

Tartars, mountain. *See* Dagestan: mountain people of

Tatars (Tartars), 72–74, *75*, 75–76, 87–88, 98, 136, 219

Tats ("Mountain Jews"), 30

Tbilisi (Tiflis), 32, 33, 40, 94, 117, 162, *163–65*, 170, 172, 218n38; Kennan's struggles with bureaucracy in, 20, 163–64, 166–69; post-Soviet ambience of, 244

Teekheenof (Tikhinov) (major, resident in Khunzakh), 210, 211

Telavi, 162, 232

Temir Khan Shura (Timour Khan Shoura), 18, 40, 41, 94, 95, 99, 106, *108*, 116, 172, 179, 183, 184, 211, 217, 239; as administrative center, 109, 111, 113–14, 120–21, 145; description of, 108–9, 111–14, 121–23

Terek (Tersk) River, 16, 35, 170

theft, 119, 137–39, 192

threshing, 129, 148, 149, 230

timber, 93, 135, 153

Times (London), 17n33

Tliarata, 134n55, 135–36, 141–42n63

Tliarosh (Tlorosche), 128

Tlokh (Klokh), 146n72, 201, 204–5

Tokyo, 11

Tolstoi, Aleksei Konstantinovich, 70

Tolstoi, Lev Nikolaevich, 13–14, 70; *Hadji Murat*, 38n91; *War and Peace* (*Voina i mir*), 14, 70

Tomburg, 157

Tomsk, 9

Tovihetti. *See* Tushetians

trade, 32–33, 57–58, 74n36, 81, 87, 197, 239, 242. *See also* markets

travel: difficulties of, xii, 6–8, 21, 121, 172–73, 176–78, 182, 235, 241–42; expenses of, 49–50, 55–56, 218, 219, 221–23, 226–27, 228, 230–32; red-tape involved in, 56–57, 122, 163–64, 166–69, 242. *See also* fleas; roads; steamships and steamboats

travel documents, 166–168; *ob'iavlenie* (obyavlenia), 167; *otkrytyi list* (atkreete leest), 122, 179, 183; passport, 59, 166–67; *podorozhnia* (padarozhna), 166; *svidetel'stvo* (svedaitelstvo), 167; visa, 56–57

Travis, Frederick, viii

Trebizond, 219

Tsaritsyn (Tsaritzen, Stalingrad, Volgograd), 84

Tsatanikh, 200n28, 211

Tsovkra, 238, 240

Tushetians (Toochets, Toovchinni, Tushuri), 118, 198, 199

Ukhtil'or River, 135n59

uniforms, Russian, 59–60; Cossack, 97, 114, 182

United States: attitudes toward Russia in, 8–11, 16–17; relations with Great Britain, 16

Untsukul, 200n28, 210–13; Muslim school in, 133n54

Uslar, Petr K., 23, 103, 115

uzden, 29

Vanno (servant of Prince Jorjadze's), 153

Vartashan Pass, 33

Vedeno (Veden; Weden), 37–38, 117, 172, 173, 176–80, 181, 187

verst, 66n22

Vesuvius, Mount, 159

village, mountain, 19–20, 95–97, 99, *104*, 104–6, 127, *128*, 130–31, *131*, 136, 141–42, 144–45, 147–48, 153, 177, 179, 181, 189–90, 195–97, 202, *214*, *215*, 217

265

viniculture, 42, 157–58, 196, 197, 212, 243–44
Vladikavkaz, 93n3, 94, 95, 106, 117, 154, 162–63, 166, 167, 170, 172–73, 218
Volga River, 29, 35, 74n34, 86, 136; scenery along, 79–84; shipping on, 74n36, 77–78, 81–82, 84, 86, 93
Vorontsov, Mikhail Semenovich, 40
vulgarity, 200. *See also* cursing
Vuoksa River, 68
Vyborg (Vweborg), 64–67, 69–70

Wagons. *See* carriages
watermelon, 72, 79, 84, 93, 107, 113, 175
weapons, 13, 53, 59, 87, 95, 97–98, 100–101, 114, 127, 135, 143, 144, 146, 153, 178, 181, 184, 192, 194, 198–99, 205–6, 208, 210, 216, 229; displayed on walls in houses, 105, 132, 180, 181, 191, 197

Westminster catechesm, 219
women: limited rights of, 139–40. *See also* dress; work: women's
work: men's, 56, 60–62, 66, 72, 76, 81, 82, 111, 114, 147, 149–50, 237; women's, 82, 112, 129–30, 147–50, 191, 202–4, 212–13, 235, 237–39
wrestling, 133n54

Yakuts, 66n24
York, 55
yurt, *85*, 85–86, 175

Zaezzhyi dvor, 112
Zakataly District (*Zakatala okrug*), 118, 121
Zamber (travel companion of Kennan's who lived in Vedeno), 173, 176, 178
Ziavdin (Frith Maier's driver in Dagestan), 236
Zoroastrian burial practices, 115

www.ingramcontent.com/pod-product-compliance
Lightning Source LLC
Chambersburg PA
CBHW031802220426
43662CB00007B/500